A Waiter in Paris

A Waiter in Paris

Adventures in the
Dark Heart of the City

Edward Chisholm

monoray

First published in Great Britain in 2022 by Monoray, an imprint of
Octopus Publishing Group Ltd
Carmelite House
50 Victoria Embankment
London EC4Y 0DZ
www.octopusbooks.co.uk

An Hachette UK Company
www.hachette.co.uk

First published in paperback in 2023

ISBN 978 1 80096 0206

· A CIP catalogue record for this book is available from the British Library.

Printed and bound in UK

12

Typeset in Garamond Premier Pro.
Garamond was originally created by the sixteenth-century
Parisian designer Claude Garamond following a request
for a new typeface for the court of the French king Francis I.

This FSC® label means that materials used for the product
have been responsibly sourced

For Morgane & George

Contents

---

waiting noun

BrE /ˈweɪtɪŋ/

1. the fact of staying where you are or delaying doing something until somebody/something comes or something happens
2. the fact of working as a waiter or waitress

Oxford Advanced Learner's Dictionary

Introduction

As I write this Paris is quiet. Her avenues empty. Her shops, bistros, cafés and restaurants all shuttered. Weeks of lockdown have reduced our worlds to the dozen or so square metres we call home.

The city holds its breath, dreaming of a return to normality, which in Paris means sitting in cafés or bistros, on terraces or in the parks. Of eating well and eating cheaply. This is the Paris we all love.

Nothing beats the luxury of the restaurant. You walk in, someone shows you to your table, a menu appears and then you sit back and relax and watch as the parade of plates, glasses and bottles appears and disappears before your very eyes – like magic.

Though Paris arguably democratized dining out, it is still a luxury, the very definition of it. During lockdown, the unceasing buying, preparing, cooking and then washing up after ourselves have reminded us of that. That's why we think so much about it. About dining out, food and of course – restaurants.

And nowhere epitomizes the world of restaurants better than Paris.

A Waiter in Paris begins in November 2011. Three years after the financial crisis and almost two years after I'd graduated from university. Fallow years during which I'd held down a string of petty jobs in London that included call-centre work, labouring, flyering, and (possibly the high point!) selling soft pornography to Eastern European TV channels. All while I applied for other, more 'prestigious' jobs. Jobs that didn't appear to exist anymore.

The question, on the surface, was relatively simple: in a post-financial crisis world, what were we, as university graduates with humanities degrees, meant to do with our lives? The answer, however, evaded me. And so, with nothing tying me to London, short on money and options, I decided to take up an offer from a wonderful French girl, Alice, to come and live with her in Paris. She was moving there from London, and I could stay with her until I got on my feet. It was the perfect solution. Fulfilling my desire to have an adventure and finally get my life moving somewhere.

When I arrived, it was with a single bag of clothes and a couple of books, including the one that arguably had got me into reading and writing and excited by the idea of Paris many years earlier, George Orwell's *Down and Out in Paris and London*. One of his lesser-known works, in which he recounts his time living and working in near-destitution, first in the French capital and then in the British. With Orwell we peered under the surface of what it was really like living in Paris back then, and it was far from the glimmering parties of F Scott Fitzgerald, or the literary salons hosted by Gertrude Stein, with Hemingway, Picasso and Matisse.

It was never my intention to work in restaurants. I naively thought I'd find a 'proper job' when I arrived in Paris but, as in London, it never materialized. And so, with time and money running out, like many, I opted for waiting as a solution. It was a way to immerse myself in the city, avoid expats, teach myself French and, looking back, prove to myself that I could do something with my life; that I could be an active protagonist in my own story, instead of just a passive casualty of the economic times.

Unbeknown to me, it was the beginning of a great adventure – slipping into the world of Parisian restaurants. A world, it turned out, that had changed little from when *Down and Out* was begun in 1929 – the year of the last great financial crash. It was an experience that started a lifelong love affair with France and Europe. But also one that taught me the values of hard work and humility. It taught me that you can do something if you put your mind to it. And, likewise, that there's a whole world of possibilities out there. You've just got to have the courage to believe in yourself and then throw yourself in.

In Paris, waiters are as omnipresent as the *tricolore* flag or the Eiffel Tower. They are everywhere: on the terraces working, out the back of restaurants smoking, propped on bars at the end of the night exhausted. They're so ubiquitous that we tend to ignore them, which is what they want. Unless there's a problem, when we let them know about it; or we give them half a thought as we chuck a few coins on the table after a meal. But have you ever wondered what it's like to be a waiter? To end up spending your life waiting tables? The truth is, it's a cruel existence. You live week to week, often under sadistic managers, with a wage so low you're fighting each other for tips. It's physically demanding, frequently humiliating and incredibly competitive. A world hiding in plain sight governed by archaic rules and a petty hierarchy – populated by the most incredible cast of characters you'll ever come across: thieves, narcissists, former Legionnaires, wannabe actors, paperless immigrants, drug dealers...

And with unfettered access to the kitchens of Paris, it certainly makes you think twice when choosing where you will spend your own pitiful wage when you do eventually eat out.

In total I spent more than four years doing various waiting and bar jobs across the city as I tried to build a career as a writer. *A Waiter in Paris* is that story, and although based primarily on an experience in one particular restaurant, it is in reality an amalgamation of all my experiences. It's not really my story; I was merely an observer passing through. 'A camera with its shutter open', as Christopher Isherwood wrote of his time in Berlin. The real heroes of this story are the people I encountered there. To that end I have changed the names of everybody mentioned in this story, including the name of the restaurant, which fortunately – and rather unsurprisingly – has since closed down.

Of course, this isn't really a story about a restaurant. It's a portrait of contemporary Paris, and by extension France. Slice a Parisian bistro in half and you will be presented with a startlingly accurate cross-section of contemporary French society. A multilingual, multi-ethnic, complicated and highly nuanced picture. With the rich and White up top, the poor and Black down below and everyone else – including you – in between. Yes, Paris may not be France, but all of France can be found in Paris.

If you don't believe me, the next time you go down those narrow stone steps in search of the toilet in a Parisian bistro, take a look in the kitchen and tell me how many Sri Lankan or Black faces you see. They're there for the same reason that I was up top, above ground, a Caucasian waiter.

As a result of my experiences – both the highs and the lows – and the incredible people I met and worked alongside, I felt almost duty bound to write this book. To give a voice to an invisible workforce. To tell it how it is.

So yes, the setting is Parisian, and the language French, but these stories are much more universal; they're being played out right now in London, Paris, New York, Berlin, Madrid, Rome and beyond. We just often choose to ignore them. Focusing instead on what we want to see: the food, the decoration – the façade.

And then there's the wonderful French language. How does someone who doesn't speak a word of French (full transparency: I don't even have a GCSE in a modern language) understand what's going on? Well, I quickly learned that, providing you understand the context of what is being spoken about, even if you pick up only one in every ten words, you can often get the gist. The brain does a magnificent job of filling in the blanks – which is how I've tried to write the dialogue throughout the book. Unless indicated, everyone spoke French to me, making no concessions to my Englishness. As we will see, I muddled through.

A Waiter in Paris is my attempt to tell the story of the people who live and work on the other side of the swinging door marked 'PRIVÉ' and a little of what it's like to live in Paris and be a waiter in a Parisian restaurant. Or, at least, *try* to be a waiter. As it turned out that – like most jobs I'd applied for since graduating university – the restaurant profession didn't think I could do it either.

If there's one thing to take away from this book, I hope that it is this: the next time you're eating something that seems too good a value to be true, spare a thought for the people who are paying the real price. And, if you can, spare them some of your change, too.

We've been told that the world post-Covid-19 will be different. I sincerely hope it is, especially for those who find themselves in the restaurant industry.

Edward Chisholm
March 2021

Amuse-Bouche

It's lunchtime and the tables in the dining room are filling up. The waiters in their smart black suits and bow ties are looking professional, busy – and distinctly French – as they scurry about handing out menus, taking orders, fielding questions and finally disappearing, like assassins, or monks, through the small swinging door at the back of the dining room.

I stand there watching it all, trying to hide my mounting panic, wondering if I should come clean with one of them – take them aside and tell them the truth: that I've absolutely no idea what I'm doing.

But I can't even do that. It would alert them to another fact I'm keen to hide: that I don't actually speak French. I'm in the middle of a smart restaurant in the capital of France, dressed – to all intents and purposes – as a Parisian waiter, and I can't even speak the language.

This isn't some small café or local bistro. This is a genuine, full-blown Parisian restaurant, replete with a terrifying woman at a lectern by the door, an army of surly waiters, a *directeur* who looks like Napoleon Bonaparte's (much taller) cousin and a spiteful manager who wants me gone because he knows the truth: I don't belong here.

I've managed to swing the job (if it can be called that) through a series of well-timed shoulder shrugs and a pre-learned monologue. If they find out now that I can't speak French, that will be it. I must fit in at all costs. If I don't, whatever this is – a job or trial shift, I'm still unsure – will be over and I'll be back to padding the frozen streets of Paris from dawn until dusk with a folder of CVs.

The present facts are these: I arrived sometime after dawn in a cheap, baggy suit and have until recently been kept away from the other waiters, like the Minotaur, in an underground cellar as I polish glasses until my fingers blister.

From the brief moments I've been around the other waiters I hear the same word, 'runner', which I assume is me. Of course, I've no idea what a runner is, and even less idea of what he's actually meant to do.

So, as the restaurant continues to fill up with elegantly dressed Parisians, I remain as still as possible to avoid being noticed; watching the other waiters for clues – anything that allows me to decipher how it all works, how the machine runs. They move like clockwork, locked in some strange choreography, moving without thought, one step ahead of their diners; adding and removing silver cutlery; slight bows; chairs pulled out; white serviettes laid across laps; wine uncorked and served with Gallic ceremony; discreet smiles, nods of the head…

Needless to say, I have neither pen nor notepad. I've no idea what's on the menu, nor how to take orders, nor indeed if I should. I've no idea where the food comes from, nor how it's made, nor even who makes it.

Quite naturally diners attempt to attract my attention, but after a couple of unsuccessful attempts at trying to understand them, I stick to ignoring them, which is surprisingly easy and gives me an air of professionalism.

Just when I think I've finally succeeded at blending into the heavy red curtain behind me, I notice the thin-faced manager in his grey suit, prowling on the other side of the dining room.

The restaurant, which is decorated in a classic French style, with high ceilings and low lighting, flaking gold-rimmed Louis XV mirrors, wallpaper with fleur-de-lis motifs and large single-glazed windows that let the flat light of a Parisian winter illuminate the whole scene, is now almost full. From the tables, light chatter, the delicate clinking of cutlery on ceramic, and expensive perfumes waft upwards to the world of the waiters, who soar above with giant silver trays, the white cloths draped across their forearms trailing behind them like an aeroplane's vapour trail.

The thin-faced manager is now closing in fast, so in a last-ditch bid to look busy I decide to make a beeline for the swinging door at the back of the dining room. The door is light and swings both ways on its hinges, depositing the voyager into a world where the air is cool, there is no smell of perfume and certainly no polite chat.

But it's more than a door, it's a threshold – beyond which lies an entirely different world, one I glimpsed this morning: a labyrinthine world of kitchens, prep rooms, storerooms, cleaning rooms, locker rooms, bin rooms, corridors, hidden staircases and more. And then there are the people who animate it. The hidden faces of Paris. The people whose job it is to toil away in the shadows so that you can have your meal at a decent price.

Ahead of me is a dim, low-ceilinged, flagstone corridor leading down into the bowels of the building. On the air drift the smells of cooking, the distant shouts of men and the sharp crashing and banging of metal.

Behind me, on the other side of the door, hundreds of Parisians are waiting to be served food in the opulent surroundings of a well-known restaurant.

It's the boundary between two worlds: the Paris you see and the Paris you don't. And I want to know what's there, what goes on behind the city's façade.

Suddenly, the manager with the thin face bursts through the swinging door and begins berating me, pushing me forcefully up the dark passageway towards the source of the mysterious sounds and smells.

'____ _____ _____!' he yells.

I've no idea what he's saying, but he's clearly angry.

'*Je suis le runner,*' I try.

'_ ____ ____ *putain runner*!' he snaps.

There's something in his tone of voice that confirms it. I am the runner. How hard can it actually be?

With each aggressive shove from behind he pushes me further along the passageway, deeper into the machine, closer to the strange noises and odours. With a last push I trip down some steps and into a small room. There's a huddle of three men, all of them waiters, crowding around some kind of opening in the wall. There's a lot of shouting going on. They push, shove and yell at one another. Finally, like spooked pigeons, they disperse, their silver trays laden with delights, the thin-faced manager shooing them up the passageway and back into the dining room.

I'm alone again, the mysterious waist-height opening in the wall is clear. The heat lamps burn red, like the entrance to Hades. In the dark room on the other side a shadow moves about.

'*Allô?*' I say.

No response. Moments later a bell rings. The shadow materializes into a dirty white jacket – the lower part of a person. Then silently a pair of hands pushes out a plate. They're followed by a voice: '*Service!*'

I stand there, frozen. Absolutely no idea what I'm meant to do. If I take the plate of what looks like *foie gras*, where do I take it?

'*Service!*' This time more insistent.

Screw it. I'm taking it. I have no idea where to – but what's the worst that can happen?

PART 1
L'APÉRITIF

EAST PARIS

Some months earlier... I settle into my new life in Paris. I live in Alice's first-floor room above a piano repair workshop in the east of Paris, near the Porte des Lilas. It doesn't look like Paris, not the one I had imagined in childhood. There are no wide, tree-lined boulevards or parks with ponds that children push toy boats around in. It's a frontier zone of pre-war factory workers' buildings and post-war tower blocks – right on the edge of the city. Beyond it are the *banlieues*, the suburbs – an industrial–residential netherworld that those living within the Périphérique, the Paris ring road, prefer not to think about. It reminds me more of the film *La Haine* than anything I've seen in the Musée d'Orsay.

Going down the Rue de Belleville, towards the centre of town, is one of the city's two main Chinese neighbourhoods. An entire street of narrow restaurants, chaotic Chinese supermarkets and small, cluttered shops. All the signs and shopfronts are written in Chinese characters. It's a bustling place. During the day the Chinese men stand outside bartering, betting, smoking and spitting on the pavement. At night the Chinese prostitutes line the streets in their droves, milling around and chatting to each other, smiling and blowing smoke into the faces of passers-by who glance at them for a second too long. '*Bon-soir-sa-va-mon-sur,*' they say phonetically. For their services they'll take you to one of the back rooms in the building, down into the cellars or even to a parked van.

The flat has a narrow brass bed in one corner, a sink in a half-rotten cabinet in another and two electric rings for cooking. Behind a flimsy door is a tiny, once canary-yellow bath that you can just about squat in to shower yourself, and on the landing is the shared toilet – a confined place with no light bulb that stinks of slurry and stale piss and always has a wet floor.

The building has periodically been divided up into increasingly smaller spaces using thin walls that do little to dampen sound. Alice and I never see much of the other residents, yet we all know each other intimately. The water flowing through the walls as someone takes a shower at 3am, the rhythmic thumping of a headboard at 5am, blood-chilling arguments at 8am. Our immediate neighbour, a tall, anaemic-looking waiter with a permanently disgusted look and a grey comb-over, takes great delight in slamming his fist or cooking pot against the wall in protest at the slightest noise. The fact that he is disturbed by an English voice only seems to incense him further. '*Espèce d'Anglais de merde!*' he'll cry. '*Sale con de rosbif! Pauvre con!*' As a result, I'm quickly picking up swear words.

The entire stairwell smells of old cigarettes and body odour because the waiter always leaves his door slightly ajar. When he shouts, I return in kind, banging the wall and yelling obscenities. Before long other residents join in. Like prisoners rioting in a cellblock or a madhouse.

'*Ta gueule!*'

'*Ferme-la!*'

If we're lucky, they'll be tuning a piano downstairs at the same time.

One evening, when the waiter has worked himself into such a rage that it feels like he will either break through the wall or suffer a heart attack, I charge into his room. He is as shocked to see me enter it as I am to see the size of it. The poor man doesn't even have a window. There is a single camp bed in the corner, made neatly with a tightly pulled scratchy wool blanket, a cheap table with an electric ring for cooking and a candlestick in a wine bottle covered in centimetres of melted wax. The source of the odour on the landing is now clear, as there are overflowing ashtrays scattered all around the room and the paint is peeling and nicotine stained.

In short it is a cell, no more than a few metres square. Where there should have been a window he's stuck up three postcards, each showing Christian saints and martyrs contorted in pain or praying.

We watch each other for a moment, across a great divide – two different worlds face to face. In his raised hand is the pot. Hanging on nails in the wall behind him are his waiter's clothes with some battered shoes on the floor below. I begin slamming my fist repeatedly against the wall like a crazy man. Telling him that if he continues to bang the wall that way, I'll do the same to him. The waiter meanwhile is sitting on the only chair he has, in front of a small oil heater, wrapped in a thick dressing gown with his slippers on, his face a picture of shocked disgust. His stunned silence tells me he's understood.

Over the following weeks I think often of the waiter. I can't understand how a man can sink so low, can be reduced to such inhumane living conditions, in twenty-first-century Paris. This isn't a young man or a student. This is as good as it is going to get for him.

Parisian Days

In Paris life costs less than in London; it's easier to be poor. For certain staples the prices are essentially fixed: a traditional baguette, €1.20; a démi bière, €1.50; a café au bar, €1.00. Cigarettes are cheaper, wine too, even the Métro is inexpensive (€1.70 for a single compared to London's £5.00).

My days take on a luxurious form. I live like a gentleman of means, rising late, reading the papers in bed or in cafés and strolling the streets of Paris, notepad in hand, picturing myself as some kind of young novelist or poet. Paris is a city that inspires you to walk, and walk I do, every day, without direction, just taking in the city. Getting lost in it. I walk until I'm completely exhausted, whereupon I take the Métro home.

For the first time since having a student loan at university I can feel my purchasing power rising. However, I still need to find work. Because, beyond some abstract ideas of wanting to be European, that is why I'm here. I have a two-pronged approach to job-seeking: at night, in internet cafés, I apply for what I call 'career jobs', then during the day I hunt for 'temporary' cash-in-hand work. This I mainly look for on notice boards in local shops and *boulangeries* or on rudimentary websites that never seem to be updated.

During my first few months, as autumn becomes winter, the 'temporary jobs' are sporadic, yet diverse: English lessons with a French businessman who keeps suggesting I meet his wife; selling gnomes at a garden fair; playing an extra in a movie; building Ikea furniture – anything for a little bit of cash. However, most of the money we have comes from Alice, who has two jobs: one in a small restaurant in the 8th arrondissement – a place where the businessmen smell of lunch – and another in the evening, babysitting the spoilt child of an aristocratic family who live in a gigantic apartment in the chic 16th. On top of this Alice is studying hard, with ambitions of becoming an art restorer. She has a single-minded determination and a sense of direction that I admire immensely. Two things I lack.

Inspired by her sense of purpose I apply for jobs with the same verve I had after university – hunting down names, guessing email addresses, sending letters. Anything. The silence, however, is deafening; no one replies.

December comes and the city grows colder, the days shorter; it's harder to spend as much time walking. The pavements are icy and the city has ground to a halt. My days are spent in the local café, or in bed trying to stay warm. I still apply for 'career jobs', but it's with so little belief in anything coming from them that I eventually just stop. There are only so many times you can keep writing to people and getting no response – you feel like a madman howling into the wind. On top of that, my funds are running dangerously low.

'It's only been two months,' Alice says. 'You'll find something.'

'Two years *and* two months. You're forgetting to count the years since university.'

Things aren't going so well between us. What had started as a brilliant romance has stagnated. The arguments grow more frequent, the reasons more obscure. The energy that had originally drawn us together is pushing us apart. She feels frustrated. Frustrated by me and my lack of belief in myself, frustrated by her own situation. She wants to work in art, not wait tables and clean up after some rich kid. We both want to go somewhere in life: the difference is that she knows where.

'I can't deal with coming back every night and seeing you look so... dejected.' She is standing brushing her blonde hair in the cracked mirror on the wall.

'Not finding a job. It's grinding me down. I keep wondering what I'm going to do with my life. If I don't find something soon, surely this is it? I'll never have anything. I'll be in my late twenties, and I'll have only done shit jobs. Maybe I'm not good at anything. But Paris, I love it.'

What Alice doesn't know is that, as a way of killing time and not thinking about my financial and career problems, I am now often spending my days in the rougher, peripheral areas of Paris, particularly the cafés and bars: Aubervilliers, Montreuil, even going up to Sarcelles. Here I feel more alive, there is no pretence, a hint of danger in the air perhaps. The prices are also reasonable, and there are plenty of other people who appear to be out of work; each in their own way muddling through the existential dread of living. These neighbourhoods feel more real, more raw – a world away from online job applications, CVs and the pressure to be someone in life.

'And me?' she asks.

'You have a job.'

'That's not what I meant. Me, do you love me?'

A moment's hesitation, a death knell droning in the distance.

'Of course.'

'You don't. And you don't even have the courage to say it. The truth is you love *the idea* of me.' She puts the brush down and turns to me. 'Don't worry, I've known it all along. I love you, yes, but I can't make you love me. Not like I want. Not like I need.'

You don't even have the courage...

She undresses quickly in the cold room before sliding into the small bed beside me.

'Put your arms around me, I'm cold,' she says. Then, after some time: 'Your lack of confidence in yourself, it's crazy.'

Alice has me sussed and knows what no one else knows: that deep down I want to write. What she doesn't know is that I have nothing to say, and that, even if I did, I lack the confidence to say it. Besides, how do you even become a writer? Or a journalist? Emailing CVs and applying for jobs doesn't seem to work. All I ever hear is that they're *firing* journalists, not *hiring* them. Sure, hanging around dive bars or rough suburbs is showing me a world I'd like to know more about, but to write about it would make me a fraud. An outsider looking in. Unless I truly lived it, of course.

The following day a friend of Alice's introduces us to some English and American expats. They've been in Paris for varying amounts of time, but they have one thing in common: none of them speaks any French.

What exactly they do eludes me. My original plan had been to see if one of them could help me find a job. However, it soon transpires that their main sources of income are their parents. They are living a cliché: one is there to write a novel, another to study photography, while the third has a moderately successful blog which tackles such important topics as 'where to find the best macarons in Paris' or 'dating a French guy'. In truth, none of them appears to be doing anything. I am not in Paris to hang out with English speakers playing at being expats, or pretend writers. I vow never to mention wanting to be a writer myself.

'You're not so different,' Alice says bitterly as we walk home. 'At least they're actually doing something. Not sitting around wondering who they're meant to be.'

'No, they're just sitting around *pretending* to be who they want to be.'

Despite my happiness at being in Paris, as the weeks drag on, my pessimism about finding work, and finding a direction in life, worsens. My days become formless, unravelling from my hand like a piece of string. Even with so much time available. Days pass and I achieve very little. Reading seems like the kind of luxury someone does in their spare time, not their entire time; the museums aren't free; and it is so cold outside and I am running so low on money that I stay in bed all day instead of doing all the things you imagine doing in Paris: old cinemas, exhibitions, bars and so on. To save my remaining funds I have reduced myself to one espresso, *au bar*, per day. It is cheaper there and conveniently also where the newspapers are left, so you can outstay the length of time it takes to drink the coffee by maintaining an intense interest in *L'Équipe* or *Le Parisien*.

My primary hang-out is the *café-tabac* just up the road from Jourdain Métro station. A narrow and drab-looking place on the outside, but always busy and full of other layabouts. With Christmas approaching they've even put up what was once probably a quite elegant fake Christmas tree, although now it would be better suited to unblocking clogged drains. The *café-tabac* is the kind of place where it's never too early to drink a beer or an *eau de vie*. And the cast of regulars paints a picture of a Paris I'd like to know better, one that seems more real than the places in the centre of town where a loud American voice will carry across the *salle* and everyone looks rather glamorous. And it's certainly more Parisian than any of the addresses in that English girl's last blog about 'the most Parisian bars in Paris'.

I even see the waiter from next door here occasionally. Although since our altercation he refuses to acknowledge me.

The patron is a bitter old French man who has ceded the *tabac* half of his establishment to two industrious Chinese brothers, and now spends his entire time behind the bar moaning about them to anyone who will listen.

'Ninety-eight per cent of *tabacs* already...' he says, as if he's conducted the research himself. 'The Chinese, they're taking over. I was one of the last, you know.'

The Chinese brothers ignore him. They're too busy doing a roaring trade with the continuous stream of people who come in to buy cigarettes and scratch cards.

The Holiday Is Over

In France you are what you studied. There are no transferable skills. You can't have done, say, history, and want to be a journalist or a screenwriter. If you studied history, you work in a museum. End of discussion. You want to work in marketing? Advertising? Finance? You'd better have done the appropriate studies. Otherwise, you need to go back to school. In France, these career decisions are made for you long before you have any idea what you want to do in life.

'I need to tell you something,' Alice says.

Her voice is quiet and her eyes wet.

'There's this job... in a gallery. It starts in a few weeks... and... well, I'm going to take it.'

Here she pauses.

'The thing is, it's... it's in London. So...'

The suggestion is implicit. We will return together. But she never asks, and I never mention it. She knows as well as I do: for me, going back is out of the question. I've only just arrived. I am in Paris, and I am going to stay. That much I do know. At least until I've achieved something – even if it's just learning French.

For the next two weeks we pass like ships in the night. Coming and going when the other is out. The temperature now begins to radically drop. The radio says it is the coldest winter in Paris in years. In the apartment the air is practically the same as outside. My solution is to spend more time in cafés, which means spending a little more. Eking out a coffee over a couple of hours on a table by a radiator. Yesterday's paper in front of me covered in biro marks, a second-hand English–French dictionary on my left.

There is a certain irony in it. Within a month or so of my encounter with the waiter next door, my life has been thrown upside down. Instead of pitying him, I now envy him. I desperately need what he has: a job and somewhere to live. And the clock is against me. Alice will be gone in two weeks.

In the days following Alice's announcement I throw myself into some profound soul-searching – eventually concluding that school and university have successfully built me up for a world that no longer exists. If anything, I am worse off than when I started university – with a large debt to remind me in case I forget. I resolve to embrace the fact that I have no money and no friends in Paris (as, in an incredible act of solidarity, the friends of Alice's whom I have met since arriving quickly disappear once they get wind of my decision not to return to London with her). I also decide that if I am going to pick myself up then I am going to do so from the bottom, which in itself, once I accept it, comes as a relief. I just need to prove that I can do it, that I can do something. I've done crap jobs already, but this time it's different. I will stay in Paris and have an adventure, see where it takes me. Besides, it is the only thing I can do: I have nothing else.

A weight is lifting – as my focus sharpens to the immediate future. Forget about the career rejections, the failures of London, the pressure to get on with life, to be somebody. Here is a chance to be somebody I am not, or at least I haven't imagined I am. And perhaps, in the process, I'll learn something about myself. Learn who I really am.

There's a moment's silence, then I hear the tall front door to the street bang shut. Then her steps again, fading into the dark city.

The bed is still warm from her. The room even smells faintly of her perfume. That's all that remains.

I assess my situation. The apartment has been paid for until mid-February. That gives me just under four weeks to find a job and find somewhere to live. Either that or go back to England with another failure chalked up on my list.

FINDING A JOB

In Paris there are different levels of eating establishment. You have the neighbourhood bistro or café, which specializes in turning out decent food at reasonable prices as quickly as possible; this is where your average Parisian office worker will go for lunch. At the other end of the scale are the Michelin-starred restaurants and those found in the palatial five-star hotels. Neither of these kinds of place will hire an untrained waiter. The former because they deal in efficiency and what they are looking for is a hardened career waiter, and the latter because they want professionals – often people who have trained at prestigious hotelier schools or climbed the ranks at a neighbourhood bistro. Of course, in between these two extremes lies a whole plethora of restaurants, from anything that is not French cuisine – which in Paris tends towards restaurants serving food from former colonies, such as Morocco, Lebanon or Vietnam – to bistros of varying types.

Having printed off a handful of CVs in an internet café – probably my greatest work of fiction to date – I begin a quest for a job. The plan is simple: in a city with thousands upon thousands of restaurants, I will get a job as waiter.

From dawn to dusk, from dusk to dawn, to every corner of Paris and always in my smartest clothes. Mornings are spent queuing in front of 'temping agencies' that have been hastily installed in recently vacated shops – overlit with tiled floors, a cheap desk and a potted plant. Only to be laughed out for being overqualified. Then the walking. So much walking. But not like before: I'm no longer that romantic literary figure

le flâneur – the Baudelairean artist-poet I saw myself as when I arrived –
I'm a jobseeker.

There is no restaurant or bar in the whole of Paris that I won't go into.
I have a dog-eared pocket map of the city and a dogged determination.

The process is, on the whole, humiliating. CVs placed in bins before
my very eyes, sniggers of pity as I walk back out. The fraternity of Parisian
waiters seems intent on keeping me out. However, on the plus side, by the
end of the first two weeks I can pass off speaking French, having slowly
learned a monologue about looking for work. With a few Gallic shoulder
shrugs thrown in for good measure I'm starting to look local.

Some cash-in-hand jobs turn up too, including one picking up empty
glasses in a busy bar. For three nights I work: 7pm to 3am. On the fourth
night I turn up and am greeted by the kid whose job I'd taken.

'We don't need you anymore,' he sniggers.

Things are starting to get desperate.

Climbing the creaking stairs to the apartment, I can see the waiter's
shadow through the crack under his door; his radio is on in the background (a football match), the smell of stale cigarettes seeps out onto
the landing. Over the last weeks my thoughts have kept on coming back
to him. The miserable creature in his windowless room. At least he has a
room. A room and some kind of job. In my desperation I decide to knock.
I hear the radio turn down, then nothing. I knock again. There's another
pause, then eventually the door opens slightly and his miserable foxlike
face pokes through the gap. Without me saying anything he launches into
a defence about the radio:

'_____ I can't listen to the radio? Eh? _____! *Espèce de con
d'anglais de merde...*'

I ask him in laboured French if he's a waiter. He looks at me as if I'm
mocking him.

'...I look for a job,' I continue in my best French. 'As waiter.'

He sucks through his pursed lips, relishing the moment; it's like he's
been waiting all his life for it. The door opens wide, and he stands up
straight in his thick dressing gown.

'You think that *you* _____ waiter?' He laughs.

A fake laugh. 'You can't _____ a waiter. It's a real *métier*. _____!'

He begins to close the door.

'*Attends.*'

'*Quoi?*' he spits.

'Where you work? Um, job for me?'

'Where I work?' he says with incredulity. 'You think _____ piece-of-shit Englishmen like you? I work _____ fine French restaurant. _____ _____ important people in Paris. You? A dirty *chômeur*? Work with me? *T'es fou.*'

And with that he slams his door and turns up the radio.

Espèce de merde d'anglais was pretty easy to understand, but *chômeur*, it's the first time I've heard that word. Back in my freezing room I look it up. It literally means someone who doesn't produce work. Someone unemployed. But it seems a dirty word: *un chômeur*. Someone who lives to do nothing.

By the beginning of the third week I've started rationing my meals to reheated tinned lentils and bread. I've taken an express elevator down to the basement of the job world in which I'm still having no luck. As an oily-haired temping man tells me, 'These jobs aren't for you. Go and get an office job.' But there are none of those. That's what he doesn't understand.

I'm about to give up hope entirely when an Irish barman working in Pigalle gives me a tip. He says he knew a girl who had worked as an *hôtesse* at 'this restaurant in town', and that she'd made good money. In almost childlike cursive he writes the name down: Le Bistrot de la Seine. It's the end of the day, my last day, I have decided, of looking for restaurant work. The Irishman's description isn't exactly encouraging. From what I can understand, Le Bistrot de la Seine is no neighbourhood bistro, but neither is it a Michelin-starred dining experience – it is somewhere in between, styling itself as a kind of mecca where fashion and fine dining meet. For the *beau monde* it's the place to go to be seen, but also where tourists have a shot at eating, too. He says that it isn't excessively expensive, but neither is it cheap. In essence, the Bistrot encapsulates contemporary Paris, its obsessions with appearances mostly. As if to confirm this he gives me a final piece of information about the girl who used to work there: 'Very pretty. Liked to say she was a model. Can't say that was true, but I can confirm that she was a total bitch.'

It's the end of the afternoon and already dark outside. The heavy entrance doors of Le Bistrot de le Seine deposit me into an even darker antechamber with a lectern and a tiny brass reading lamp glowing. Leaning over it, as if in study, a tall man in an incredibly expensive-looking suit.

'*Bonjour,*' he says inquisitively.

He's the *directeur*, he corrects me, not the manager. '*Schweeler le directeur...*'

As I give him my monologue he remains silent.

Eventually, lips pursed and followed by a haze of rich perfume, he steps out from behind the lectern and looks me up and down – the way a farmer might regard a disappointing stud at a cattle market.

'_____ _____ *commencer quand?*' he says curtly.

Gone is the servile manner in which he'd whispered *bonjour* when I arrived.

I can start immediately, I tell him.

'*Bon. Faut qu'* _____ *à six heures.*' He speaks with a clipped tone now. A hint of disgust at my presence, of having to breathe the same air as me, an *Untermensch*, a former *flâneur*, now *chômeur*. A wannabe waiter.

'*Le matin?*'

'*Evidemment, le matin.* _____.' The second phrase is not said in a friendly way.

I thank him and turn to leave.

'*Attends,*' he barks.

I turn with a touch too much servitude that surprises even me.

Looking down his nose, the *directeur* raises his glance from my feet to my face and adds – while looking at my brown boots, grey trousers, blue shirt and grey jacket: '*Avec des chaussures noires, un costume noir, une chemise blanche et un nœud papillon noir.*'

I bid the *directeur* farewell. I haven't understood if I have a job, or perhaps a trial shift, or even an interview with someone else. All I know is that I have an hour before the shops close, and I need a cheap black suit, a white shirt, black leather shoes and the last thing he had asked me for – a black-something-butterfly, which turns out to mean a bow tie. I know the word for butterfly because I've recently finished *Papillon* by Henri Carrière, in which he recounts his time sentenced to hard labour on a French penal colony. On the front cover was an enormous butterfly. Looking back, the universe may have been trying to tell me something.

La Descente

Bitterly cold, 5.45am. At the bottom of the Rue de Belleville where the road turns to *pavés*, there are still a few Chinese prostitutes in fake furs standing in dark doorways. I rumble past them on Alice's old bicycle. Their dark eyes watch me, silently. There's a smell of cigarette smoke and then the odourless cold again.

Outside a cheap hotel a night porter smokes under a streetlamp, collar up around his ears, hands thrust deep into his pockets. In the Marais a smell of croissants fills the air. People say Paris smells of piss, but in the morning it smells of croissants.

The rhythmic clicking of the bicycle as it echoes off the old stone walls. Suddenly flashing white light spills into the street. Inside an expensive lingerie boutique, the lights are all on. Below towering television screens of half-naked goddesses, an old Black man in a blue waistcoat vacuums the floor. He doesn't once look up. I sail past, a shadow.

Silence again.

Over the Rue de Rivoli. A couple of taxis with their green lights on, stalking, looking for a ride to finish the night. On the metal vent in front of a department store a man lies face down as if he has just fallen there. There's no movement, only his knotted black hair blowing slightly in the stale warm air that breathes out of the vent. It was minus seven last night.

Back into the 4th arrondissement, pedalling hard. I hear it before I see it, that straining, whining sound. Then the orange bursts of light on the walls, the coarse shouts of the men and the slamming shut of plastic lids. The smell as you approach the truck is always the same, a sour reek, as

Orwell described it. The men in their green overalls hop up onto the metal platforms, the bin truck lurches forward and disappears around a corner.

Silence again.

Now the Seine. The horse chestnut trees are bare and lifeless. You can smell the cold river on the *quais* below. A river barge noses its way into the current, barely moving. Its cargo is so heavy that the gunwales are almost at water level. To the west, below a starless sky – Paris, in all its twinkling, dirty, majestic, slumbering glory.

Soon after, a slow, deliberate, scratching sound. Under a streetlamp a figure dressed in green is hunched over a broom, moving along the gutter between the cars.

Paris, early morning, still night; February – an enormous theatre devoid of its main cast. Only the stagehands working in the shadows, setting the scene.

I lock the bike against the iron railings, then hurry past the brass plaque with the restaurant's name. Stretching out before me is a long terrace. Hundreds of chairs aligned in perfect order. The small square below is completely empty. Just the orange streetlights, ablaze in the thin haze of the dark morning.

Inside the restaurant there's a lone light on behind the lectern, but the front door is locked – like a shrine. I knock. A woman – tall, black, elegant, indifferent – walks to the door in a tightly wrapped shawl and opens it with a quiet '*Bonjour.*' She has a face from a Modigliani portrait, slender and melancholic.

'*Ça caille.*' It's freezing, I say, blowing on my hands. It's something that Alice always said in the apartment when we could see our breath in the air.

'*Oui,*' she responds. 'You _____ be the new runner. Valentine,' she says in French and holds out a cold, slender hand. '*Enchantée.*'

I follow Valentine up the red-carpeted stairs I saw yesterday and into a large dark space. It's the dining room: silhouettes of tables and chairs. A smell of wood polish mixed with the perfume of flowers.

'*Attends ici,*' Valentine says.

She disappears, an exaggerated swinging of the hips as she walks, and I wonder what on earth a runner is. Perhaps it's what they call the waiters here.

When Valentine returns it's to yesterday's paper at the bar at the far end of the dining room. She says nothing to me. It's so quiet in the restaurant that I can hear the pages falling through the air as she turns them. I'm about to remind her I'm here when the old parquet flooring creaks under the carpets. I turn to see someone walking towards me.

'*Viens avec moi,*' he says.

We head towards a black door marked '*Privé*' at the back of the dining room. A tingle of excitement: I'm finally going through – I'm passing to the other side.

The door closes behind me. The two of us make our way along a passageway with whitewashed walls. Halfway along is a small opening leading to a narrow stone stairwell. Before there was a restaurant here this building must have had another use, and we're now in the service area of what was probably once a private mansion or a palace. Without turning around the guy says something to me about never going upstairs. '*Interdit,*' he says, pointing as if towards heaven, or the surface world of mortals.

We take the steps down. Turning a corner, we suddenly hear noises drifting up from deeper underground: muffled voices, shouts, clattering. The kitchens, perhaps? But we never get there. Before reaching whatever lies at the bottom of the stairs, we turn off and step down into a small whitewashed cellar.

'Wait here,' he says.

When he returns he has a plastic bucket of boiling water that smells strongly of vinegar and has a handful of sliced lemons floating in it. In the dim light of the small cellar I can see now that he's probably only a little older than me. He has a handsome, wide face and dark brown hair with a fast, expressive mouth under a large Gallic nose.

'_____?' He points to a dozen grey plastic boxes of cutlery stacked in the corner of the small stone room. '_____ cleaning. No _____ soap _____.'

I guess he wants the cutlery cleaned.

'Coffee?'

'Sure.'

'I'm Lucien,' he says indifferently.

We shake hands.

'_____ accent?' he asks.

'English.'

'*Anglais, chic.* Good luck,' he says in English.

Lucien leaves me alone in the small, cold, whitewashed cell. A closer look at the cutlery and it's clear it needs polishing to get the soap stains off, not to mention the dried food that whoever cleaned it missed. It's an endless job that involves plunging my hands into boxes of knives and forks, a process that punctures my waterlogged skin, before plunging them into the vinegar and lemon water, which makes them sting like hell.

From somewhere below the unmistakable noises of the kitchen continue to float up: clanking, hissing and the slamming shut of doors. Occasionally voices, too, indistinct, unintelligible...

I look forward to the coffee that Lucien said he'd bring, but he never does.

Opening Up

At 6.40am Lucien returns and we head back up to the dining room. The lights are all still off and Valentine has disappeared. Lucien says nothing, we work in silence, me copying him. First the shutters. Enormous wooden things that creak as they open to reveal the end of the Parisian night. Our hands are cold, the heating is not yet on. We work in the dark, by the sulphuric orange of the streetlamps that radiates through the windows. There's something relaxing about it, as though we are still asleep or dreaming – ghosts in the city. Outside, the occasional taxi rumbles down the boulevard, lights begin to come on in windows high up in the building opposite. Paris awakening. It will be a grey day, a cold mist hangs in the air.

'*Putain, il fait froid.* _____,' says Lucien. 'Unless you are in zee office. Zen you 'ave a nice little 'eater,' he adds in English for my benefit.

I look in the direction of 'the office', towards the darkness and the mystical source of heat. I assume that's where Valentine is, Valentine with the pretty face and swinging hips, but I don't want to ask Lucien as he'll realize how bad my French is. I stick to my well-rehearsed Gallic shrugs.

'_____ smoke?'

I don't particularly want to smoke at this time, but if I understand Lucien correctly, he's telling me it's the last break we'll have for the next few hours.

'If you don't smoke… start,' he says in heavily accented English once we're outside. 'You sink you can take a pause if you simply say you want to stand… *comment dire?* outside? Never, *mon ami*. Never.' He laughs.

31

'To smoke, it is to be free.'

I smile.

Delicate plumes of blue smoke rise up from our cigarettes in the bitingly cold air which stings the ears. The small road behind the restaurant is quiet. Elsewhere the city is coming to life. You can feel it. The sound of Paris as she wakes. Traffic, sirens, the occasional deep rumbling from a Métro train somewhere.

A small delivery truck covered in graffiti appears with a screech and stops in the middle of the one-way street. A lean-looking driver steps down with a clipboard and a lit cigarette and opens up the back. He begins hauling a massive sack onto his shoulder when suddenly, from out of the small black door that leads to the back of the restaurant, a short, Indian-looking guy appears and shouts at him in a mixture of broken French and some other language. The delivery is late, is about as much as I can understand. The two men proceed to shout at each other with an incredible amount of violence.

Lucien doesn't seem to find this remotely interesting, and when his cigarette is almost finished he lights a second with the glowing nub of the first and stamps his feet for warmth. With nothing left to distract us he asks me if I've worked in restaurants before. He asks me in English. I answer with all the insouciance I can muster. He doesn't probe too much; in fact he doesn't really seem that interested in me, which is a relief. I desperately want to ask him what the hell a runner is and what I am meant to do today, and even if I'm on a trial shift, but I'm also terrified that I'll get rumbled for being a complete fraud with absolutely no real experience of restaurant work. So instead I stay mute and just pray to God I'll get through whatever it is I'm expected to do, and that this is indeed a real job and that I can stay in Paris and everything will be all right.

'Coffee?' Lucien asks for the second time this morning.

'Sure.'

We finish our second smokes and head back inside. However, before I can set foot inside, Valentine has appeared.

'What are you doing? Take this. Go. Go and clean the terrace. It's a
_____.'

I take the brush and turn for the terrace.

'Not like that. _____. We're opening soon.' And
with that she's gone.

Thankfully, Lucien clarifies. 'When the restaurant is open, you have
to be in uniform.'

I look at him blankly.

'No jacket.'

I reluctantly hand him my trench coat, from which he takes my wallet
and cheap Nokia phone and, handing them back to me, says something
about being suspicious of waiters, but to trust him. He then closes the
door behind him. As I work, the frozen air of Paris washes over my cheap
synthetic jacket like an ice-cold river. I really hate the suit. It doesn't fit
correctly but it was all I could find last night. I diligently sweep the terrace
and the pavements until my hands are blue and stinging from the cold and
my teeth are chattering. Eventually I head back in.

For the remainder of the morning I'm sent by either Valentine or
Lucien to do various tasks, often in subterranean caves and always alone,
such as polishing the rest of the cutlery, polishing the glasses and finally,
sorting, ironing and folding all of the white tablecloths and serviettes,
which are in such a state that I can only assume they've been ironed by
some primitive robot that is being trained to perform some kind of giant
textile origami. I am quickly learning the French concern for the appearance of things. All the while, from elsewhere in this underground ants'
nest – deeper underground, closer to hell – come shouting and the strange
smells of food being cooked. They increase in intensity as we get closer to
lunch. Becoming more potent, more mysterious. I fight a strong desire
to go and have a nose around. To fill in the blanks of the mental map I'm
creating of the restaurant.

By 10am I'm hungry and very thirsty, but I've no idea where I go to get
water and I'm keen to keep a low profile, so I continue working. Perhaps
this is the job, polishing and ironing. That suits me fine, although the
request that I wear a black suit seems a bit excessive.

Eventually Lucien returns and, with a cynical smile, simply says, '*L'Anglais*, come. _____. *C'est l'heure.*' It's time.

This sounds incredibly ominous. I put down my iron and follow him. My watch says 11.30am.

The Waiters

Among waiters your worth is measured according to two criteria: tips and covers – how much money you made in the course of a 'service', and how many people you served. The more of both the better.

Lucien leads me to the low-ceilinged room we passed earlier when he led me down to the cellars. Before it was empty; now, however, there are half a dozen men standing there, going through their final preparations before the lunch service.

'*Hé! Les gars. Voici le nouveau. L'Anglais.*' Hey, guys, meet the new one. The English guy. Lucien introduces me.

The men ignore me, like veteran pilots would a rookie. I figure they know that I probably won't survive beyond the lunch shift, let alone long enough for them to bother learning my name. But I remember theirs – who could forget such a group of misfits? They look more like a well-dressed street gang than waiters in a posh Parisian restaurant.

'This is the Pass,' Lucien says, pointing to a low rectangular hole in the back wall of the small room. It's about two metres long, half a metre in height, runs along at waist height and glows red, like the gates of hell, from the heat lamps that hang there. Beyond it is another room, but the Pass is so low it's difficult to make anything out in there.

The atmosphere in the Pass area is one of nervous expectation: like actors in the wings before a performance, or soldiers in the trenches before an attack. The air is bitingly cold, just as it is outside, but there's also a reassuring smell of coffee and stale cigarettes.

'Right, that's De Souza,' Lucien continues in French.

A short man, impeccably dressed with gelled-back dark hair and a handsome, slightly large and tanned face with a nose that was once broken. Full of nervous energy – always on the balls of his feet and moving. His suit clings tightly to his body and shines in the orange half-light of the caged bulb in the Pass. He's using a knife from the dining room to scrape dried stains from his jacket front and sleeves. Occasionally it catches the light with a flash. De Souza looks up and I feel his eyes scan me from head to foot as he takes the measure of me.

'*Ça va?*' he says.

'There you've got Jamaal.'

Jamaal is kneeling down on the floor, pouring olive oil from one of the table sets onto a white serviette and polishing his battered shoes. His hair is thinning.

'*Ça va, mon frère?,*' he says.

Jamaal stands up with some difficulty. He's overweight, with sweat on his temples. His suit looks cheap next to De Souza's. Jamaal is North African-looking, possibly Algerian, with a receding hairline and bulbous, slightly crossed eyes, under dark, heavy lids.

'*Alors?*' He catches my eye and throws a glance down at his shoes. The old leather has taken on an aqueous sheen, like they're wet or freshly painted.

'Give it here,' De Souza says.

The blackened serviette is thrown among the men before being tossed into a bag where the other dirty serviettes will go during the service.

'Tomorrow all white again and back on the tables.' Jamaal winks.

'_____.'

'_____.'

'_____.'

The men at the Pass all laugh. I've no idea what they're saying, or whether they're laughing at me.

'Hey, Renaud,' Lucien says.

A large pot of gel sits on the side, and Renaud is dunking his dirty fingers into it before running them through his short black curly hair while trying to catch a glimpse of his reflection in one of the dull metal refrigerator doors. There's something instantly dislikeable about Renaud. His eyes are almost black, like a ferret's, and he's poorly shaved. He's older, late thirties perhaps; a career waiter, with a round head, weak chin and an untrustworthy mouth. He doesn't say anything, just nods with a sharp upward motion. I watch as he pulls his waiter's wallet from inside his jacket and begins counting the notes, the way an assassin might check a loaded gun. He takes a ritual pleasure in it. Knowing that I can see: 'This is what I made last night,' he's saying, as the thick wad of notes flicks across his soiled fingernail. The others begin to do the same.

'At least two hundred *couverts* yesterday...' Renaud seems to be talking to no one and everyone.

'Bullshit!' De Souza cuts him off.

' _____,' Lucien adds.

Renaud catches me looking at him.

'*Quoi, l'Anglais? T'as un problème?*' His thin lips recoil to reveal a miserable set of teeth.

'Oi, got any fives? I'm out.' Jamaal hits up Renaud. He'll need them to give change, I guess.

'No, mate,' he lies.

A man with a mop of dirty, almost greasy blond hair and a pitted face arrives in a cloud of smoke from a cramped hole-in-the-floor toilet just off the Pass. He has a wiry frame, yellow teeth and a bellicose disposition.

'Hey, Adrien,' Lucien slaps his back. '*Voici l'Anglais.*'

Adrien shakes my hand limply and talks to Lucien as if I don't exist.

'*C'est qui?*'

'*Le nouveau runner.*' There's that word again.

Adrien is uninterested. He leans down to the hole in the wall and shouts aggressively while banging his hand on the aluminium top so that the silver ring he is wearing clanks loudly: 'Oi! Where's my coffee?'

Words drift out, I can't quite make them out, they don't sound French. Moments later a hand from the other side slams an espresso down and disappears. Adrien takes it, drinks it in one go and bangs it back down on the metal surface.

A barrage of shouts erupts from inside the dark room beyond the hole. The same hand picks up the dirty cup and throws it into a plastic box at the other end of the Pass. The cup shatters.

'*Putain!*' Adrien leans down and sends a torrent of violent abuse into the darkness. It's met with equal ferocity, though again the words are not French, or at least I don't think they are. It's hard to say because Adrien repeats them before walking off, leaving the voice coming out of the dark hole.

'He's the head waiter. The Untouchable,' Lucien says with a smile. 'Coffee?'

Lucien leans down and shouts into the dark room, 'Oi, Nimsath! *Deux cafés...*'

'*Tre,*' the tall, well-built man leaning against the wall filing his fingernails interjects in what sounds like Italian.

The coffees appear. Bitter, acidic stuff.

'*Caffè de merde francese. Cazzo,*' the man with the accent says into the hole before smiling at me.

He's Sicilian – Salvatore. Bright blue eyes and thick brown hair. Big, like a bear. As he stirs his espresso I feel his cold eyes upon me. He nods his head towards the hole in the wall and smiles again. 'What's this shit _____ coffee, hey?'

'*Ta gueule,* Sal.' Shut your face, comes the foreign voice from the darkness beyond the Pass.

Salvatore leans down: 'You know that we love you, darling.' He blows kisses into the dark like a circus chimpanzee.

Something indecipherable comes out.

From one of the passageways a small old man with a quick step, bushy white eyebrows and thick glasses appears with a worn copy of the sports paper *L'Équipe* under his arm.

'Franjo, can I introduce—'

The old man raises his hand to stop Lucien talking. He puts the sports newspaper on the Pass and disappears with his small, fast footsteps. The waiters rush to grab it.

'The sommelier,' Lucien says to me. 'Franjo.'

'Which team?' Salvatore the Sicilian asks me.

I shrug my shoulders.

'*Un Anglais qui n'aime pas le foot!*' Renaud says with exaggerated incredulity.

'_____' Jamaal adds.

'_____ PSG,' someone says, referring to Paris Saint-Germain, the leading local team.

The rest laugh at me before going back to ignoring me and preparing for the service. I drink my coffee and watch, unsure what else I should do. Unsure of what my role is here. Unsure for the most part what they're saying, or indeed doing.

The waiters take immense pride in their appearance. From looking at them you can see that almost all of them have had their suits adjusted. They look fitted and expensive, even if they are not. I'm even more conscious of mine, a cheap, ill-fitting thing. I look like an '80s accountant, whereas these guys look like they've just stepped out of a Dolce & Gabbana advert.

Lucien shows me his ornate cufflinks and asks me to look closely at his bow tie. 'My grandfather's,' he says. 'Hermès.'

'Hermès. Hah,' Adrien, the head waiter, the Untouchable, taunts him. He turns to me. 'You know that Lucien _____ church now? _____ *bon petit catholique.*'

'Bullshit. It's real. _____ *putain de serveurs,*' Lucien replies.

I have no idea what they are talking about. So I just nod. The waiters begin to crowd around me.

'*Ça, c'est mon truc.*' De Souza points to his black shirt studs. '*D'accord?*'

'*Regarde-moi ça,*' Adrien says, encouraging me to touch the floral stitching on his lapel.

Salvatore, I think, tells me that his suit shoulders are soft, in the '*style napolitain*'.

De Souza mocks his shoes as being too pointed.

'*Va fan culo, stronzo!*' Salvatore responds.

They're each showing me the little *something* that is their sign, but it's also a warning: 'Stay off my territory,' they're saying.

One of the waiters tugs at my suit, and the rest of them begin laughing and pointing at it. '*Pitoyable,*' someone says. Another waiter even pretends to light it with his lighter.

Suddenly the sound of high heels echoing off flagstones. In the background a blonde woman with a heavy face and large jaw, perhaps mid-thirties, wearing too much make-up and holding a big leather book, appears.

'Ah, Pauline...,' Lucien says.

Her searing look silences him. She opens the book and tells the waiters sequences of numbers that mean nothing to me. They huddle around the book, the reservations book I think, muttering names to each other and smiling or cursing. I recognize some of the names she says – famous people, politicians, actors and the like. Salvatore pinches Pauline's bum, she raises her eyes and glances quickly around the Pass to see me looking at her and asks him who I am.

'Dunno,' Salvatore says with a smile.

'*T'es qui?*' she demands coldly.

'*Le runner,*' I say.

But even as I say it, I'm not sure if I am, or indeed what exactly it entails; it's just what everyone has been calling me since I walked into the restaurant this morning. The runner.

'*Et le dernier?*' she asks Salvatore.

Before he answers more footsteps – the squeaking of leather – echo down the corridor. This time slow, purposeful – ominous. Pauline closes the large reservations book with a snap, turns and leaves, shooing the waiters out of her way with a tired '*Dégagez*' as they make last-bid attempts to convince her to change her mind about the sequences of numbers.

'*Cazzo! Il direttore,*' Salvatore says. Again, that smile.

He must mean the *directeur*. The man I met last night.

There's a quick glance between the waiters; something changes, they're men now, not boys. They turn to each other and check their bow ties with a fraternal tenderness. Coffee cups disappear. They stand together, me apart.

Suddenly the door bangs against the wall. The *directeur*, with his large head, mass of thin hair and chest pushed forwards, marches down the steps like a Napoleonic general bellowing something which finishes with '*Il y a du monde déjà!*' Which I roughly understand as 'There is already the world', but soon learn means 'It's already busy.'

The waiters head for the still-swinging door. Back across the threshold to return to the surface world and the dining room. The *directeur* stands there a moment in the weak light watching them disappear, a touch of pride, a touch of pity; finally his eyes fall upon me. As he takes in my cheap suit, his mouth pulls taut like someone who has just drunk sour milk.

'You've definitely worked in a restaurant before?' he asks again; there's a touch of worry in his voice.

'*Oui,*' I assure him for the second time.

'_____ work with Lucien. _____. *D'accord?*

'*D'accord.*'

He smooths down the front of his suit. It is a light blue colour, finely cut, with a powder-yellow silk tie. Eventually he inhales deeply, draws himself up tall and disappears into the dining room with one hand ahead of him and the other trailing slightly behind.

Adrien, the head waiter, who has hung back, pulls me aside. '*L'Anglais,*' he slips his hand into his pocket and removes his wallet, 'if you want, I can get you one. A nice waiter's wallet. Real leather. If you want to be a Parisian waiter, you must.' He grins. His teeth are like small yellow crystals. Inside the wallet there must be three hundred euros. His breath smells of old fags and coffee.

'*Combien?*' I enquire.

'*Pour toi,* forty.'

'I'll think about it,' I lie. I may want to be a waiter – in fact, no, from what I've seen this morning, I really do want to be a waiter – but not at that price.

Lunch

The lunch service is beginning. Groups of customers are threading through the busy dining room in the wake of what look like off-duty models but in the restaurant are known as *hôtesses*. The customers can't help but watch their impossibly long legs, scanning them from their high heels to the short skirts that cling to their hips. The giant windows that look down onto the small square below are covered in condensation from the radiators, filling the room with a strange kind of ethereal white light. It's warm in here now and the smell of wood polish has been replaced by the perfumes of the customers, of hairspray, cologne; outside, the frozen city is forgotten to us. The dining room is opulent, with large marble fireplaces at either end. The carpet that covers the dark wooden parquet floor is thick and a deep red like the hostesses' lipstick.

'You worked in restaurants before?' It's Lucien who asks this time.

We're by one of the service stations in the main dining room. A kind of relay post where supplies are stored: glasses, cutlery, serviettes and so on. The cutlery I spent three hours polishing this morning. I recognize the host from the evening news show being led to a corner table. He's smaller than I imagined, but more tanned.

'*Oui*,' I say.

'*En* _____ *runner?*' he says.

To change topic, I deftly mention the news presenter and say that he has nice hair.

'*Quoi?*' Lucien responds.

I later learn that he thought I said the TV presenter had nice horses. 'Anyway, where's your *plateau*?' he asks.

'My what?'

'*Viens.*'

We return through the swinging door and down the long, narrow whitewashed passage, back to the room with the Pass. Lucien takes a giant silver tray in his hand and shoves it into mine. He's clearly resentful that he has been landed with me.

'This. You know how to hold it? Yes or no? Wait.'

He takes one of the olive oil-covered serviettes from the laundry bag and polishes the *plateau* until it shines like the shield of Perseus. He puts it on my upturned hand and begins to place empty wine glasses upon it. The tray feels ungainly.

'Always start in the middle.' The glasses tickle against one another. 'Then work your way inwards – towards the arm.' He pushes down on the inside of the tray to make his point. The tip of the tray rises upwards and the glasses in the middle slide towards me. '*Attention.*' He pulls it back down, then continues to load the tray with glasses until it is completely full.

I go to ease the weight with my right hand.

'*Non!*' he snaps. 'Never two hands. Only one hand ever holds the *plateau.*'

Finally, he takes a clean white serviette, folds it lengthwise and places in the crook of my arm that's holding the tray aloft. The tray, with its delicate cargo, is an accident waiting to happen.

'*Bien.*' He stands back and looks at me, happy with his work – I must look something like a waiter.

'I do what?' I finally ask in halting French.

'*Quoi?*'

'The runner. What does he do?'

Lucien laughs. It's a sinister kind of laugh.

'*C'est simple:* you run!' He sniggers and pats me on the shoulder patronizingly.

I look at him blankly and finally see a touch of pity in his eyes.

'Listen,' he continues quietly in English, not wanting anyone else to know he's telling me this, 'you come here… to the Pass… you collect glasses, cutlery, drinks, plates, food… everything. Then you take them to the tables. OK? When you come back you bring anything dirty. Everything dirty. As fast as possible. You never stop. *Compris?*'

'*Oui.*' I go to put the tray down, my arm is aching.

'*Non. On y va.* Oh, and one last thing: if you _____ your salary.'

Lucien disappears into the dining room. I try to follow but it's impossible. There must be at least sixteen tall, incredibly delicate wine glasses on the tray. And every time I try to move they slide perilously close to the edge – taunting me with their jingling sound. Whoever thought of using a giant metal tray to transport fragile glasses must never have used one. Unable to go forwards and hunched over like Quasimodo, gripped by a fear of all the glasses falling and shattering into thousands of tiny pieces, I finally give up and take the tray in two hands. Backing awkwardly into the swinging door like an elderly driver.

Once out in the restaurant I see Lucien. He's a world away and the room is suddenly a lot busier, with tables of customers talking animatedly, waiters darting about, hostesses parading with clipboards, managers prowling. It's a gauntlet. I literally shuffle through the room, staring intently at the glasses as the other waiters play a game with me which involves flitting past me as close as possible to see if I'll drop anything while making snarky comments. It's a cross between sledging in cricket and the kind of training a Spitfire pilot had when he arrived at his squadron and the aces would fly out of the sun and 'buzz' him. My dreams of becoming a waiter are about to shatter with these sixteen oversized wine glasses.

'Here. And one hand. What did I tell you?' Lucien snaps before turning and smiling at the customers.

I lean down to put the tray on the edge of the table.

'*Putain*, what are you doing?' He says it under his breath, then looks around at the table to make sure no one heard. 'Never put the tray on the table. *Jamais.*' He glances over my shoulder, whisks the tray out of my hand and says something which ends in 'table'.

Unsure, I begin to place the glasses on the table when, from nowhere, there's a voice in my ear.

'*Très bien.*'

The *directeur* is leering over my shoulder with his hands together like a priest. He smiles, a thin smile. '*Plus vite,*' he says, and with this he's gone. Sashaying between the tables serving stone-cold smiles to the seated guests with the occasional squeeze of a shoulder or hand resting on a diner's back.

'He's right. You're too slow,' Lucien grumbles.

As we leave the table the elderly sommelier is presenting wine to the customers with an immense sense of importance and occasion. Even the manner in which he holds the bottle, like a vicar performing a christening, makes it seem like something of great value.

Lucien and I make several trips to the Pass and back, working together. He takes the orders, then we collect the drinks from the Pass and head out to the table, whereupon I stand in silence like a footman as he places the drinks on the table from my tray. I can tell he doesn't like it. He's embarrassed and the other waiters keep making jibes at him – '*le babysitter*', they're now calling him. Meanwhile they go about their business with the elegance of matadors. Pirouetting between the tables, their *plateaux* aloft and gleaming, stacked in gravity-defying ways full of drinks orders. The way they handle their *plateaux* is admirable. Swinging in all directions, even when they're fully loaded.

I watch Adrien, the head waiter, exit the Pass, his tray heavy with drinks, yet perched upon the tips of his fingers. Coming towards him at speed, his *plateau* also fully loaded, is the little pretend-boxer with the broken nose, De Souza. They seem set for a collision, but at the very last moment, choreographed to perfection, they swing their trays to almost vertical in opposite directions and glide past each other – like a fighter-jet display team. All this is going on above the customers' heads, yet few seem to notice. Nonetheless all the waiters are at it. Playing their roles exquisitely in this vast culinary amphitheatre.

After the drinks are out and the food has been ordered there's a lull and we're all back at the Pass. Lucien gives me a crash course in the layout of the restaurant and the table numbers – I now understand what Pauline was saying earlier. All those sequences of numbers. She was giving out the tables. Each waiter has his own territory, or *rang*, as they call it here: rank.

'You see a ticket with my *rang*, you take it,' Lucien says.

'*Hé! Moi aussi, mon ami*,' De Souza adds, between shadow-boxing upper cuts. 'Keep your guard up. Always keep your guard up.' He lifts my hands in front of my face and proceeds to shadow-box, which includes landing a few punches on my head.

'Eh, he works for all of us,' Adrien, the head waiter, with his pitted face and red eyes, snaps.

The waiters come at me from all directions with demands that I work for them, spitting sequences of table numbers and what I understand to be offers of split tips. I nod in agreement and keep saying, '*Bien sûr*', of course, with absolutely no idea what they're talking about. There's something vaguely threatening about the way in which they speak to me when they're not ignoring me.

'You see mine, you take them,' the evil-looking Renaud hisses.

'Don't be slow. Don't fuck it up,' Lucien says. 'You heard the *directeur*.'

'*Comme le dernier!*' Adrien grunts.

'*Espèce de runner de merde*,' Salvatore adds. His opinion of the previous runner is clearly very low.

'What happened to the last runner?' I finally ask.

No one answers.

A number of small, elegantly arranged plates are pushed out of the wall by the hands. The waiters crowd in, digging their elbows into one another.

'*C'est à moi*,' Salvatore says as he scoops them up and onto his tray and heads out.

More plates begin to arrive: smoked salmon, duck *foie gras*, pumpkin soup. Occasionally the sauces have spilt or the contents moved. The waiters carry out final touches with their fingers or serviettes lying about before taking them out to the dining room. Some plates arrive with Lucien's numbers on them. Before I can take them, he pulls me aside: 'You've never worked in a restaurant before, have you? Hey?'

'*Non*,' I finally admit.

He shakes his head and then laughs, that same sardonic grin as earlier.

'I knew it. The others said it, too. What is it then? Student job? Holiday job?'

'No. It's a real job' is all I can articulate.

'You want to be a waiter?'

I shrug my shoulders. 'Yeah.'

'You've got a long way to go.' He takes the starters and puts them on his tray. '*Mais, bon courage.*' He pats my shoulder. '*C'est parti.*' And with that he disappears into the dining room, leaving me alone in the low corridor that leads to the Pass.

Then, for the first time, I see a face lean down and look out of the Pass. It's the small Indian-looking guy I saw earlier. He hands me a coffee. It's the same coffee they serve everywhere in Paris: bitter, rancid stuff. Although this one is cold, clearly one that has been forgotten.

'Engleeshman,' he says in English with a smile.

His name is Nimsath. 'Tamil. Not Indian.' His voice is slow and lyrical. His large eyes and brilliant smile the most welcoming things I've seen since getting in here.

'Engleeshman,' another voice repeats from the other side of the Pass, really drawing out each vowel – as if simply saying 'Englishman' is a great pleasure. But I don't see the face. Just a large midriff. From here I can see that there are three of them on the other side of the Pass. But before I can ask them any more, they've gone. Faded back into the shadows of the room beyond the opening in the wall.

I soon find out why. Corentin, the rodent-featured manager, is standing behind me: 'What are you doing there, *l'Anglais*? Drinking a coffee? _____! _____! Take these... Four-nine-three.'

He shoves me through the door with a boot up the arse and suddenly I'm back in the hushed luxury of the dining room. The place has changed from earlier: it's abuzz, electric; there's a palpable energy as the lunch service is now in full swing. The clicking of cutlery on ceramic, loud conversation. The waiters stalking the aisles like crows, guardians of their individual domains; in the corner the *directeur* surveying the scene; down by the entrance at the ornate gold lectern with the little reading light and the reservations book, the blonde woman, Pauline, looking hostile; a smile when the reservation is confirmed and a glamorous hostess, like

Charon, is given the nod to ferry her cargo up into the dining room. I meanwhile have no idea where 493 is. And after two circuits of the restaurant Corentin reappears. Cursing, he takes my *plateau* and goes to the correct table. Afterwards I see him exchanging words with the *directeur* and eyeballing me.

The entire service passes like this. Back and forth between the tables and the Pass. With every sortie a waiter hisses at me to help him clear a table or to go and get an order. Back and forth, back and forth – it's non-stop. On top of that the waiters seem intent on my downfall. A number of times during the service I'm given dishes, then deliberately sent to incorrect tables – much to the confusion of the customers, who can't understand why I've brought what I have to their table, and on top of that why I can't seem to speak beyond saying I'm sorry and *d'accord*. Naturally the waiters play this game with the others' orders, not their own, which only helps my popularity.

Débarrasser is probably the word I hear most. The waiters say it and point at dirty tables. It means clear the table, I think.

'It's bullshit,' Renaud is saying to Jamaal at the Pass as I hurry down the steps to collect another order. 'I'm telling you, he forgot everything.'

'He won't last,' the overweight, slightly cross-eyed Jamaal assures him in my presence. 'If it was me...'

They both give me a resentful glance, then disappear back into the dining room. Later I hear Adrien slagging me off to De Souza, something about me costing him his tips: 'If he thinks I'm giving him anything, he can forget about it. *Connard*.'

Even Lucien avoids me.

And so it goes on; there's always too much to do, not enough time and never a break. The work continues unabated until early evening, when suddenly Pauline pulls me aside and whispers into my ear, '*Bon, stop*. You can go now.'

And that's when I know it is over.

I put my tray down at the Pass and walk back through the narrow, whitewashed corridors, glad not to see any of the other waiters. The only one I see is Adrien, who respectfully ignores me. There's no sign of Lucien, or the others. None of the aforementioned tips for helping them, either. Not finding Lucien is a problem as it means leaving without my jacket. I try asking after him. But no one can help. He's gone. In the end I leave without it.

I'm fairly certain I'm not even going to be paid for the day, which makes me even more depressed, as the awful suit and shoes cost me €154 or, more precisely, a little under half of the money I have left in my bank account. Passing back through the now almost empty restaurant, all I can think of is that I have literally no idea what I'm going to do next. I can't even keep a trial shift as a runner.

At the entrance the *directeur* is looking over the reservations book with Pauline. They hear my footsteps and look up with polite smiles that disappear the instant they see that it's only me. I stand in front of them as they discuss, in hushed whispers, the contents of the sacred reservations book. 'No, he cannot be sat near them; no, this is not possible; that's not her table' and so on.

'*A demain,*' the *directeur* finally says without looking up.

'*Six heures,*' Pauline says.

Outside the frozen air of Paris hits me in the face like a fist. It's already dark and beginning to snow. I walked in the same door exactly thirteen hours earlier. I haven't eaten since last night and I'm starving. But that's not important. It would appear that I have finally – finally – found a job.

Frozen Out

The following morning, whiteness everywhere – the city has gone. Snow is piled on the roads and perched delicately upon the points of the iron fences around the parks. Paris has been replaced by a soft memory. Everything feels asleep, there is no one, no noise. Everything is frozen; water no longer flows, the clouds, the silence. Everything is in suspense. My cheap leather shoes crunch in the snow, I can't feel my toes, I can't feel anything. The cold has stopped life; it feels like it's just me moving through time. The world of the dead.

It's 5.20am. I'm in a *bar-tabac* on the Rue Saint Honoré drinking a *café allongé* to kill time – I'd woken early because of the cold and, on seeing the snow, been terrified of not being able to get in to work, so left almost immediately. It turned out that the Métro hadn't been affected and now I am half an hour early. On the television in the corner of the room they're talking about the presidential race later this year, though no one can hear because of the hissing of steam from the coffee machine behind the counter. Finally, it stops. Two men come in; I feel the sharp air on my ankles. My toes are still numb from walking on the snow-covered pavements outside, but the café is warm. Since I've arrived in Paris it feels like nowhere is warm, apart from my bed, and I reflect that I badly need a winter jacket instead of my ludicrous second-hand trench coat, which is currently somewhere in the restaurant, or just outright stolen by Lucien.

It's still night outside, long before the city awakes. In the café I take in the reflections in the glass behind the bar – labourers, taxi drivers, delivery men, road sweepers, me – this is the Paris I have come to know.

The woman behind the bar is wearing a black shawl, thick cream socks and rubber sandals. She bangs the metal handle down heavily on the open bin to eject the spent coffee. Once, twice – Bang! Bang! Then she shuffles back over to the little heater to prepare the coffee. One of the men at the bar next to me – a short man with dark eyes and thinning grey hair – is already drinking a *demi* of beer. He looks exhausted, like he's just finished a night shift. He keeps the glass resting on his bottom lip between sips and his eyes fixed on the reflection of the TV in the mirror behind the bar. We watch it together in silence. The hissing restarts, then stops again – Bang! Bang! The news anchor says France is expected to get even colder.

'*Encore plus froid, putain!*' The man finally puts down his beer and picks up yesterday's *Le Parisien* newspaper, starting with the sports pages at the back. By the time he's finished, the current French president's face on the front page is unrecognizable, soaked in the stale beer on the bar. The man orders another *demi*.

Running through what I learned yesterday: the names, the words, the rules. I try and imagine what's going on in the rest of the restaurant, but it's still a blank. But I'm happy: I have a job. Eventually I pay for the coffee, breaking one of my last notes, Alice's apartment keys on the bar in front of me – a sharp reminder that in a week I'm homeless.

'*Bon courage,*' the tired man at the bar says to me as I leave.

'*Merci. Bon courage,*' I reply.

A few of the other men gruffly wish me good luck and a good day. They all say it to one another, knowing that, no matter what we're doing, we're in it together. There's no other reason you'd be here this early.

The street is still, completely empty. The coins in my pocket clink together. My feet slip and crunch through the treacherous snow. The boulevard is deserted, an endless field covered in white scarred by dirt-brown lines. Everything is still. The air is so cold that it stings my face; it has no smell whatsoever. On a plaque above a school, *Liberté – Egalité – Fraternité*, the foundations of the French Republic.

The door to the restaurant is closed and the lights are off like last time. I knock and eventually a face appears from the shadows, the same face as last time, Valentine's – a beautiful face, completely symmetrical, like the bust of Nefertiti.

'*Bonjour,*' she says, hurriedly shutting the door behind me, pulling her shawl tight.

She disappears up the steps, the swinging hips. I follow her into the large dining room in the hope that it will be warmer than outside: it isn't. The heating is not on yet. Along one side of the restaurant the line of tall windows: single-glazed and cold. Beyond them the terrace and then the small empty courtyard covered in virgin snow.

'*Assieds-toi,*' Valentine says.

Seated at a table, watching with his dark shark eyes, Renaud.

'*Salut,*' I say, sitting down and hugging myself for warmth.

Renaud says nothing. Adrien, the head waiter, appears in the background and sits down at a different table, wrapped in a large overcoat. Behind him the door to the Pass and kitchens swings back and forth lethargically on its hinges. When it's open – the sound of plates being stacked; when it shuts – the mysterious sounds are muted. We're back in the restaurant again; dawn hasn't quite advanced.

Adrien grunts, shoves his hands deeper into the pockets of his overcoat and closes his eyes. Eventually Valentine returns with Corentin, the other manager – the skinny man who looks like he's always in a hurry. The one I heard the other waiters refer to as '*le Rat*'. She's saying something to him about me not being on the planning and he's shaking his head.

'What are you doing here?' he asks threateningly. He has a small diamond earring which glistens. 'Stand up.'

A knot in my stomach. Corentin's a short man with a thin face, long teeth and a vulgar grey suit that shines in a way that can only be acceptable for a waiter when he's convinced he's on the way up. He also stands too close when he speaks and his breath smells of stale garlic.

'What you doing here again? You? In this restaurant?'

I want to tell him about the conversation with the *directeur*. However, by the time I've worked out how to say it (lots of past tense and reflexive verbs), the conversation has moved on. He was clearly not consulted when the *directeur* asked me to come back today.

'*Je suis le runner*' is all I manage.

'The runner! You don't look like the runner!'

'Eh,' he says over my shoulder to the other waiters. 'You guys know him?'

'*Oui. C'est l'Anglais,*' Adrien says, sounding half-asleep. It looks like I'm only ever going to be known as that, *l'Anglais*.

There's a silence. Thin-faced Corentin is seething with resentment. He comes right up close, his warm garlic breath on my face.

'*Le directeur—*' I try again.

'Shut up!' He cuts me off. 'I know your type. I don't know what the *directeur* was thinking. _____ _____ _____ _____. Working in a restaurant is a real *métier*. Now piss off.'

He turns to Valentine, says something out of earshot and disappears up the stairs.

I look at her blankly. Have I just been sacked? Why did the *directeur* not tell them he'd asked me to come back today? I feel sick to my stomach.

'*La neige,*' she says.

'*Quoi?*'

'Not everyone's come in. Because of the snow. Your lucky day.'

The managers disappear. Adrien and Renaud say nothing. So much for *fraternité*. We get back to sitting in silence and waiting for something; our breath hangs in the air. My heart beats incredibly fast. In my head I'm trying to piece together a coherent but simple sentence to get clarification from the others about what's going on. Eventually Valentine returns with a phone in her hand.

'Lucien called, he can't—'

'Bullshit.' Renaud stands up. In the dim light you can see his two-day stubble. 'I _____ _____ _____ _____ _____?'

That's a spanner in the works. At least with Lucien I could have spoken a little in English, clarified what's going on. With the others I get the distinct impression that they don't like me. That they don't want to help out. That actually they'd be happier if I was gone. Besides, I don't think they would speak English to me even if they knew how to.

'I'm gonna smoke,' says Adrien.

'I come,' I murmur.

Adrien shrugs. 'Where's your jacket?'

'*Je ne sais pas.* Lucien...'

'You're not cold?'

'Yes.'

Adrien raises his eyebrows, accepts my jacket-less attire as an English quirk, even though it's snowing outside. Perhaps he thinks I'm just really proud of my terrible suit and want to make sure people can see it. God, it's frustrating not being able to express myself.

Pushing his greasy blond hair back Adrien smokes quickly as if he doesn't want to be caught. Adrien is the head waiter, or *maître d'hôtel*. I assume this is why he is referred to as the Untouchable. He has a troubled look. Under the streetlight I can see that his eyes are ringed black from fatigue. There's not an ounce of fat on his body: he's all skin and bone apart from the chaotic mop of greasy blond hair upon his head. The skin on his face is pitted, as though he has severe chickenpox. As *maître d'hôtel* he is higher than the waiters and his word is law. I need to make him like me.

'No one's coming.' Adrien spits a yellow jet over the balustrade and into the snow. '*Putain de merde,*' he adds with frustration, between sucking on the wet end of his cigarette. 'Not good. Not good at all.'

Renaud comes out. We stay grouped together, smoking, waiting. Our ears red from the cold; sniffing and wiping our noses on the backs of our hands.

'Where's your jacket, *l'Anglais*?' Renaud asks, notably more smugly than Adrien.

I shrug my shoulders and try and limit my shivers. The small square in front of the restaurant remains empty, covered in untouched snow, not a single mark. Still no sound from the city, no cars, no sirens, nothing. Everything is white, everything feels dead. *The ghosts of Paris.*

'So, *l'Anglais*, how old's your queen?' Adrien asks. And while the question is bizarre, I appreciate that he's trying.

I make a number up.

'*Sacrée femme,*' he grunts. Incredible woman.

I offer the two men a cigarette. They take two each.

'*Pourquoi il a un problème avec moi?*' It's the simplest construction I can find about the Rat.

'What?' Adrien is elsewhere.

'Who? The Rat?' Renaud says, baring his little dirty teeth.

His head, with his short black hair, is like a giant snooker ball, completely spherical.

'Yeah, Corentin.'

'He's a manager,' Adrien says. 'They're all dicks. _____.'

'Manager! Only just!' Renaud adds bitterly. '_____ _____ _____. Not long ago he was a waiter. One of us.'

'More of a waiter than you'll ever be,' Adrien says.

Renaud squirts a stream of yellow saliva from between his teeth into the white snow.

'Fuck you, *l'Intouchable*.'

'Don't call me that.'

The door opens. Valentine walks out with the phone still in her hand: 'We're opening.'

'*Quoi?*' Renaud says.

'We're opening,' Valentine repeats and goes back inside.

Renaud follows her.

'Corentin. He has problem? With me?' I ask again.

Adrien shrugs. 'Corentin doesn't like you. _____ _____ _____. What do I know?'

Before he finishes his cigarette, I make a last desperate attempt to win the Untouchable's favour.

'I'll take a wallet.'

Adrien's greedy little eyes flash – it's the first hint of life in them I've seen this morning.

'Sure. Black?'

'Black.'

'Give me the money tomorrow.'

'End of the week. I don't have money now. Twenty euros?'

He laughs; he knows my predicament.

'No, forty. It's real leather.'

Forty euros. It's a rip-off. But if I owe the Untouchable forty quid he may just stop me getting sacked this week.

I'm about to walk back inside, where it's marginally warmer, when Corentin comes out in a blaze of fury.

'What are you doing? You're not paid to smoke. Piece of shit. _____ smoking on the terrace? Hey? Look at this _____.' He points at the long, abandoned terrace, and begins marching me down it pointing at imaginary things, his hand on my neck pushing it towards the floor. Eventually we go down the steps to street level. 'And this... it's not possible,' he says of the snow-covered pavements. Although, from his reaction, he could well be talking about the whole of Paris.

'Don't come in until it's finished,' I think he says.

'I don't have a jacket...'

Corentin, the Rat, the manager who was recently a waiter, almost trembles he's so angry. His face getting redder as it gorges with blood. He's saying something to me, something about a winter jacket not being uniform and that working warms us, but all I can focus on are the blotches of red now flourishing on different parts of his face like small nuclear detonations. My eye darts between them, and then to the tasteless earring glistening in his right ear – why does he hate me so much? What do I represent to him? What am I upsetting deep within him?

As I sweep the terrace and clear the snow in my polyester shirt, bow tie and synthetic cheap black suit my teeth chatter, and eventually my hands go blue and have trouble holding the cigarettes I'm smoking for warmth. When the shivering becomes uncontrollable, and holding a lighter under my palm becomes ineffective, I head back into the Pass.

Before the service the Rat takes me aside and says something to me which I don't quite understand. I notice that the nuclear blotches have diffused, their toxic radiation moved on. I assume he's talking about my shift, so I ask him what time I'll be finishing. I need to find a place to live, I tell him. He's oddly friendly now, and mumbles something about me finishing after the lunch service. That's good, that gives me the afternoon. Afterwards, I follow him out towards the dining room when suddenly he turns around and asks me what I'm doing.

I see the first bruising of red on his chin: the nuclear war has begun...

'Go! Clean the cutlery. Are you stupid?' he says, as if he's talking to a child.

For the rest of the morning I stay hidden in my cellar like Edmond Dantès, polishing cutlery or ironing tablecloths. I think about what the Rat said earlier, that I'll never be a waiter, that it's a real *métier*. It's just as the waiter in my building had said. By now the other waiters no doubt know what Corentin said, too – and they probably agree. I'm an impostor and I'm not going to last. Lucien said as much yesterday. Perhaps I've mis-understood the whole exchange and today's my last day? It's possible. Not being able to express myself, having been rendered an imbecile, is incredibly frustrating. Everything I know is locked in my head. Twenty-four years of life experience. To these people I am nothing but a bumbling, almost mute, English guy. They're right, I don't even merit a name. And as guardians to this ancient Parisian profession, they don't think I merit being a waiter either.

At the end of the breakfast service the *directeur* marches into my cellar, followed by the Rat.

'What are you doing?' he asks curtly.

I stand up, try to say something, but only stammer.

The *directeur* looks at the Rat and laughs, says something about me being a good soldier and the novelty of having an English runner. The Rat does not laugh, just says, 'Never trust the English.'

'It's a joke,' the *directeur* says to me. '*Hein, Corentin?*' He pats his back. 'Better today, *l'Anglais*. Adrien says we might make a real runner of you. Finish the week and you've got a job.'

The *directeur* turns ceremoniously on his heels and marches out. The Rat waits until the footsteps have disappeared, then leans into my face and whispers, '*T'es personne ici, d'accord?*' Initially I understand 'You're someone here, OK?' which, considering the context, seems incorrect. But then I realize it means I'm no one. If he wasn't so scrawny, it would be slightly intimidating.

Despite Corentin's promise that I would be finishing after the lunch service, he doesn't let me go until dinner is well under way. That's a fourteen-hour shift, without a break and without a meal. Reduced staff? Perhaps, but I get the distinct impression he's simply trying to show me who's boss. However, the fact that both he and the waiter next door said the same thing – 'You'll never be a waiter' – has only strengthened my resolve. I will be a waiter. I will succeed in this old-fashioned Parisian world.

It's night again when the restaurant returns me to the city. Darkness to darkness. The snow is no longer white, but dirty, heaped into piles on street corners. The pavements, now salted, are wet. Traffic hisses down the avenues, buses splash through the slush. Outside the school that famous refrain again: *Liberté – Egalité – Fraternité.* There is fraternity in the restaurant, I can see that, even if I'm not part of it. As for liberty and equality, they seem less likely. Let's see.

A simple meal and I crawl into bed, exhausted. I curse the Rat, and also Lucien because I still don't have my jacket. If I can just get out for an hour when the shops are open and get to somewhere cheap, I can buy a new one. But that's the least of my problems, as I still have nowhere to live. On the upside, if I can survive until the end of the week, I may officially be a runner.

Bon Dimanche?

The Sunday service is not restaurant work, it's attrition. And waiters are in the frontline. The sheer scale of the operation means that it is physically impossible to carry off without a hitch. Around 650 covers need to be served within the space of a few hours – and that's just the beginning. The Sunday service never lets up; it's all day, as wave upon wave of customers scramble up the steps as if they were a Normandy beachhead demanding to be fed. And all of them are surprised, and then angered, when they're asked to wait; convinced that they were the only people in the entire city who had had the idea of going out to a restaurant on a Sunday.

For the next six days I work non-stop. From before dawn until after midnight and usually without a break. Always terrified of losing my job. The role of the runner is becoming clearer thanks to the patience of Lucien, Salvatore and De Souza. Yet, despite their tutelage in the ways of waiting, nothing has prepared me for the Sunday lunch service.

It turns out that Lucien's dodge has been to pretend he's a devout Catholic in order to miss the beginning of the service as he's attending another type of service, at church. That was what Adrien's comment on the first day meant, about him being a good *catho*.

Even before it begins there is a different feeling from the previous days, with the waiters seeming more on edge than usual. As if they all know what is coming; it is just a matter of when. There is a feeling of fatalism about it. As if it is already too late.

The Sunday service is like a storm: it builds out of sight, slowly gaining energy as hundreds of orders make their way from the waiters down into the various parts of the kitchens. In the kitchens the panic has begun, but in the restaurant, on the other side of the wall, all is calm – disconcertingly so.

The service begins slowly, plates rattling their way up and down the dolly lifts, the waiters up and down the aisles. Illegible tickets soaked in sauces stuck to dishes are decrypted by the Tamils, who begin putting the orders together at the Pass. When they're ready, there's a cry: '*Service!*' And a waiter will swoop in and back out.

'*Va chercher le seau!*' Get me a wine bucket, a waiter calls as I pass.

I run back to the kitchen and fill a bucket; re-serve some more wine; plunge the bottle into the ice.

'*Il me manque un Perrier sur la trois cent.*' I'm missing a Perrier on 300; another waiter this time.

I see the glass of Perrier and grab it. However, the diner doesn't want a slice of lemon, but they do want ice. I go back to the Pass with the glass. One of the Tamils barks at me to take another drinks order with me. I ignore him and fish the lemon out with my fingers – I suck it before chucking it in the bin.

The service advances. Plates are now rattling their way up from the kitchens at even greater frequency. Side dishes, sauces, salads. All put to one side of the Pass, stacked one on top of the other, thanks to rigid plastic coverings. Kept warm by the lamps. The drinks are still coming out; the tables aren't ready for the food yet.

Now the baskets of bread. With their bare hands the waiters scoop rolls into baskets and place them before the impatient customers who greedily tear into them.

Back and forth we go: wrong wine; corked; drinks forgotten; no lemon, no ice; ice, lemon; different glasses; 'Excuse me, sir, these are dirty.' I pad my way at speed between the tables, silver tray aloft with a dozen of the restaurant's finest wine glasses. They tinkle, like a shiver, as you walk – a forest of crystal. Renaud turns too quickly.

'*Chaud derrière!*' I cry in warning, which is something I've picked up from the other waiters.

Up the *plateau* goes almost vertical. I hold my breath; the glasses slide slightly. A delicate ringing sound. I'm getting the hang of the *plateau* now. Mastering its centrifugal forces.

Back at the Pass the men wait, occasionally popping heads out into the dining room to check their tables are OK. There's a calm. The drinks are served and most of the orders for the first service are in. De Souza is leaning over the metal Pass.

'*Allez. Allez.*'

Half his *plateau* is ready to go.

'Nimsath, *putain?*'

'*Ta gueule!*' Nimsath gestures.

On the other side of the door the restaurant is humming along quietly with polite conversation.

At the back of the Pass a small buzz. Nimsath unloads the service lift while one of the other Tamils shuttles plates to the Pass. *Sole – sauce à part; steak tartare 'aller-retour'; bavette à l'échalote...*

De Souza has already taken the sole. He pours the sauce onto the fish. Sticks his finger into it, licks it to check it's still warm.

'*Bon,*' he says.

He's gone.

The service lifts are buzzing non-stop now. Waiters wait impatiently over their plates at the Pass, elbows out, covering them. The Tamils keep stacking unfinished orders under the plastic covers to one side. The lids are high enough to not touch what's on the plate, so the towers gain height quickly and take up less space on the Pass. Nimsath, meanwhile, reads what he can on the soaked tickets, trying to piece it all together and organizes the plates into coherent table orders. The waiters take advantage of the confusion, stealing plates to fill their own orders. The quicker they turn their table round the better. Everyone works on the assumption that their order has been stolen. They wait there, with their *plateau* almost fully loaded. Peering over the Pass into the darkness, trying to see what's coming up. Feet tapping, fists clenched. A constant repetition of '*putain, putain*' on their lips. As they wait they continually stick their fingers in sauces, prod pieces of meat, nibble vegetables. Checking everything is still hot enough to be served. All while doing small calculations in their head: if I leave the Pass now, can I be back before another waiter steals my order?

'*L'Anglais! Tu m'aides.*' You help me, Adrien says.

It's the big table; he's already loading up my *plateau*.

'*Ça va?*' He doesn't look at me, just carries on arranging the seven plates on the tray.

The upper part of my arm is burning from the strain. He turns, so I go.

'*Attends. Putain!*' Wait, fuck.

More plates. Now they're dangling over the side. Stacked so intricately that I've no idea how I'll get them off. He slaps me round the head.

'*Fais attention.*' Pay attention.

The *sauce au poivre* from the steak has run onto the plate of *ravioles*. I steady the silver tray with the other hand while he uses the nearest thing – a serviette from the used bin – to wipe the plate clean.

'*C'est bon.*'

Back into the dining room. Like a diver, swimming along channels. All my upper body is trying to offset the weight of the laden plates stuck out in front of me.

'*À une main!*' the Rat snaps as I go past. He swivels on his heels to watch me.

One hand again. My arm burning. Every fibre wanting to let go. Adrien, the Untouchable, is right behind me. I can feel him. He walks a little like a spider crab with his feet out and his knobbly knees visible through his trousers.

'*Allez! Allez!*'

We fly through the restaurant single file – like migrating birds or formation fighter pilots. At the table Adrien dispenses his dishes first. I wait. One-handed. The pain now excruciating. With all my concentration I focus on pushing my arm up. Adrien comes over. He takes the first two plates from the farthest edge of my tray. The sudden change in weight sends it tipping upwards. The remaining plates slide towards me. I counter, just in time.

'*Putain,*' I hear him say before he turns around. '*Alors, le bœuf, c'est pour vous, monsieur. Les ravioles, ici...*' You can hear the smile as usual.

'*J'avais commandé des légumes de saison aussi.*' The woman at the corner of the table tells us that her seasonal vegetables are missing.

'It's coming, *madame.*' Adrien's response is almost immediate, automatic, polite. He turns to take my *plateau* – 'Go and get them' – and spins back round to dispense the remaining dishes.

Head down, heels driving into the floor as I ignore the raised hands of other customers and make it back to the Pass.

Breathe.

'There are no fucking vegetables on the order. *Punday.*' Nimsath waves a slimy piece of paper in my face. 'Reorder! Reorder!'

I can't reorder Adrien's food as I don't have a till key and if the woman doesn't get her vegetables soon there will be no tip and Adrien will kill me.

Nimsath ignores me. There are enormous stacked towers of assembled plates under their plastic covers either side of the pass now, some seven or eight plates high, every conceivable order, ready to go out, just awaiting the final few to complete the table. Meanwhile, waiters flit in and out depositing dirty plates in the remaining space between the towers. Dirty cutlery slides into the soapy water of the metal box with a terrifying crash.

'Reorder on machine,' Nimsath shouts again.

Behind me Salvatore slices the remains of a barely touched burger into bite-size pieces.

'*Tiens, les gars.*' He offers it to the waiters, who scoff it down.

'*De la haute cuisine, hein?*' De Souza jokes.

'You should have seen her. She was never going to eat it. Miserable-looking *dame,*' Salvatore says. 'Her husband was telling her they've got money problems and that they'd have to sell the...'

'No. Now, Nimsath!' I say.

He explodes; he will not put the order through. I turn to see Adrien, who's heading into the Pass. 'For fuck's sake!' he says.

They argue until Adrien takes another side dish that's sitting on the pass and forces it into my hand.

'*Vas-y.*'

By the time I'm back at the table the woman has eaten half of her meal already.

'I don't want it now. *Ça ne sert à rien.*'

Her husband tells her to take it anyway. Whether she ordered it or not is irrelevant. Adrien won't see a tip. As far as he's concerned, the sooner they're out the better.

At the Pass there's now pure contempt. The language between the waiters and the Tamils has reached new lows. Physically the waiters are jostling between themselves for plates.

'*C'est à moi, ça.*'

'*Non! C'est à moi.*'

The dolly lift buzzes – more plates. The waiters scatter like pigeons.

The full force of the kitchens is spewing out of the lifts like fires at the gates of hell. On the Pass finished entrées begin to accumulate; unfulfilled orders are stacked higher and higher; the orders that are ready are taken down from their towers and assembled into small clusters of plates on waiting waiters' *plateaux*. But they don't go out fast enough. There's always something missing. And with each new delivery of dishes from the kitchens, the towers of food slide forwards like coins in a penny-pusher at an arcade.

Back and forth, back and forth. Too many things to do, never enough time. Aching heels, sore feet, dry throats. I throw the remainder of a large glass bottle of Perrier Fines Bulles down my throat. It froths. I'm hungry. When there are no waiters at the Pass I take a roll of bread, rip some off and stuff it into my mouth. My fingers are sticky. The rest of the bread I put in a coffee cup at the back of the shelf. It's so dry. The *directeur* comes around the corner.

'What are you doing?'

'Sweet potato purée,' I manage to say.

'Where is it?' he demands of Nimsath angrily.

'*Ça arrive, ça arrive.*'

The *directeur* takes one from another cluster, bangs it on my tray and pushes me out forcefully.

When I come back all the waiters are pushing and shoving to get close to the Pass.

And that's when it happens.

The force, the storm that has been welling up. A tower to the left goes over first, like a cliff collapsing into the sea. There's a hideous noise of crockery smashing; every waiter knows what this means. From the Pass you can feel the lull in conversation in the dining room. You can imagine them all looking. But they can't see what we can: half a dozen main courses, and another load of side orders, which two seconds ago were ready to go out to the tables, now lie smashed together on the floor. Jamaal shouts first. Then Renaud. They're right up in each other's faces. One blaming the other. De Souza pulls them apart. I begin to pick up the mess. The *directeur* appears. Pulling me up he holds me against the wall and spits violence in my face. His face redder and redder, the top lip glistening. I try to tell him it wasn't me. Renaud shoots me a look that silences me.

'You're finished!' he screams in a whisper. 'Nimsath! Coke Lite! Now!'

Three of us are on our knees as the *directeur* drinks his Diet Coke. When he's suitably calmed he spins on his heels and is gone. Back to the restaurant to pirouette between tables and bow obsequiously to guests like a dancer.

A sense of complicity. New plates are taken and, using our hands, we pick from the floor what we can still make use of. The hands that have been dealing with the dirty plates and shoving our gelled hair back into place are now rearranging duck breasts and pushing haricot beans around. It's over in an instant. What's missing – a handful of beans, a spoonful of mashed potato – is taken from other waiting orders while Nimsath barks for replacements into the intercom. The waiters disperse. The order is gone. The table is none the wiser.

Renaud comes back into the Pass with a *coquelet avec pommes dauphine* in his hand. He slides the dauphinoise into the bin with the back of his hand, then licks it. He wipes down the plate with a serviette that's knocking around, then, by hand, puts French fries on the plate from a selection of others that have yet to be claimed. He disappears for a moment, leaving the plate on the Pass, only returning to collect it once a suitable amount of time has passed and he can take it back to the table.

'I spoke with the chef, he did it specially for you,' I hear him say to the diner. 'Rushed it through.'

On the other side of the restaurant Lucien's table is leaving. '*Bon dimanche,*' they say cheerily to him.

'*Bon dimanche,*' he replies politely.

The truth is that there is no good Sunday when you're a waiter. Waiting work is hard, unrelenting and mindless. Yet we work as if our lives depend on it; nothing is more important than the specific task we are doing. Hunger haunts us, but we cannot eat. Forced to chase it away with snatched cigarettes, cheap coffee and bread rolls. We work together but apart. No one cares if you lose your job; it's their own they're worried about. Waiters can be sacked on the spot for the smallest of reasons: stealing food, slow service, a complaint from a customer; everything hangs in the balance. On Sundays you keep your head down and work and pray to God you're on the schedule for the following week.

And for the time being, I am. I am officially a runner. Or, at least, that's what I understand. I still don't have anything in the way of a contract and have no idea if I am going to be paid, and if so, when, and also, how much. Which feeds into my other problem: I am quite literally in the soup. The entire week I've not been let out of the restaurant. As a result, I've not had a chance to look for somewhere to live, and time is up. Tomorrow I am homeless.

Before leaving I ask Valentine if I could have Monday off. She laughs. It's not possible, but as a favour she will let me come in before lunch instead of doing the opening.

'You owe me,' she says coquettishly as I walk into the night.

But my relief at having been given the morning off is short-lived. When I return to where I left Alice's old bicycle, it is gone. As if to taunt me, a police car drives past, its blue light beating silently.

PART 2
LA SOUPE

Voyage Au Bout de Paris

Renting in Paris means navigating a myriad of administrative hurdles. The first of which is 'le dossier'. Before you can even visit a place you need to put together a dossier in which you must provide a bounty of personal information, including previous tax returns, your last three payslips, bank account details and, importantly, a guarantor's details – someone who will pay your rent in the event you don't. It has to be someone in France, and they have to be willing to share their tax returns to prove they earn at least three times what both your and their rent is, and then they have to handwrite a letter that takes up an entire side of A4 paper. As such, every advertisement I've contacted has declined me – I don't have a complete dossier. Some simply decline on the sound of my accent alone – it isn't worth the stress for them to rent to a foreigner; it is hard enough to find a French person with a complete dossier.

It's 5am: the building shakes as the Métro passes underneath, the first of the city's faceless workers sitting drearily in near-empty Métro cars as they snake unnoticed under the city. I've hardly slept a wink. In the small room it is dark and deathly cold. Breath hangs in the air. My bags by the door, just like Alice's a few weeks ago. One minute I'm up, the next I'm back down. The euphoria of having finally found a job has worn off at the same rate that it's worn me out. I'm exhausted. And during the lonelier hours of last night, I have been over the options available to me.

My situation is that I have just over one hundred pounds in my UK bank account, eighty euros in cash in my pocket and nowhere to live.

In theory I have a job, but I still haven't been paid and, as far as I'm aware, I don't have a contract. In any case, without a contract and payslips I have no proof of a job and therefore can't rent a room, and I can't open a bank account; and without a bank account I usually can't get a job, as there's no way to pay me. And without an address I can't get a national insurance number, and therefore can't pay any social security contributions and therefore can't see a doctor if needed or get a contract. It's a very tidy French administrative catch-22.

Plagued by doubts, I shoulder my bag and leave Alice's room for the very last time. As usual there's a thin strip of light under the waiter's door, and I can hear him moving about – it's like he never sleeps. I stop for a moment and listen. He stops, too. I can picture us as some kind of weird mirror image, either side of his door. Young and old, lost and found.

Outside in the still night air of the city, steam rises from the apartment buildings' small metal chimneys. It's bitterly cold and dark and everything is closed apart from the *bar-tabac* near the Métro station with the two Chinese brothers and the grumpy former owner. I sit there barely able to keep my eyes open, physically exhausted. I can't for the life of me work out what I am going to do, nor indeed where I'm going to go. I need to find somewhere I can stay, and I need to sort it out before work. I think of hostels, shelters and even the other waiters, although I don't have their numbers, and frankly, seeing as I don't know them, asking to crash would be incredibly odd.

Orwell would have stayed in the dosshouses on the Left Bank, but these no longer exist; instead of exiled Russian émigrés, you're more likely to meet exiled Russian oligarchs there now. I think of phoning someone in London, maybe Alice – borrowing money and getting a train back. It's only a few hours' journey but it feels a world away. It also reminds me that, since Alice left, I'm essentially living in my head; I don't really have people speak to. In a French-speaking world, the English me, the one who thinks and feels, is redundant, disappearing; he has no use. My contact with anyone is via the fog of the French language; and this new 'French me' currently has the communication skills of a three-year-old.

With the coming of dawn and the coffee and the early-morning workers – Paris in all her bustling matutinal glory – I am rejuvenated. This was never going to be easy; to leave now would be to fail. Also, what would I do when I got to London? Where would I stay? The problem would be the same. At least here the bread is good and I have a job, of sorts. On top of that, even if I'm still terrible at French, I am better than when I arrived and, importantly, I am slowly but surely getting under the surface of the city – sinking that little bit deeper. This is just the next step. A leap into the murky water, the point of no return.

I decide to head out to the north of the city, where I've seen a number of rough-looking hotels on my rounds looking for work. Places beyond the Place de Clichy, towards the Porte de la Chapelle and Porte de Clignancourt. I've no idea what they are like, but I'm certain they'll be cheap. The romantic in me tells me it will be a good fit as Henry Miller used to live somewhere around there.

At the end of Line 4 of the Métro I begin walking. This is the very northern edge of Paris proper, the turbid urban estuary where the rivers that run from the suburbs deposit their human sediment in the sea of the city.

There's a brown fog over the city, litter-strewn pavements, uninviting-looking cafés with North African men sitting at plastic tables, talking fast; halal butchers, garages, a giant food market just getting into swing that feels like it's been transplanted straight out of Africa; shops selling knock-off sports brands, convenience stores selling international sim cards. The only other Caucasian person I see has a small cheese stall in the market. He looks at me hopefully – his is the only stall without people in front bartering and shouting. Eventually I turn off the Boulevard Ornano and into a short quiet residential street of five-storey buildings built in architectural styles that span the last 150 years. In the middle of the street a sign hangs: Hôtel du Simplon.

There are hundreds of this kind of dwelling scattered around the rougher edges of Paris. Pitiful-looking places with dirty signs hanging over small doorways that lead straight back to the innards of the building. Uninviting doorways that take you beyond the organized façades of Paris and into a world of inner sanctums, shadowy courtyards and buildings within buildings. In some parts of the city, these hidden places are oases of calm; others resemble the Paris of yesterday, the one Baron Haussmann thought he'd destroyed when he and Napoleon III vowed to clean up the city – warrens of sloping-walled buildings with sunken floors and hovel-like rooms accessed by tilting staircases, the wood black from years of grit. The Hôtel du Simplon is one such. From the grimy sign it is unclear if it has one star, or simply the shadow of a recently departed one.

The entrance is a long, narrow corridor, at the end of which is a severely scratched Perspex window at shoulder height, something like at passport control or a police station. From here I can go no further; there is a locked door of cracked, reinforced glass. Behind the Perspex is a miserable little office where sits an overweight woman smoking and watching a small television showing what looks like an Eastern European tele-shopping channel.

As I stand by the screen waiting, she makes herself look busy by shuffling some of the strewn papers on her desk and acting as if I can't see the small television that she is watching beyond the blue haze of cigarette smoke. Eventually, she stands up and inspects me with a squint through the almost opaque Perspex. Her face is round, with acne on her chin, and her dark greasy hair is scraped back and tied up with a ragged pink scrunchie. She looks more exhausted than me.

'I'm looking for a room.'

'No,' she says, before tapping her cigarette in the overflowing ashtray on the desk and sitting back down.

'You have no space?'

'*Quoi?*' She peers at me through myopic eyes.

'Do you have any space?'

She leans close to the glass to get a better look at me. I have pushed my bag in front of my feet so she can't get a look at it. I feel that appearing desperate might reduce my chances.

'That depends,' she says.

'On what?'

'What you want.'

She lights a second smoke with the end of the first and looks at me expectantly.

'How much is a room?'

'Twenty, with private shower.'

Her accent is strong, definitely Eastern European-sounding. Lucky there are no French people within listening distance to hear us butchering their language.

'You have cheaper?'

'Police?' she finally says.

'Police?'

'If you police, you must tell me.'

'I'm not police.'

'If you police, you have to tell me,' she repeats. 'It's law.'

'I'm not police.' I assure her. 'I'm not even French.'

She calls to someone in a back room, whereupon a deep voice booms something back in another language.

'Cheaper? Only for single. This is ten per night.'

It seems ludicrous that I can sleep in Paris for this little. Things are looking up.

'No private shower,' she adds, after a moment's hesitation.

'Can I see the room?' I ask.

After much deliberation with the deep voice she slides me a key to a double room on the first floor with strict instructions not to go anywhere else and buzzes me through the reinforced-glass door. I climb the impossibly narrow stairs, which are so low there is a dark stain running up the middle where people's dirty hair has rubbed. There is the familiar smell of stale cigarettes, body odour, food and dope. The room on the first floor is small, horribly decorated, but nonetheless fine. Indeed, it is warmer than the place I have just left. I sit on the electric radiator for a minute and turn it on. The smell of burnt dust rises upwards.

'I'll take the room,' I say, when I am back downstairs.

'In single room, there is already other man. You pay first two night now.'

'Other man?'

'Room is divide. Private sleep area. First two nights, twenty euro.'

I pay in cash and leave my bags with her. As I am leaving she asks, 'British?'

'Yes.'

'I never go to England.'

And at this point she takes a long pause. She clearly has something highly important that she wants to know about England. Perhaps if I can answer her I'll get a better room and won't have to share with 'the man'. Since starting in the restaurant, I have managed to up my knowledge of the Royal Family – this, strangely, seems to be the main thing that anyone I meet wants to know about England. What would it be this time? How many children the Queen has? How old is Prince Charles? Or perhaps something more important about the minutiae of living in London, the kind of things Nimsath asks…

'Tell me,' the myopic lady eventually says. 'Tell me. Do you have the machines… the machines that sell the cigarettes there, in Britain?'

'Cigarette vending machines?'

'Yes.' Her enthusiasm is at best non-existent.

'Um, yes.' I hesitate. 'Actually, no, I don't think we do anymore.'

Before I can finish stumbling through my ignorance on the matter of cigarette machines she sits down. I can only see the top of her greasy head and the smoke rising up.

The Hôtel du Simplon doesn't aspire to much, but at least it will give me a bed until I can work out a more permanent arrangement. And with the loss of the bike, the Métro nearby is useful. There is also a small tailor's opposite, a tiny little place, no larger than a cubicle, an Aladdin's cave with suit jackets hanging everywhere. Among them, seated behind a small desk, peering closely at his sewing machine as he works, a slightly overweight man, with a shining bald patch. Upon my arrival he springs up, opens his arms and squints at me before taking off his magnifying glasses.

'Please, sir, take a seat,' he says with great fanfare. I feel like Odysseus on his return to Ithaca.

From among the rows of hanging jackets a stool appears. 'One moment.' He returns with two glasses of hot water with fresh mint in.

His name is Youssef, he's Egyptian and he likes to talk. Before I can even tell him that I simply need my trousers adjusted, he's giving me his entire history and that of the street.

'...and I wouldn't usually be here so early, but my wife. My wife, she left me, and sometimes she comes back to where we live... unannounced. I have no choice but to sleep here. My whole building is laughing at me. It's terrible.'

'You sleep here?' I said, picturing him camping out on the floor below the canopy of suit jackets.

Youssef laughs, the flash of gold teeth at the back of his mouth. Later we stand by the door and he points out where certain characters on the street live.

'Here you must always look up before passing. The lady that lives there, she is old, very old. And likes to stand at her window with a pot of boiling water, which she pours on people. It does not matter if you are Muslim or not.'

'What?'

'Very old. Very old,' he says, as if this explains everything. 'And here, opposite, you must not go. Here drugs.' Outside the building stand a huddle of young guys. 'See, they keep moving it to different bins.' Watching them is like watching one of those cup-and-ball tricks – it is impossible to say who has the drugs and where exactly they are at any one point.

'In these buildings, many prostitutes,' Youssef continues. 'That place, on street level, you will see, has a man who never leaves, never. Always at his window. And in his room, so much stuff, piles and piles – newspapers, rubbish, bottles, all sorts of junk. Sometimes, he shouts out the window and waves his cane. But he's nice. Cédric, he's called.' Youssef is suddenly seized by something, 'But wait, where do you live, my friend? You do not live here?'

I tell him about the Hôtel du Simplon. His face looks grave.

'Hmm, this is an interesting place. You are a heavy sleeper, I hope?'

He will not elaborate, so I tell him about my intentions to get my suit adjusted. Jacket and trousers. I don't have the money for the jacket yet, but he says he'll do me a favour and do the trousers straight away. Eleven euros. What a relief not to have to go back to work in the clown pants. From behind some hanging jackets a mirror appears and Youssef gets to work. Pinning the trousers, narrower, shorter.

'But like this, we will see your socks. No, no, no. It is not possible. We ruin a perfectly good pair of trousers here.'

Youssef clearly does not understand the waiter's style but eventually acquiesces. As he works I look out of the window to the street. From one of the parked cars a woman gets out, followed by a child. Their breath hangs in the air. They look cold. Upon closer inspection I see that the beaten-up car is full, as if they have all their belongings in it.

'Those people?'

'Ah, they are awake. One moment.' Youssef disappears; when he returns he is holding two cups of tea. 'Please, my friend, open the door.'

He crosses the road and hands the lady and her young daughter the teas. He points to the shop, but she shakes her head. Youssef returns.

'It is very sad. Yes, they live in this car. Can you imagine how cold it is? I insist they come into my shop; sometimes the little one will, but not the mother. All of their belongings are in that car, she will not leave them. In the morning their faces are blue. Look.'

I watch the two of them. The woman must be in her thirties, the girl about six. The woman looks absolutely terrified, just standing there, wide eyes taking in the frozen street. What misfortune has brought them here? And why, of all the streets in the world, has she chosen this one?

'*Voilà*, my friend.'

The trousers fit perfectly. Youssef draws the curtain back from the mirror again. Staring back at me is half a waiter.

I'm getting there.

Life In the Hôtel du Simplon

'I was almost stabbed myself. There were three of them. Lucky, I had this.'
From his trousers Stéphane pulls out a flick knife.

The last three evenings have been the same: when I get back to the
Hôtel du Simplon, usually sometime after midnight, the man who sleeps
in the bed on the other side of the screen is at the small sink by the door
that we share, preparing to go out. The sink is also where he urinates, as
he often can't be bothered to go to the toilet, which is down the hall. I say
'man' – he's probably about the same age as me. He calls himself Stéphane,
but it's not his real name, he says. He likes to talk, conspiracy theories
mainly. I've no idea what he actually does. He goes out after midnight,
always in a black silk shirt carrying a briefcase. He returns sometime in the
morning, occasionally before I get up, but often after I have left. I know
very little about him, but I'm fairly certain that he's completely deluded.

As I change out of my waiter's clothes Stéphane carries on talking
about the complicated network of dealers who stalk the underground
passageways of certain stations and how they should be avoided at all
costs. He is getting ready to go out to 'manage his affairs', as he likes to say.

He's a small guy with the face of a vole and little eyes that squint at you
from behind small rectangular glasses. He speaks no English, but he's
patient with my French and helps correct it.

'What happened?' I ask about the knife fight.

'I shouldn't say.'

'*Allez*,' I encourage him. Knowing full well that he's happy to have an
audience.

78

'You tell no one, OK? I don't need *les flics* on my back. Not now.'

'Sure.'

He sprays a sickly-smelling perfume onto the collar of his shirt and his hair, but continues to hold the knife in the other hand. We've been living together in this room for the last week and I've never felt threatened, even if he gives off the vibe of someone who is slightly unhinged; however, now, seeing the knife, I'm reminded that I really do need desperately to get out of this place. The harrowing but slightly amusing thought that I'm living with a serial killer passes through my mind. Perhaps that's what he does at night? Goes out and kills people?

'...all I'll say is... it cost them a lot...' Stéphane makes an awkward slicing motion with the knife.

Clearly disappointed by my underwhelmed response, he turns from the mirror to see me staring in exhaustion at the enormous dark stain on the floor, which has intrigued me since I arrived.

'It's blood. A man was killed here. Perfect place, if you ask me. You know in Paris the police don't have time for murders – not here in the 18th arrondissement. My friend's brother works there. They don't care. If low-lifes kill each other it makes their jobs easier. Less paperwork. Honestly, when have you seen a *flic* here? You don't. They pass in their cars sometimes, but they never get out. The only time you see a Parisian policeman out of his car is when he's buying a kebab.'

'What about the ones on roller skates?'

'They're not policemen. They're an embarrassment. You know I once did the entry exams for the police, got the highest marks they'd seen...'

Stéphane goes to his bunk and slides his briefcase out from underneath, making sure to open it so that I can't see in. Stéphane calls himself a 'businessman', but from what he's told me I can only deduce that he either works in an illegal casino or is part of a cult. Perhaps both.

'You think Paris is dangerous, *l'Anglais*? Try Marseille. I've spent a lot of time there... for my work. I won't go back anytime soon. But there are opportunities down there, for someone of the right mind.' He taps his temple. 'Great for you lot, too – waiters, I mean. You want to be down there in the summer. Good money to be made. Guess that's your plan, right?'

I don't know what my plan is. But I think he's right about the blood. To hear Stéphane call me a waiter feels quite strange. However, he's right: he knows nothing of me except that I work as a waiter, and as far as he's concerned that's it for me. I can't tell him the truth, that I'm not even a waiter. I'm a runner. If he knew that, he'd probably lose what little respect he has for me.

Stéphane gives his pointed black leather shoes a final polish.

'Working tonight?' I ask.

'*Oui, comme toujours*. You're lucky, *l'Anglais*. It's the advantage of being a waiter – you don't work nights. And you can travel. Every city needs waiters. A truly international job.'

He slides on his enormous Russian army overcoat and picks up the briefcase.

'Where did you get your jacket?'

'The flea market. Porte de Clignancourt. There's an army shop. But you can get more than jackets, if you know what I mean. If you go, say I sent you. Say "Jean-Jacques" sent you.' He winks.

When he's gone there's a lingering smell of marijuana from the corridor. I wash myself in the sink and think about what Stéphane said – he's right, I am a waiter. I go back to bed and try to fall asleep to the sound of a man getting his money's worth with a prostitute in another room. It's so loud it's as if the walls don't exist. As far as I can deduce, the Hôtel du Simplon, along with its primary activity of hospitality, also provides rooms to the hooker bar in the street below. Eventually I pass out. My sleep, most nights, is interrupted either by fighting or by fornicating.

The Hôtel du Simplon is situated on a sort of triple frontier at the very top of the 18th arrondissement. To the north, towards the Porte de Clignancourt, is the Maghrebi area and beyond that a Roma shanty town built on disused rail tracks where the air is thick with smoke from the fires used to heat the huts; to the east, the Goutte d'Or, the sub-Saharan area, *l'Afrique Noire*; and to the south, the slowly expanding frontier of what the French call *les Bobos*, the *bourgeois-bohèmes*. A world of organic supermarkets and charming cafés, and people like those I met with Alice who run blogs or work in jobs that probably carry the prefix 'marketing'.

All these worlds exist within a road or two of the Boulevard Ornano. The change is often sudden and, just as in the restaurant, zones are clearly defined: crossing from one side of a road to the other, you can quite literally move into a different social class or culture. Central Paris is unique in this way, a compressed version of a larger city. Different cultures and economic classes all squeezed together, suffocated by the tight belt of the Périphérique and the slowly expanding gentrified areas. The 18th has always been a working-class area; Stéphane says his great-grandmother worked in a vegetable shop not far from us – she came from Germany, fleeing Nazis, having worked in a factory making bombs. It's an area that is now predominantly Maghrebi, a reflection of the changing diasporas of the city.

The Rue Boudelière, for better or for worse, is like a concentrated version of the 18th: it has all the residents, although they're notably spread out according to the cardinal points closest to their respective areas. On ground level most of the shop spaces are for rent or boarded up. At the southern end there are three sub-Saharan African hairdressers, followed by Youssef's. In the middle of the street a laundrette, and on the other side the Le Seau, the bucket, a tiny space that has been converted into a sort of bar where the working women hang out. Beyond them, to the north, are three more hairdressers, this time for North African men and women, and lastly a garage, a halal butcher's and a PMU bar – a café with TV screens showing horse-racing all day, and a terrace where men stare into espressos with their feet among spent betting slips. Cars are parked bumper to bumper, and though in theory anyone can park there, if you happen to take one of the places that is 'reserved' you'll come back to find your wing mirrors smashed off.

Apartments and rooms don't stay empty for long on the Rue Boudelière. Within a day of the elderly lady's body – the lady being the one who would pour scalding water on people – having been carried out of her apartment, there were men to be seen queuing outside her door.

'African girls,' Stéphane says, as he gets out of bed.

'What?'

'The men queuing,' he says dryly. 'You can tell the type of prostitutes that have been set up by the type of men going in and out.'

Prostitution, betting, hairdressing and drugs; the Rue Boudelière has its own economy. People leave unwanted objects in the street: mattresses, a toilet, an old microwave, a shoe. Throughout the day men and women will pass to collect them, either on foot or in vans, and by evening most of the objects will have disappeared. As for the squatting, the girls who have been set up in some apartments are long-term residents, whereas other times they're hastily bailed out. However, it's never long before someone notices another empty room and they're back up and running again.

Night Life

The Rue Boudelière, five o'clock in the morning. An eruption of male shouting from down below in the street; harsh syllables – violent, staccato. There's a bang and the sound of something smashing. More voices join the mêlée. Now a woman's voice, hysterical. Down below my room, outside of Le Seau – the seedy-looking hooker bar – a number of young men are collected into groups being kept apart by the elder ones. A youngish woman, dressed in a short red satin negligée and heavy make-up, is being restrained as a lone man sits on a parked car with his head slumped forwards and his hand to his eye.

The shouting picks up again. From one of the windows opposite, a woman leans out and screams, '*Ta gueule! C'est dimanche! Y a des gens qui veulent dormir!*' Shut up! It's Sunday. Some people want to sleep!

Her cries only anger the men: '*Ferme-la, salope.*' '*P'tite bourgeoise de merde!*' they howl.

Presently, from inside the Le Seau steps a larger woman, much older. She's wearing a low-cut top to reveal enormous sagging breasts, a short leather skirt and has a cigarette clamped between her fingers. Her thighs are trussed up like hams in fishnet leggings and she sports a pair of leather boots that stop above the knee. I see her during the day sitting outside the bar on a dirty white plastic chair, smoking and chatting in Arabic and dressed normally; but right now, there is no doubt that she is the madam of the joint. During a lull in the fighting she takes one of the men aside and gives him something from inside her bra.

After consulting with the older men the madam fires off a barrage of commands and sends the young ones off in different directions. A few even disappear into the building next door, where soiled bedding hangs from the windows. The injured man is eventually lifted to his feet and marched in the direction of the Boulevard Ornano, his head still slung forwards like a marionette with its strings cut.

Calm again on the Rue Boudelière as the remaining men go back inside Le Seau. The madam casts a look up at the windows where some of the residents – like me – are looking down. She makes a hand gesture, screams, '*Quoi?*' and disappears. Moments later there's the harsh metallic scraping sound as the shutter goes down, leaving just enough space for people to come and go from Le Seau. Silence again. In the car with the mother and child, there is no movement.

I lie back on my bed and close my eyes. I'm exhausted. I feel like I've just dozed when off I'm jarred back into the present by a deafening hydraulic wheezing sound and a banging of plastic lids. The stench of rubbish momentarily wafts into my room. It's 6.30, the first bin truck of the day. The noise is incredible. The shouts of the men working feel like they're in my room. Stéphane arrives, his eyes dark circles.

I fall back to sleep. Half an hour later my alarm goes off. Nothing has changed, it's still dark outside. I'm still tired. The sheets are ice cold when I turn; Stéphane snores behind the partition that separates our rooms. The remaining euros from yesterday jangle together in my pocket as I slip on my trousers in the dark room. These are my days.

HOTEL TOILETS

On the rare occasions when you're given a break from the restaurant it's usually only for an hour or so. Going home is out of the question, you don't have time. Besides, most kitchen staff may work in the centre of the city, but very few live there. The problem is that in winter, or when it's raining, there's nowhere you can go to sit, rest or sleep, without paying. Exhausted, you look for anything, anywhere to rest, as close as possible to the restaurant to avoid losing time walking. The clock is against you too: the hour begins the moment you're told to leave. In summer it's different; you can sleep in the Tuileries Garden, in parks or on benches. But in winter you must find something else.

Bang! The door slamming open in the next cubicle wakes me. My mouth tastes disgusting – stale coffee, cigarettes and yeast. It's 5.40 in the afternoon. Preparation for the dinner service began ten minutes ago, and I'm late. This is not good. I'm currently in the depths of a palatial five-star hotel in the centre of Paris – in the men's toilets, to be precise. On top of that, the newspaper that has served as my pillow – *The International New York Times* – is stuck to my face.

I listen impatiently to the person outside going through the laborious task of washing their hands. Mercifully, I finally hear the sound of the outer door opening and closing; and then silence, the hum of the giant building.

I explode out of the toilet cubicle like a rocket.

Hastily I remove my bow tie, undo my shirt and begin washing under my arms, behind my neck and then furiously trying to scrub the ink from my face, listening the whole time – over the sound of the water pouring out of the brass dolphin faucets – for the slightest sign of the door to the toilets opening. If someone catches me doing this, I'll be escorted out in no time. I look like a homeless person, washing myself in the sink.

Outside the city is blanketed in an ice-cold mist, but for the time being this hotel is the warmest place I've found to go. It's also my connection to the outside world; my source of free international newspapers – the ink of which doesn't appear to want to come off my face right now. Despite my world being reduced to restaurant work and limited sleep, I'm still trying to keep up to date with current affairs, although they seem increasingly irrelevant as time passes and my world shrinks.

My stomach grumbles. The last thing I ate was the crust of a quiche Lorraine that a diner hadn't touched, not with their hands at least. God knows when I'll next eat anything.

I focus on desperately scrubbing the sauces that have spilled onto my hands after a relentless day of carrying dirty plates. The soap in the hotel is expensive and smells of vanilla, there's even a perfumed hand cream and fluffy white towels. I've learned that in Paris you can get the measure of a place by its toilets. In Le Bistrot de la Seine they have thick paper towels, a cut below the hotel. But then I'm learning that a restaurant is always trying to save money and only gives the appearance, superficial though it is, of luxury. However, not here, never in a palatial hotel. Here the bathroom is warm and spotless, and all the surfaces are clad in light-orange marble, like a tomb. The tomb where I sleep. Yet the true beauty of these toilets is that they're so deep inside the hotel there's rarely anyone here.

On my way out of the hotel a waiter approaches me: 'Can I help you, sir?'

I mumble something about a *rendez-vous* and keep walking towards the exit, *The New York Times* tucked nonchalantly under my arm, certain that he knows my secret. We can tell each other a mile off: even in the street I can recognize a waiter now. There's something about the tired suit, the haunted look, the hurried yet fatigued walk, the worn shoes, the slick haircut, the thin frame.

Outside it's dark. The end of the day and Paris is alive. The streets clogged with traffic, the pavements with people hurrying home or tourists shuffling along in groups. The cafés are abuzz. The air tastes cold. Under orange heaters groups sit huddled together, blowing plumes of blue smoke into the frozen air and drinking steaming *vin chaud*; inside, behind misted windows, silhouettes move about in the warm light; taxis honk, a woman in fur on a scooter shouts at a taxi driver for cutting her up. The Métro rumbles along underneath our feet; streams of people are swallowed and disgorged from the ornate station entrances. A siren wails as an ambulance tries to crawl through the immobile traffic towards the Place de la Concorde and eventually up the Champs-Élysées towards the Arc de Triomphe.

Five minutes later and I've arrived at the quiet backstreet and the low black door that lets you into the Pass. I can already hear the noises from the other side. The shouts, the bangs, the clattering. Another waiter coming in for the evening shift disappears inside ahead of me. No one special, an ordinary Parisian. You wouldn't recognize him in the street. There's nothing remarkable about him. He's one of the many people behind that door. From waiters to line chefs, cleaners, hostesses, night porters, *plongeurs* and more. We all find ourselves here, toiling night and day out of sight. Making this great city turn.

Of course, none of us really see ourselves like this. These are temporary jobs, we tell ourselves. Our real lives are just around the corner.

So, in the meantime, well, we wait.

Lᴀ Lɪɢɴᴇ 4

What most visitors to Paris don't know is that there are two Métros: that of the day and that of the night. After midnight, despite the harsh artificial lighting and dirty white tiles, the Métro has a dark, sinister air about it. To descend into the Paris Métro system is to delve into the id of the city's identity, to experience the 'other' Paris. Among Parisians the northern end of Line 4 is infamous. Drivers have been known to refuse to stop at certain stations, and some of the deserted subterranean walkways are notorious for being stalked by dealers selling crack and heroin, with their clients, quite literally, littered about.

Having snaked its way under the Rive Gauche and Saint-Germain, with its expensive shops and luxury apartments, the Line 4 Métro makes a quick stop on the Île de la Cité and the Paris town hall at Châtelet, before beginning its trajectory north towards its final destination: La Porte de Clignancourt.

On the Line 4 train ghosts of men and women wander the carriages: the homeless, the addicted, the mentally distressed. With failing voices, they wearily recount their lives with little regard to the deafening noise of the squealing brakes or the train passing in the opposite direction, before passing down the line of carriages with their hands out, bumping into exhausted passengers. The demographic of travellers changes almost entirely depending on where it stops, for Paris is still segregated racially, socially and culturally.

At Les Halles, underneath the subterranean misery of the neglected shopping centre there's a mass change of people. It's here that you find the connections with the RER trains – the suburban commuter trains rammed full of the poor, whose tunnels are even deeper than those of the Métro, even closer to hell.

This is where I get on. It's been a fourteen-hour shift, with a one-hour break in which I slept in the toilets of the Hôtel M____ for thirty minutes before walking back and beginning the dinner service. I've eaten four bread rolls, drunk nine coffees and smoked a dozen cigarettes. My fingers are dark under the nails, my feet ache and I just want to sleep. At Château d'Eau a French-African man, in the most wonderfully coloured clothes, sits down opposite me and smiles. He has a dead chicken in a plastic bag on his lap. The body is limp, still covered in feathers with a small amount of blood collecting in the bottom of the bag, which occasionally drips onto the floor. He, with most of the other French-African and African passengers, gets off at the Gare du Nord – no doubt to take one of the many RER trains that pass through here, too. When the doors are open the carriages are filled again with the unmistakable smell of the Paris Métro: a heady, sulphuric, rotten egg, old shoes, brake dust and urine-tinged infusion.

After the Gare de l'Est and Gare du Nord comes Barbès-Rochechouart, a frontier town where everything is for sale: hash, black-market cigarettes, voodoo doctors, stolen phones. Groups of Maghrebi boys with closely shaved haircuts are on the platform. Some get on, some get off; elaborate handshakes, small packets exchanged. Beyond here it's fairly lawless. At the next station, Château Rouge, a man with a hollowed face wearing ripped trousers tied at the waist with string stumbles on without looking up. The carriage is filled with the smell of his still-lit cigarette and the musty, ammonia-tinged odour of a man who hasn't washed for some time. As the train pulls away, another man, giggling, chasing a marble that is being propelled along the floor by the train's speed, finally picks it up and holds it in his palm, mesmerized. He offers it to the man next to me, then to me.

'Take it,' he implores us, 'it will protect you. *Regardez.*'

He stares at it. The train slows abruptly to a screeching of metal, causing the marble to fall from his hand again and thus he begins his mad, haunting, giggling pursuit of it back up the carriage. The next station is

Marcadet–Poissonniers and the man with the haunted face in the soiled clothes stands up, but the doors do not open. There are six men sitting along the floor of the platform. Two are loading crack pipes. One is passed out, half on a cardboard mat, half on the dirty floor. We hear shouts from further along the platform, a fight. We can't see anything, but some of the addicts on the floor have the energy to look up; one even stands and cries something unintelligible in the direction of the shouting. Meanwhile the man standing at the door is getting agitated, pulling tirelessly at the little metal pulley that opens the doors, but nothing happens. His cigarette is almost finished; from his jacket pockets he fishes out a handful of smoked cigarette butts, harvested from ashtrays around the Métro stations. He sorts through them quickly like a factory worker, throwing those with nothing left on the floor. When he finds one with enough tobacco left he lights it off the last one, just before it goes out. Eventually the train moves off without the doors opening. The man, pained, slams his fist against the door and runs towards the back of the train as if he might be able to get off there, pursued some seconds later by the madman with the marble. The remaining passengers crane round to see where the voices are coming from. On the platform there's some kind of fight – a man pushed up against a wall, another on the floor – but we only glimpse it before we're plunged into the blackness of the tunnel and our own reflections.

The Métro is a very different place early in the morning. It operates like a dark vascular system, pumping people to where they're needed so that the city may live. Before dawn there are the office cleaners at the end of a night shift, on their way back to the suburbs; kitchen staff, labourers, road sweepers; then, of course, there are the men and women who sleep there – stretched out on pieces of cardboard on the platform floors, oblivious to the world, not far from their small puddle of pungent urine. Rough sleepers are welcome to seek shelter in the Parisian Métro system. Then there's everyone else, exhausted by their existence, going through the motions. In the carriage we sit there in silence, half nodding off, shadows underneath the still-sleeping city, waiting to be spat back out momentarily before crawling back underground to our jobs.

PART 3
L'ENTRÉE

TAMIL TIGERS

One could be forgiven for thinking that a Parisian restaurant was a thing of great beauty, a well-oiled machine, like a well-drilled army, that has been running smoothly for centuries.

It's not.

A Parisian restaurant is a twice-daily exercise in crisis management and maximizing profitability, and, quite frankly, having seen how it works from the other side of the swinging door, I can say that it's nothing short of a miracle that your dishes arrive at your table with all the elements you requested, and that, on top of that, they arrive at exactly the same time. The truth is, a Parisian restaurant is an inefficiency-riddled structure that's manned by underpaid and underfed slaves.

A Parisian restaurant is like a hive, with you, the diners, at the top, and the kitchens somewhere down below. But the nexus of this operation, the place that connects these two worlds – and where I have spent most of my time these last three weeks – is the Pass.

This low-ceilinged, six-square-metre purgatory is where all food and drink will pass; either on its way out of the kitchens, or back in in the form of dirty plates and glasses. The Pass is the gateway to the Underworld, replete with its own Cerberus, in the form of three tough Sri Lankans who take no quarter, and work lit by a naked bulb in a cockpit-sized cell. They wear soiled, once-white lab coats, which bulge at the buttons because of all the layers of clothes they have on underneath. Even if these men are the guardians to the infernos below, they are condemned to work the Parisian winters in glacial temperatures, for the Pass also has an opening onto the terrace for the summer. During the winter, however, the hole has been thoughtfully covered up by a thin metal shutter.

The leader of the gang in Le Bistrot de la Seine is Nimsath – a small wiry man with deep lines on his face, an intense stare and a snappy attitude that's always ready to boil over. He is dark, sinewy and muscular. He could be late twenties or forty – you couldn't say for sure from looking at him. He makes this wonderful growling sound when he's angry.

'Tamil Tiger, Freedom Fighter,' he'll bark. 'Not Sri Lankan. Not Indian, *Ingleeshman*.'

The second Tamil is a giant of a man – the waiters all call him Baloo – with very dark features. He has kind eyes and slow, deliberate movements, as if he's afraid of breaking something. The third is called Mani. I've not seen him before; he doesn't speak – just watches me and smiles.

The men running the Pass, it turns out, were all members of a guerrilla fighting organization that the European Union has had blacklisted since 2006. Conversations with Nimsath and the other Tamils reveal that they are all hardened soldiers, with enough gruesome tales to get the waiters through the slowest of services. It's hard to imagine sometimes that the men stacking plates and shouting at the waiters are adept at hand-to-hand combat and know how to plan and execute a guerrilla attack on an armed convoy. My respect for Nimsath is probably the highest of anyone who works in the restaurant. No one works harder. He's 1 metre 60 of pure muscle and aggro. The waiters may shout and throw tantrums about their lost plates, but they all know Nimsath could more than kick their arses. He doesn't need to say it, you can tell from the look in his eyes. But there's also something immensely comical, almost childish, about him. Of course, sometimes the management, with their petty rules, will try and crush the spirit of independence that exists among the Tamils. However, they underestimate them and are probably ignorant of exactly who they're speaking to. Because, no matter how hard it gets, the Tamils will not be put down. They will not break. In idle moments I like to imagine Corentin coming into the Pass to reprimand them, only for the Tamils to surge out, as from a foxhole, carving knives clamped between their teeth, in order to 'neutralize the threat'. Possibly Baloo dragging Corentin's still-warm corpse back into the Pass to be disposed of appropriately.

As the only English person in the entire restaurant, I've quickly assumed the name, or perhaps identity, of *l'Anglais,* the English guy. *L'Anglais,* I have learned, is a name that can be said in many different ways: with disgust, admiration, intrigue. But there's no one who takes more delight in calling out my name than Nimsath, who prefers the anglicized version, which makes it sound more like *Ing-gleeesh-maan.*

Beyond this fairly superficial persona, no one knows anything about me. Nor do they seem to care, which suits me fine. We're here to work, and all I'm judged upon is that. However, for Nimsath, I hold a certain amount of fascination. As if, even though our lives are wildly different and our reasons for being here even more so, Nimsath sees us as the same – we are both foreigners in France. He also has an obsession with London. This is an advantage, as I'm discovering that the key to a successful service as a runner is having the Tamils onside, particularly Nimsath. To push the military metaphor further: if the restaurant is like the board game Risk, then the Pass is like Kamchatka; if you've got it onside, you're in with a chance of winning.

As a diner you believe that you are going to a restaurant to eat food, but what the restaurant is really selling you is an illusion – it's theatre, pure and simple. And your waiter, as the first and last link in the complicated chain that connects you, sitting upstairs, to the poor sods sweating and swearing underground, is the greatest actor of them all.

Remember, the waiter has one objective: to ensure that your exact order arrives at your table in good time. It seems so simple. That's why you sometimes berate him for not being polite or neglect to leave him a tip. Yet for this straightforward objective to be achieved, your waiter needs to ensure that Nimsath and the other Tamils at the Pass are prioritizing your order. Put simply, this means that he will charm, pressurize and bribe the Tamils to take dishes from other orders, while simultaneously stealing dishes from other waiters' orders so that he can fill his own and get it out. This process is complicated by the fact that every single other waiter is doing exactly the same thing. And they're doing it because they want your tips. As the runner I'm on the receiving end of a lot of this stress. The waiters are often so busy fielding requests from their tables that I'm regularly sent into the Pass under strict instruction to obtain something that is missing from a table's order. There's always too much to do, and I struggle to keep everyone happy. If there's any problem, it's instantly my fault: such is life at the bottom of the food chain. And whenever I need to sort something out quickly, it's to Nimsath I must address myself.

The restaurant layout means sod all to Nimsath: it may be just beyond the door, but it's nothing more than a concept, about as vague and undefined as London. Nimsath's world is the six square metres that he works in. Some Hollywood celebrity may be awaiting her seasonal vegetables, and Adrien the Untouchable may be on the verge of killing me, but Nimsath doesn't give a shit. His job is simple: food comes up, he does his best to stack it into complete orders, without too much interference from the waiters; dirty plates come in, he sends them back down. And if you want special favours from him, well, you're going to have to earn them.

You're going to have to share your tips with him; you're going to have to accept that sometimes he'll have given your dishes to someone else; so you're going to have to argue with him, and accept that being called every single Tamil profanity under the sun is part of your job; and finally you're going to shout back at him, and you'll do it in Tamil, because any Parisian runner or waiter worth his salt knows a smattering of Tamil. But when the service is over, and the casualties have been counted, you're going to drink a coffee with him again and see if there's any food knocking about that he can give you because you haven't eaten for eight hours. And then you're going to talk about everything and nothing until the same thing happens again at the dinner service. A repetition of repetitions.

As a runner my position with the Tamils is weakened by the fact that I don't earn tips, and as such can't share them, although I get the impression that they think I'm just tight. The waiters, in theory, are meant to give me three euros each for my work, but they rarely do and it's humiliating going around at the end of service with my hand out like Oliver Twist, asking for it. The consequence is that when they scream at me to go and get the missing *pommes dauphinoise* for table 487, Nimsath couldn't care less.

I need more of the hard currency which makes this world go round, I need to start making tips – and not just for bribing the Tamils, for living, too. However, in the meantime, when it comes to Nimsath, I have one card up my sleeve: London. But how long this will last, I've no idea.

'London good, Paris bad' is a common refrain of his.

To Nimsath, the idea that I would leave London – where, according to him, everybody is friendly and they don't treat you like a slave – is inconceivable.

Perhaps he has a point.

For Nimsath, the likelihood of ever getting to London is slim, and he knows it, so he contents himself with asking me questions in broken English, and feeling that, by speaking to me, a real Englishman, he is somehow closer to his dream.

When the shift is over Nimsath – like the other Tamils – wraps himself up in further layers of clothes and heads off to the forgotten suburbs. I'm not sure exactly where he lives, but he describes a place of neglected tower blocks where the lifts no longer work and the residents haul their shopping up to their apartments using ropes. No wonder he thinks London will be better. Besides, he can never return to Sri Lanka, he says.

'Tamil Tiger, Freedom Fighter,' the Tamils mutter to themselves when the going gets tough.

Nimsath may no longer be a soldier, but he's still fighting for his freedom. Who knows if he'll ever truly find it? He's been in Paris for ten years, most of them in this Pass – the gateway to the Underworld.

The Underworld

Though your passage through the restaurant may only last an hour or so, the truth is that there are people preparing for it from the crack of dawn, long before you arrive; and then there are others dealing with the fallout from it, long into the night.

To reach the Underworld – a place officially known as the prep kitchen – you must take the stone steps from the Pass all the way down to their terminus. Already as you descend you can smell it: an intense combination of humidity, stale cigarette smoke, gas flames, body odour and decaying vegetables wafting up to greet you. Walking down the steps you submerge yourself in it, you can feel the air change, become thicker; it's like wading into a bath of warm filth. No matter what the temperature is above ground, here it is always hot and humid.

I squeeze past Jamaal, going back up to the surface world, already changed into his waiter's clothes. Beyond the prep kitchen is the locker room. A grim place, and the only one where all the men of the restaurant really mix.

'*Ça va, mon frère?*' Jamaal says with his strong accent. The *frère* is almost a cough. I ask him if he knows when we get paid. He just shrugs his shoulders and hurries upstairs. Getting paid, getting a contract – my two primary concerns right now.

Contrary to the waiting staff, who are European or North African, and the men at the Pass, who are all Tamil, in the prep kitchen they are all African or French African. If the waiters are a well-dressed street gang, then the cooks are more like pirates. Replete with a uniform of dirty white cooks' clothes, headbands, sharp knives and rubber shoes. Like the waiters they have their own language, which they shout to each other across the stoves. It's short and brutal because of the environment they find themselves in; a mixture of African patois, French and pidgin English. As a rule, the cooks don't talk to the waiters. Such is the division of the crews. The cooks prefer to keep to themselves. There's an atmosphere of distrust as you pass through – like you shouldn't be there; you can feel the eyes on you, the lull in conversation. As far as the cooks are concerned the waiters are made of money and work as spies for the management; and as for the cooks, the waiters see them as untrained idiots, whose main aim is to cut corners and provide inedible filth, which the waiter, with his own sense of decorum, must fix before letting his customers eat it. Put simply, if you're a waiter, the kitchen is trying to screw you; and if you're a cook, the waiters are getting rich off your work.

The prep kitchen isn't a glamorous place; on the contrary, it's a place where the floor is always partly flooded, where the men spend most of the day standing in water and rotting vegetable peelings. And the noise is overwhelming. Even at this time, long before the service starts.

On my way to the locker room via the prep kitchen I hop between the islands of dry floor as a man with a brush slops hot soapy water and vegetable discards towards a drain in the middle. When it blocks he rams his hand in and pulls out a fistful of gloopy detritus that he slings into a large open bin. In the prep kitchen we are below the river's surface; hidden yet vital, a relic from another time, like the canal.

At the back of the prep kitchen are the lockers and the changing room. The door to the tiny hole-in-the-floor toilet opens and out wafts a smell of cigarette smoke and shit followed by the menacing look of a cook.

'*Quoi?*' he demands aggressively.

Another man takes his place in the toilet, and the cook goes back to chopping; he doesn't wash his hands. The cooking will sort out the germs – despite what the signs everywhere about cleaning hands say. Besides, there's no sink in the toilet. Same in most French apartments. Usually because there's no space.

In the prep kitchen the men deal with the fundamentals of what will be served. True to its name, they are concerned with preparation: peeling, slicing, dicing, cooking, grilling, cleaning and baking. They may prepare the meat and fish, but their main jobs are the side dishes: there is another kitchen, the upper kitchen, where the meat and fish are sent up via the dolly lifts to be dealt with. I have an idea where the upper kitchen is, but I have repeatedly been told that we're not to go there – under any circumstances. In the kitchen hierarchy, the men in the prep kitchen hold low-ranking grunt jobs.

The locker I left my waiting clothes in last night is full of someone else's stuff. I panic and look around. In a pile on the floor in the corner are my shirt, suit jacket and shoes. I pick them up. The shirt is damp from the floor. It smells faintly of mould. I hang my coat – a recently acquired Russian military overcoat like Stéphane's that I picked up in the flea market not far from the Hôtel du Simplon – in another empty locker and stuff my bow tie and wallet in my pocket. Lucien has said often that you should never leave anything in the lockers, describing it as a 'nest of thieves', but then this is coming from the guy who stole my trench coat.

On the one short bench between the lockers a man lies on his back trying to sleep with one hand shading his eyes from the harsh strip light. Here we are truly in the depths of the machine. The noise is unabating, his exhaustion complete. He catches me looking as I stuff my wallet into my pocket. I can see his eyeball staring through his fingers, then he closes his eyes again. If only he knew that the wallet is completely empty, that, as of this morning, apart from change in my pocket. I have no money whatsoever.

Fortunately, Adrien, the Untouchable, hasn't remembered about the waiter's wallet I requested in my first week. That's the last thing I need. An overpriced faux-leather waiter's wallet. Besides, as I'm still not a waiter, I don't handle money.

Yesterday's shirt is damp. The inside of the collar is yellow and the neckline edge is almost brown. As I button the shirt I watch the man lying on his back again. He must be in his fifties. There are dark patches on his face, blemishes, and a hastily shaved, greying beard. His hands are all shrivelled, as if the skin is too loose and bunches like a glove. The sleeve of his stained white jacket looks soaked and he's wearing wellington boots – must be a *plongeur*. A guy who cleans dishes. The lowest of the low. The very bottom of the food chain. The banging of the toilet door again raises him, and he disappears inside with a thinly rolled cigarette between his lips. It smells like death down here. Despite the rotting humidity it is a dry smell that sits in the back of the throat and lingers after you leave. Finally, I slip on my cheap black jacket. In the harsh light of the locker room I can see how dirty it is, particularly the sleeves and the lapels where the plates and sauces slide onto my chest. I've been wearing it solidly for almost four weeks now with no time to wash it. Once the jacket is on, what can be seen of my shirt is OK. On a bench is an almost-empty bottle of cheap perfume which I spray on my jacket. It smells sickly, but no doubt better than whatever the jacket smells of.

Then lastly the shoes. My feet sting in protest at the reunion. Since I've been working here my feet have blistered all over, and the toes are even beginning to take the form of the cheap shoes. It's time to return to the surface. To pass back through the prep kitchen and the souls who toil there with little chance of returning to the mortal world. I count myself lucky to be one of the waiting staff. To have the uncomfortable winged shoes of Hermes, the runner, the shoes that allow me climb back up to the surface, to the Pass, the gateway to the Underworld, and eventually out into the restaurant.

PUNDAY

A Parisian restaurant runs on strict, yet unspoken, rules. And the most important rule is that everybody only does exactly what they're paid to do. Nothing more. That's why you will not see a waiter stacking plates at the Pass; you will not see a Tamil putting the dirty cutlery in the bucket of water; or a cook touching anything to do with the waiters' service. The reasons are twofold: firstly, you're paid so little that you have no interest in doing anything more; and secondly, if you start doing someone else's job, and you do it wrong, you could get sacked. It is a communist division of labour, presided over by ardent capitalists and enforced by the individual's sense of fear.

At the Pass I hustle another coffee from the Tamils as a way of putting off going to see the management about my contract. I've been in the restaurant for almost a month now, and I'm concerned they could just boot me out and not pay me a dime. Not only do I desperately need the money, but I actually genuinely want the job. The strange, hidden world of the restaurant has intrigued me. I can feel myself slipping into the shadow realm, sinking deeper, leaving my 'surface self' behind; and, in a way, I'm slowly being accepted by the fraternity of men who work here: the real Parisians. If I was looking in some way to get truly down and out, and experience the real Paris, then surely being completely broke, living in a peripheral hotel slash whore house with a croupier slash sect member, and working as a runner in a restaurant is pretty good. Money would help, I can't deny it. How on earth I'm going to eat for the next few days is beyond me.

'Nimsath, how do we get paid?'

Before he can answer there's a blast of frozen air as the small door to the back road opens and a delivery man enters. Félix, the *gardien de nuit*, also appears from the stairwell, hunched over and dragging two large sacks of rubbish in the opposite direction. The two men pass: the drained-looking delivery driver with his crates of fresh vegetables; Félix with his bin bags of rotting detritus. Félix must be in his fifties, from Côte d'Ivoire. A man of few words and a thousand-yard stare; a man whose shift has just finished and who is dressed to leave. He arrived at midnight; all night he's been here, completely alone. His job is to clean the kitchens and dining room. The other waiters say he's rich because of all the lost jewellery and dropped banknotes.

'Be careful. All that comes in fresh leaves rotten,' Félix says flatly to the delivery man as they pass like night trains with their cargos. He makes the same joke every morning. 'I don't know what they do with the place while I'm not here,' he'll add. You ask Félix anything and he'll pretty much always reply with 'I don't know.' It's the best way to stay out of trouble, he says.

Félix returns, the door is still open, the cold Parisian night blows into the Pass.

'*Bon,*' he says, 'I'm off.' The words are slow, fatigued.

We shake forearms and he disappears up the steps, back into the other world, the one outside the restaurant. Perhaps he'll be home before it's light. Perhaps not. The delivery man tries for a free coffee, but the Tamils refuse. '*Trop tard livraison. Toujours trop tard,*' they shout to him. He calls them a number of names and slams the door shut behind him.

'Which manager is here this morning?' I ask the Tamils.

They smile: 'Corentin.'

'Corentin no like Ingleeshman.'

Salvatore, the Bear, arrives looking half dead and is handed a coffee – in a ceramic cup, on a saucer, I note – by Nimsath. He drinks it, mechanically, eyes glazed over, desperate for the caffeine within. Salvatore, most days, like many of the people who work here, is a picture of modern-day exhaustion. It's deeply physical, but this morning it goes deeper than that – all the way to his liver. To get within a couple of metres of him is to realize that the poor guy is in terrible shape. His eyes bloodshot, his breath a heady concoction of booze and cigarettes, and his hands trembling like an old lady's.

'Why do you get a ceramic cup and saucer?' I ask.

'*Cazzo.* I'm Sicilian. To drink coffee from a plastic cup is not possible. Even this French coffee.'

I like Salvatore's style. I too ask Nimsath for another coffee, specifying that I also want it in a ceramic cup.

He shouts something back at me in Tamil: '*Punday!* _____. Anyway, Sal, Sicilian,' is about all I understand.

'You know *Sicilia*?' Salvatore says, his eyes screwed shut in pain.

'I've never been.'

'Then you can't imagine. Paradise. None of this... grey. None of this... eh.' He looks at his coffee with disgust and lifts his shoulders. 'My friend offered me a job this summer. Beach restaurant. Down in the south. Avola – where the wine comes from.'

Salvatore's body bristles. As if all the cells in his body awaken at the thought of his Mediterranean island. Warmed simply by the memory of the sun.

'Imagine, *Inglese*, you spend all day on the beach.' He closes his eyes again and inhales. 'Beautiful women... in bikinis... everywhere. And you, you are tan, healthy... and importantly...' His eyes open. '...you are not in *cazzo Parigi*.'

'*Cazzo Parigi*,' I repeat, adding the hand gesture. There's a real satisfaction to Italian swearwords. Also, something quite elegant about being called *Inglese*. This feels like a small but significant step in my mission to be accepted.

'*Essato*. Instead, you are in *Sicilia*. Where the people are real. Where the people treat you like a human. *Non animali*, like here.' He squeezes his temples. 'In *Sicilia* the people are not rich,' he finally says, 'so they are not *stronzi*. You know this word? Very good, it means "arseholes".'

'*Stronzi*,' I repeat.

'But this is plural. *Stronzo* is if there is only one. Like Corentin.'

'Corentin, *che stronzo*.'

'*Stronzo!*' The big bear smiles. 'In Italian we have many good words like this.'

'What's the worst?'

'Ah, probably *porco dio*. This, you must not say. But you can say *porca Madonna*. They basically mean that God or the Madonna is a pig.'

I hear Nimsath repeating the words from the other side of the Pass.

'Nimsath, what's the worst word in Tamil?'

'*Punday*. Very bad word.'

'*Punday*.' I see Baloo and the other Tamil smile as I say this.

'No, Ingleeshman, you must not say this. Very bad. Very bad word.'

This is funny, because since I arrived I have been trying to make sense of the words I'm learning. In the evenings I'll look up what I heard during the day, often spelling them phonetically and often not finding them. If Stéphane is there, I'll ask him, but usually he's adamant that the words are not French. I insist, telling him they must be, that all the waiters use them. *Punday* is one of these words. Possibly the word I hear most – after *débarrasser*, of course.

'Nimsath, another coffee.' Sal turns to me: 'You want one?'

'Sure.'

'Adrien here?'

'I don't think so. Why?'

'His stuff would help. More than this coffee.'

I'm not exactly sure what this is about, but my guess is that the Untouchable might have some kind of side business.

With his wry smile, handsome face and melancholic blue eyes Salvatore is one of those rare people in life who you really want to like you. His flirting is legendary in the restaurant: he seems to have a way with women and often finishes a service with at least one phone number, even though, by all accounts, he's in a relationship with Pauline, the girl with the reservations book. But it's not just women: the men also want his affection, which is evident in the way the other waiters treat him. He's a genuine presence among them. Even the usually taciturn Adrien has a soft spot for Sal, who regularly makes him laugh with tales of his sexual escapades. Becoming friends with Sal would give me a useful ally.

But, more importantly, a friend in Paris.

Yet all is not always rosy with him. Below the bright surface lurks something darker; like a Roman god's, Sal's mood changes are often extreme and instantaneous, and can leave him brooding and isolated. In an instant he can go from being the warmest-hearted of the waiters to someone you are certain you have committed some unforgivable act against. On numerous occasions during the last few weeks he has completely lost his shit with me and had to restrain himself from physical violence. In times like these, looking into his eyes, you're unsure of who you are talking to. It is night and day, two completely different people. His psychological state and mood swings make me wonder if he's perhaps slightly bipolar. Of course, the other issue Sal has with me, and consequently probably the reason he has so little respect for me, is how poorly cut my suit jacket is. It's an affront to his Italian sensibilities. But until I get some money, I can't do anything about that.

'Ingleeshman, time to go and see Corentin,' Nimsath baits me.

'That piece of shit Corentin,' Sal says. 'He's here?'

'In the office, I think.'

'Too scared to show his face in here, I bet.'

'*Stronzo.*'

'*Un enorme stronzo. Porco dio.*'

It turns out that Salvatore is sore because today was his day off and last night he went out drinking, but because one of the other waiters didn't show up, Corentin chose to call Sal as a replacement – this was an hour ago, apparently. Hence his current physical state. How he will get through the entire day is beyond me. Although, whatever Adrien's 'stuff' is will clearly help.

'Eh, and *Inglese*, I don't know why you're laughing. Corentin, he doesn't like you either. I don't know what you did,' Sal says.

'Nothing. I did nothing.'

'Hah! That's what my uncle always says. And he's in Ucciardone prison. But screw Corentin, he's a piece of shit.'

Salvatore clearly doesn't like Corentin either, which makes him attractive as an ally in my campaign for a contract and acceptance.

'You like diving, *l'Anglais*?' he asks me.

'Diving?'

'Beautiful sport. This summer, I go to Egypt. There's this place in the middle of the desert, a deep blue hole. The most beautiful diving spot in the world. And no one knows about it. You want my advice? You take as much money as you can from these rich *pezzi di merda* – and you piss off. This is why waiting is good – wherever you go, you can find a job. You're a man of the world.'

In a bid to get him to give me some money for yesterday's work I remind him that as a runner I don't make tips unless the waiters give me three euros each, which he ignores. Instead, he talks about diving some more, but the idea of this bear of a man being graceful in the water eludes me. Fortunately, he eventually he returns to his hatred of France and rich people, which this morning is embodied by Corentin. I think Sal's main problem is with authority, so we soon hit it off and he begins telling me I should meet some of his 'friends'.

It turns out that Salvatore is an active member of the Communist Party in Paris. And even if he can't vote, he often tries to canvass for recruits in the kitchens. His great-grandfather, he tells me, was one of the key figures in Italian post-war politics. 'A leader in the Sicilian Communist Party.' Who, Salvatore says, was present at the celebrated Portella della Ginestra massacre in 1947, in which the famous Sicilian bandit, also called Salvatore, but this time Salvatore Giuliano, is said to have opened fire on the May Day parade. Salvatore's activism, by the looks of things, still takes on quite a physical form, as the cuts and bruises on his knuckles attest. I point out that it's strange he has the same name as someone who he says killed fellow communists, but Salvatore is adamant: Giuliano did not do it. 'Giuliano was like Robin Hood.' So, when he says I should meet some of his 'friends' I'm pretty sure he's talking about fellow communists. Most of them, it appears, work in similar jobs to us. I agree, naturally. And, by lightly suggesting I too would like to be part of 'something', rise in his estimation.

'Wait. Give me your coffee.' His large paw of a hand squeezes my shoulder.

I hand Sal my coffee. He leans down and asks Nimsath, incredibly politely, to fetch the grappa. Nimsath hesitates, but this is Sal, and it isn't long before he's returned with the bottle. Salvatore pours a healthy dose in both of our coffees. A shot directly in his mouth and then he hands the bottle back to Nimsath with a five-euro note.

'In Italy, we call this *caffè corretto*.'

'*Cazzo*, that's strong.'

As the grappa courses through Sal's veins he feels an increased need to vent his anger about Corentin. Naturally I do my best to spur him on, painting Corentin as a symbol of bourgeois oppression in the restaurant, a man who single-handedly seeks to crush the proletariat's spirit, and – finding my stride now – that we should seek to eradicate him and liberate ourselves from the yoke of oppression. With my dismal French, exactly how much of this gets across isn't clear. Regardless, Salvatore understands the sentiment – I can tell as his bear paw almost never leaves my shoulder now.

'*Bene, Inglese. Bravo. Fantastico,*' he keeps on saying.

I'm making progress with Salvatore and suggest that perhaps we could go and see Corentin together. In my mind, Sal can be my enforcer. Help me stand up for my rights as a runner.

'...in the spirit of fraternity,' I say. 'A true socialist France.'

This sets Sal on a roll again: 'France? A socialist country? They should come to this restaurant. See how we work. If it was a real socialist paradise, the *patron* of this place would be in jail. Yesterday, I finished at 2am. 2am! Naturally, I go for a drink... maybe two. To help me sleep, of course. And now look. I'm already here. I slept, what?' He looks at his watch. 'Maybe two hours. *Porco dio.*'

The Tamils laugh. '*Patron* in jail,' they repeat. '*Porco dio.*'

Before I can remind Sal that we have a meeting with 'the man' he has started rolling a cigarette – a task that is slightly impeded by how much his hands are shaking.

With the breakfast service soon to be upon us, time is of the essence if I want to see Corentin, and emboldened as I am by listening to Sal and his lamentations about middle management and the crushing of the working man's spirit – and having my own spirit fanned by the fumes of the grappa on a very empty stomach – I put the plastic coffee cup down and turn to go and catch the Rat.

'*Punday* bin!' Nimsath explodes. '... *Punday* Ingleeshman.'

Nimsath growls and eyes me with hatred as I return and put the plastic cup into the bin. It doesn't matter that it's right next to him. 'Do *your* job. I do mine,' he spits.

'You'll make a good communist, Nimsath,' Salvatore assures him and raises his fist.

'No communist. Tamil Tiger,' he says bluntly.

Jamaal returns to the Pass, pats me on the shoulder in a faux-friendly way as I leave. Jamaal is your archetypal Parisian waiter: lazy, duplicitous and greedy. He's meant to be doing the *ouverture* with Salvatore but has changed quickly so as to take the tables that are closest to the Pass while Salvatore drinks coffee and talks with the Tamils – as he often does. This way Jamaal will have less distance than Salvatore to travel during the service. That's why he looks so suspicious, I figure – his forehead already sweaty, the fat bottom lip protruding slightly – because he knows that for the breakfast service the *rangs* are taken on a first come first served basis, unless Adrien is here, which he's not.

'*Bon service,*' I say.

'*Inshallah, frère.*'

It's said that the waiters in Le Bistrot de la Seine are chosen on looks, but Jamaal and Renaud prove the exception.

Out of the Pass I work my way towards the back of the shadowy dining room, past the small bar in the back room and along a dark corridor. There's a door hidden in a carpeted wall which takes you back into an overlit stone administrative area with a low ceiling. There are doors along the passageway, but the only one that interests me is the final one: the *directeur*'s office.

As expected, when I do find the Rat – tucked behind the *directeur*'s desk in a space that can best be described as a void between walls, with a ceiling so low you have to stoop, and files strewn everywhere, an enormous safe, a bookshelf upon which sit dozens of pairs of high-heeled shoes (the hostesses', perhaps?) and a heady whiff of Hermès perfume, cigarette smoke and burning dust from the fan heater on the floor – he is less than pleased to see me.

'You! What do you want?'

'A contract. For renting. You said—'

The Rat almost spits out his coffee. 'Ha! You'll have a contract when _____ ready, which in my opinion is never. _____!' He stands up, his bony fists clenched by his side. 'Tell me. Why does a runner need a contract? Hey? A runner only lasts a few months. _____. It's not worth the paperwork. We have to pay for that. _____. Why would we pay for someone like you? You won't be here long enough. Come and go, that's a runner. Come and go. Come and go,' he repeats, clearly happy with the expression.

Me arguing my case only infuriates him further. The odious little man in the tight suit shouts something about wanting to fire me on the spot, and how even this morning one of the other waiters had come to see him about me, about my lack of professionalism. Not being able to argue back to this jumped-up former waiter is incredibly frustrating. Until I can speak French well enough, I'll just have to take the abuse. Eventually, he sends me out of the office under the pretence that the pavement needs sweeping. While I'm out there freezing, I conclude that Jamaal must have said something to the Rat, that's why he looked so suspicious when I just saw him. He's always so smarmy, so untrustworthy. But why, exactly, is beyond me. Surely it's helpful to have a runner?

Regardless, with a contract out of my control and, for the moment, my wages also, the only thing I can really influence is getting tips. I just need to work out how. Because, as far as I can understand, tips are only for waiters. And the three euros the waiters are meant to give me each day as a runner are often 'conveniently' forgotten.

So, in the meantime, *punday.*

OVERTIME

The French word for a tip is pourboire, *which literally translated means 'for drinking'. And you can be certain that, when you leave your* pourboire, *the waiter will spend it correctly. The reality is that the* pourboire *is the money waiters live off. It's the money left over from their wages that they hope to save, after the rent and all living expenses have been covered. It's the money they believe will free them. However, they always come back – the restaurant ensures this by paying them the strict minimum. In time I would learn that waiters are an itinerant class; they work like dogs and spend like idiots. With wallets often stuffed with banknotes, they have the illusion, temporary though it is, of being rich. The rule is that you spend your tips on the ephemeral, which in reality means alcohol, cigarettes and food. To say you've spent all your tips is a good thing. Which is why it is so important, imperative even, to keep earning them every day.*

It's after the dinner service and De Souza and Salvatore are going through their takings. Salvatore is talking about a Frenchwoman he served and that he thinks he's now in love with. This makes Nimsath snigger. 'Bad man Salvatore,' he keeps saying.

'And *la famiglia del mondo?*' De Souza laughs.

'Family of world, Ingleeshman,' Nimsath tells me eagerly.

'What's *la famiglia del mondo?*'

'It is magnificent,' Salvatore says.

Since this morning he's really picked up, helped in no small part, I'm sure, by the little wrap of something Adrien gave him at lunchtime.

'*C'est une blague.*' It's a joke. De Souza can't stop smiling.

Salvatore goes on to describe his plan to have children with women of many different nationalities. The idea is that all the children will grow up knowing many languages. He describes Christmases in Sicily with children talking in a mixture of Swedish, French, Argentinian Spanish and Lebanese-accented Arabic, which, according to him, is the sweetest of all the Arabic accents.

'He even has a theme tune, *l'Anglais*,' De Souza says.

Salvatore whistles something which sounds like a radio jingle, then sings '*la famiglia del mondo*' to the same tune before winking at me.

'You're ridiculous,' I tell him, laughing.

'I love children, *l'Anglais*. But not marriage. My parents have both been divorced three times. Twice to each other. This is not good for anyone. With *la famiglia del mondo*, everyone is happy.'

'What about the women?' It seems like an obvious question, but I ask it anyway.

'Yes, what about the women?' De Souza repeats.

'They will like it. They know what I am like. I will love them all. That is my superpower, everybody has one. Mine is that I can love many women at the same time. Whoever said you cannot love more than one woman at the same time was wrong.'

'I only love my fiancée, Sal. And when she's my wife, I'll still only love her. It's impossible to love more than one woman,' De Souza says. 'Not if it's true love. You, Sal, are an Italian cliché. A discredit to your countrymen.'

'Pfff. People love more than one of their children, De Souza. Besides, women today, they don't want marriage either, just *la famiglia del mondo*.' Salvatore's blue eyes sparkle. 'Marriage was made by men to trap them. Women, like birds, must be free. I am a modern man. I do not wish to suppress women in the institution of marriage...'

'Sal, please.' De Souza pinches his fingers together, Italian style, by his waist. 'I'm killing myself with extra hours for this wedding.'

Salvatore apologizes; he knows he's overstepped the mark. 'Too much work, *fratello mio*. You look exhausted,' he says with a fraternal tenderness.

'You want some you-know-what?'

'Not for me.' De Souza replies.

It's true, there's rarely a day that goes by when De Souza isn't working. And when the restaurant is short-staffed, he always puts himself forward for a double shift. Salvatore tries to tell De Souza to take fewer shifts.

'I have to, though,' De Souza replies.

'Why?'

'I'm scared.'

'Of what?'

'Losing them. You can't understand how much I love them...'

With his wedding later this year, and his baby daughter growing up fast, De Souza is petrified he won't be able to support them. They currently live in a bedsit together in one of the suburbs, but soon enough they'll need a bigger place, and he's worried he won't be able to afford it.

The conversation subsides. To the hum of the fridges and the whistle of the theme tune the two remaining waiters begin to scribble with cheap biros on the small pieces of paper which the restaurant gives them at the end of the day. They are counting all their takings, marking every single credit card ticket or the cash in their wallet against a long printout of all their orders for the day, or at least the ones they passed through the till. What's left will be theirs. Their tips.

Of course, the waiters all have little tricks of ensuring you leave something. That's why they prefer certain denominations of notes, particularly fives. Coins, too, which in France means the two-euro coin. The reasoning is simple. If the change from a meal comes to ten euros, the waiter will want to leave two fives. The hope is that you'll think it's easier just to leave a five, whereas, had they left a ten, you may not have left anything at all. Among the waiters there is also an informal list of which nations are the best tippers, and ensuring that the hostesses sit these people at your tables greatly increases your chances of making more money. Among the top tippers are the Brazilians, Japanese and, occasionally, Americans. Although of late the waiters have remarked a tendency for Americans to believe that 'in Europe they don't leave tips'. Among the worst tippers are the French, who somehow believe that the minimum wage is sufficient payment for the waiter's work. It is rare that they leave anything at all, despite often being the most critical of diners.

The waiters have finished their calculations.

'*Pas mal,*' De Souza says. '*Et toi?*'

'*Oui, ça va,*' Sal responds.

Neither wants to show his hand. Both are being discreet, perhaps because Nimsath is there. Because of this I also don't ask for the three euros they each owe me. Even though the other waiters have already snuck off without paying me.

'*Tiens, Nimsath.*' Sal hands Nimsath a ten.

'*Attends.*' De Souza hands him a twenty.

De Souza made more today; now they both know it. But Sal's next move is to give me a ten, which De Souza then does, too. The second set is a draw. But thanks to the waiters' perverse sense of pride and competition, I'm now twenty euros up.

As for Sal and De Souza, after a day with wallets bulging full of the restaurant's money, finally their wallets are full of what they see as theirs. Next, they must go into the back office where Corentin the Rat will count out the takings, marking them off against what has been through the tills and been paid by card. If the waiter has made a mistake, he'll be asked to hand over more money. But waiters rarely make a mistake when it comes to tips. Their salary is so low that their tips are what they live off. Worn-out banknotes that have been left to them among the dirty plates and empty glasses.

I stand in the small back office watching the Rat double-check their calculations with a blunt pencil. When he's finished he puts the money in crumpled envelopes and locks them in the small safe. The two waiters disappear, wallets full of short-term freedom. I want some of what they have: tips. Tips to eat. Tips to buy me favours with Nimsath. Tips to get my jacket adjusted. Tips – the possibilities are limitless. Especially with the amount these guys appear to be making each day.

'What time did you start?' the Rat asks me.

'Eight. But I arrived before.'

He takes down a large blue folder, notes something with the blunt pencil and mutters the word 'eight'.

'Why?'

'For your hours. To make sure you're paid correctly. I note down if you do overtime.'

'I worked non-stop,' I tell him. 'You do this since from when I started?'

'*Si, si*. It's all here.' He hisses like a snake as he speaks.

'What happens with overtime?'

'Are you stupid? I said I write it down here.' He slams the folder shut for dramatic effect.

'But then what?'

This sends him into one of his usual fits: 'Then... then... if you have worked overtime, you can take it back, as _____. Not that you're _____! You haven't _____ anything.'

I still don't really understand what overtime is. Or how my salary is worked out. I ask again when I can have my contract as maybe this will clarify the situation.

'Leave that to the accountants,' the Rat shouts and dismisses me from the little back office. 'Have you given us your social security number yet? Have you? No, I didn't think so. Get out of here.'

I walk back to the Métro feeling hungry and tired – and with one thing on my mind: money. *Du fric, des sous, du pognon, du blé, du pèze, du cash, de l'argent, de la monnaie, de la thune, des billets, de la caillasse, des ronds, du flouze, de la maille...* You hear it mentioned all day. It's the thing lurking in the shadows, permeating every decision anyone makes around here. Because it's all anyone needs – the invisible force that keeps them chained to their station, yet also the very thing that will set them free.

In a desperate bid to enrich myself I spend half the money that De Souza and Sal gave me on scratch cards in the PMU bar that is still open at the end of the street. The other half on cheap whisky, which will first take away the dull feeling of hunger, then make me forget it.

Methodically I go through the scratch cards, slowly, as if somehow this will influence the outcome. I use the largest denomination coin I have for exactly the same reason.

Alas, no luck. No win. Just the two-euro coin left in my hand and the assorted coins in my pocket. With that tomorrow morning I can buy a *pain au chocolat*. Or, right now, I could buy a *démi* of 1664 and still have some left in my pocket for the Métro tomorrow morning – I just won't have breakfast, again. Then I'll need tips at lunch in case I am given a break and can eat. Then the following evening…

Money. It is starting to obsess me, too, specifically tips – the waiter's panacea. With a pocket full of cash each day, Paris can be yours.

Know Your Rank

Before each service there's a briefing in the corner of the dining room. The staff stand to attention as the *directeur* walks up and down the line of degenerates that the restaurant has put in bow ties and black jackets and called waiters, his expensive perfume embalming them like incense from a priest's swinging chain censer. To see them here in the magnificent dining room, their suits looking fine, their bow ties straight, you could almost call them gentlemen.

Today the *directeur* wears a fine navy-blue suit. His face is pudgy, almost baby-like, and glistens slightly from cream and perspiration. He lives in the 16th arrondissement, *'le Paris des riches'*, as Salvatore calls it. The *directeur* makes a couple of bad jokes. Like me, he too wants to be part of the gang, wants the waiters to like him. But he never can. He's not one of them, and they know it, even if he doesn't.

Next the Rat reels off the day's specials. Some waiters scribble in their notepads, the old hands commit them to memory. A waiter's short-term memory is a considerable thing and taking orders without a notepad is a sign of prestige; the game is to keep a straight face, act completely unfazed as order upon order comes your way – only the pros can manage it. If you have to go back to the table and clarify something, you've failed. When the Rat is done with the specials, he looks to the *directeur* like a gun dog.

Finally, Pauline gives out the *rangs*, the ranks. The groups of tables each waiter will work for the service. I'm now understanding that this daily ceremony, on the surface so simple, belies a system that is much more complicated than first meets the eye, and clearly one of the sources of

Pauline's great power in the restaurant. The distribution of the *rangs* is not arbitrary. It is the result of numerous machinations. Any waiter worth his salt will make sure to bad-mouth his peers to the right people. To advance and be strong here is to ensure that others are weak, not that you are better. And the management are well aware of this; the daily division of *rangs* acts as a kind of bellwether on how they view you. So in between each service everybody is on a quiet campaign to discredit the others to their own gain. No two ranks are the same, and there are a limited number. This is to do with how the diners are divided and seated and how the restaurant is physically arranged. As a runner I need to know every *rang* so that I can take the plates to the correct tables. However, for a waiter, the *rang* he is allocated is of crucial importance and dictates how his service will go. Of course, some *rangs* are more prestigious than others. And as the keeper of the reservations book, Pauline is the most important person when it comes to a waiter's hierarchal mobility and chances of making tips.

For example: if Pauline gives you a *rang* with tables closer to the Pass, you can work more quickly, and therefore turn more tables, thus having a higher chance of earning tips. However, this isn't where the wealthier diners are seated, so it's a numbers game – like cold-calling. Serve enough and eventually you'll strike gold; in Le Bistrot de la Seine, the *rangs* nearer the windows have a better clientele, which is to say people who outwardly appear to have more money, or indeed are just better looking than those nearer the Pass. The understanding among the waiters is that the tips are better here, which is attributed to a kind of middle-class guilt – the customers do it as they think it's expected of them. As you get closer to the centre of the dining room the *rangs* increase in importance until they reach their zenith. This is the *rang* that the restaurant refers to as the 'VIP zone'. The focal point of the restaurant, the stage upon the stage, the altar, the centre of the mandala, of the universe. It's considered so exclusive that during some services it will remain completely empty – even if there is a queue outside – as Pauline and the hostesses haven't deemed anyone good enough to sit there. Besides, leaving it empty – with menus laid across each place to suggest they are reserved – creates the illusion of exclusivity. If you do happen to be someone rich or famous, then you get to enjoy the pleasure of swanning through the swamp of proletarians who have the demeaning fate of waiting for a table, and sitting right down. However, because the VIP zone will often be empty, most waiters loathe to be given it – it could potentially mean an entire service without a table, and therefore no tips. Though they tell me it's different in summer, as the VIP *rang* on the terrace is always busy.

As a rule, the very rich, powerful, famous and beautiful are not the greatest tippers; they believe something is owed to them and are used to getting things for free. It's here that you'll most often hear diners talking about 'how well waiters are paid' when one of the table mentions the tip. However, occasionally, one will get drunk and make a gesture to impress his table. It's from this *rang* that all the legends spring, tales that waiters pass around like snatches of gospel, stories of tips that were great enough to retire on and the like.

There is another *rang*: it's at the opposite end of the restaurant from the Pass, tucked around a corner. This special place is saved for the groups of tourists, poorly dressed or just downright ugly.

Renaud licks his lips in delight when he's given the 700, which is to say all the tables numbered 700 up. This is the last *rang*, where the hostesses will seat the large tables of Chinese who come in. These tables are so far away that it's hard to really consider them part of the actual restaurant.

'*Les chinois* give big tips, *mec*,' Renaud says when Lucien laughs. Confusingly for a runner the waiters refer to anyone Asian as 'Chinese'.

We're about to be dismissed when a towering figure of a man in soiled chef's whites with an enormous knife in his belt bursts out of the swinging door and speaks with the *directeur*. When he's done, he gives us a disdainful look from a lazy eye and heads back inside like some embittered Cyclops. This man is the head chef. A Corsican of unbridled fury, who rarely comes down from the upper kitchen – a place, Lucien is at pains to regularly explain to me, that is strictly out of bounds for waiters.

'Get rid of the trout,' the *directeur* says to us, before walking off towards his cramped back office.

We're finally dismissed. Salvatore tries to talk to Pauline but she turns away angrily. Lucien catches me see Salvatore touch the small of her back.

'You should try next,' he whispers. 'That way you'll have the good tables. Like Sal.' He winks.

'Sal's still with Pauline?'

'Come on,' he says in English. 'Why you think 'e still always 'as the good tables? Whichever waiter is with Pauline, it's their *récompense*. How do you say? Little bonus? Sal is a true pro.'

Despite her imposing presence in the restaurant, Pauline suddenly takes on a shade of the tragic.

The preparations completed, now it's the waiting game. The waiters at their posts in the magnificent dining room; the Tamils at the dolly lifts; the cooks on standby; the hostesses at the velvet cord; managers prowling, looking for problems; the runner, desperate for money, his hangover receding thanks to grappa and paracetamol. The entire restaurant ready. The calm before the storm.

I hear Lucien with an elderly French lady who's peering at her menu:

'*Les deux sont bien. Mais pour moi...*' Both are good. But for me..., he says, and you can hear the smile in his voice, 'I would advise the trout. A beautiful fish. I saw them delivered this morning.'

'*Bon, je prends la truite alors!*' she says confidently.

The lunch service passes like most before it, with too many things to do and not enough time to do them. There is, however, a glimmer of hope: a Brazilian couple. Brazilian, the proverbial waiter's unicorn, the highest of the high tippers. They don't speak French, which is a bonus, so we chat in English. They want to know where to go in Paris, where to avoid the tourists. I rise to the challenge, giving them everything I know, all my keys to the city. I even take time to point things out on their map and give them the number of an English-speaking taxi company that arrives quickly. They are more than grateful, almost deferentially so, and I can see why waiters can become so snooty: you're literally looking down your nose at people, people who treat you (occasionally) as someone of great knowledge and power. Before leaving I see them conversing to one another. I watch as the husband draws a twenty-euro note from his wallet, and with a wave and a smile to me places it under a bottle on the table. Like the grateful slave that I am, I'm practically kissing his feet as I escort him and his charming wife to the door. We speak during this short journey, but all I'm actually thinking about is what I'll spend the twenty euros on. Oddly, adjusting my suit comes to mind before giving my body nutrients. Not wanting to seem desperate, I haven't taken the money immediately but left it on the table. It wouldn't have looked good to snatch it up before their very eyes – I am above that. However, when I return to the table, the money is gone, yet the table hasn't been cleared. Someone has stolen my tip. Renaud, whose table it is, looks me in the eyes and says he has no idea what I am talking about, that there was no money, before proceeding to berate me for not having already cleared the table so that more people can be seated there. He even has the audacity to fix me with his deceitful eyes and suggest he is *losing tips* because of me; later on, at the Pass, he reminds the other waiters that a runner should be running, not chatting, to which they all readily agree.

'Listen to him complaining. When did you hear of a runner earning tips? Open your wallet, *l'Anglais*,' he's saying. 'We want to know how much you've taken from us today.'

'That money was mine. You stole it,' I say, which is ignored.

'Stole it? Runners don't make tips,' Jamaal eventually says.

This seems wholly unjust, as without my help most of them wouldn't have managed to serve half as many tables as they have. They have tips to show for it; all I have are more blisters, and now a thinly veiled criticism of my work. I make a point of going around them all after the service and asking for my three euros. Reluctantly some give them to me. Jamaal hands me just under a euro in small coins, and Renaud says he'll give me something later as he doesn't have anything on him. No ten-euro notes like the other night when De Souza and Sal were in good moods.

Mercifully I am given a break later in the afternoon and take myself off to a five-star hotel for an hour's kip in the toilets. The coins I have I spend on a much-needed sandwich, although because it is no longer lunchtime the *boulangerie* refuses to serve me the cheaper *menu midi*. Understanding how *rangs* are given out, I can now see why they want me to stay a runner, and not become a waiter. There are only so many tables to go around. But not getting a share of the tips seems distinctly unjust. I need to, in the words of the French, *mettre du beurre dans les épinards*, to put butter in the spinach, which roughly means earn more.

I need to get close to Pauline.

SAINTE PAULINE

A restaurant is a contained universe with a universal language, which everyone, no matter who they are, understands: the restaurant layout. A waiter may not want the tables in the centre, but a diner certainly does. Because they know that as you go outwards from the core, the tables diminish in importance until you reach the wings where the least desirable tables are found. The restaurant, and the city in this respect, are incredibly similar. The difference with the restaurant is that occasionally you can jump your social station, and for the duration of your meal enjoy the luxury of being part of a better-looking or richer caste. The key is to impress the gatekeeper.

Before you can even set foot in Le Bistrot de la Seine, you need to get past the door. Or, more specifically, the person at the door, which in this case is Pauline. Pauline is like a hard-faced version of Saint Peter, if Saint Peter was unforgiving, stone cold and ruthless in carrying out his duties at the gates of heaven. As head of the hostesses Pauline holds a rank that is inferior to that of the managers, yet, because she is also the keeper of the reservations book – the person at the front of house, and therefore the 'face' of the restaurant – as well as the person who gives out the *rangs*, in reality she sits somewhere between the *directeur* and the managers. Below that comes Adrien, the untouchable head waiter, then all the other waiters. Finally, me, the runner, somewhere below.

I say she comes below the *directeur*: there are scurrilous rumours among the waiters that Pauline has often spent time at the very top of the food chain, which is to say on top of the *patron* of the establishment himself.

Pauline's job is to make sure that you, the diner, are seated where you belong. In that sense her job is unique: she is there to judge you. You could say it is the most Parisian of jobs – passing judgement – and you could easily imagine there being thousands, if not millions, of great candidates across the city, but it is not so. Even her team of terrifyingly beautiful hostesses – who look and act like off-duty models, and as such see talking to the waiters as beneath them – often make mistakes. Indeed, the turnaround of the hostesses appears to be quicker than that of the waiting staff, so high are the standards Pauline holds them to. Although it may also be a tactic for ensuring she is never replaced.

Pauline's skills are famous. She can get the measure of someone in a matter of seconds, often without having to talk to them. I ask her how she does it, how she can so instinctively tell where everyone belongs in the Parisian caste system.

'It's the small details they miss.' She is talking about the hostesses. 'They think that because something looks expensive, it is. Maybe it is, maybe it isn't. This does not interest me. What's important is *how* you wear something. Any man can wear expensive shoes. The hard part's wearing them like you're *meant* to be wearing them.'

We are behind the restaurant smoking before the dinner service. She looks exhausted and slightly drunk. Although at a glance you would say she was incredibly well presented, with expensively dyed blonde hair and a black dress that is loose enough to be sophisticated yet means she doesn't have to worry about competing with the younger hostesses, whose statuesque physiques appear to have been hewn on Mount Olympus by the gods themselves.

'What about them?' I ask of a passing couple.

'Hah!' Smoke pours from her mouth as she laughs. '*Petite bourgeoisie.* He's a lawyer, and she...' There is a look of revulsion on her face as she looks the woman up and down. '...dressed like that? Wants to go back to Brittany, or Normandy, or whatever miserable place she's from.'

'They're not coming in?'

'They'll come in, but they are so lacking in class or beauty that I'll put them out of the way.'

'So, it's about beauty?'

'Not always. Serge Gainsbourg was not beautiful.'

'He was famous.'

'Certain people have something. It's hard to explain. But when I see them, I know. It is in the way they walk, the way they look at the world...'

'Confidence?'

'Perhaps, but not always.'

'Class?'

'You could say that.'

'What about me?' I ask.

'What about you? You're a runner.'

I try to ask as casually as possible about my chances of getting a *rang* – even at the furthest reaches of the restaurant.

'No chance,' she says. 'If I give one to you, I take it from someone else.' She takes a drag on her long, thin cigarette. 'You're not ready yet. Besides, your chances aren't being helped by someone telling the management you're up to no good.'

'What? Corentin?'

'Not only.'

'Jamaal?'

'My lips are sealed.'

'I need tips. I'm broke.'

'You can earn tips as a runner,' she smiles.

'The waiters never give them to me.'

'You ask for them. That's where you're wrong. The key is to make some-one *want* to give you a tip.'

On the other side of the road a woman strides past with immeasurable confidence. Her high heels ringing off the building fronts.

'She has it. You see?' Pauline continues.

'She's beautiful.'

'No, she's elegant. It's about elegance. You're English. You wouldn't understand.'

'Define elegance.'

Despite answering almost immediately, she finds enough time to look my terrible suit jacket up and down once before saying, 'Never too much; never too little.'

And with that she crushes her cigarette under her high heel, gives me a look that says the conversation is over, and disappears inside.

Pure elegance.

Pauline's judgement was brutal, and I wondered what she would say if she scrutinized herself in the same way she judged others. She gave up little of her own story. What I could ascertain came from fragments of other people, such as Salvatore, who said she had no real friends or family in Paris that he knew of. Like the people she now criticized, and many French people, Pauline too once moved from the provinces to the capital; with dreams of working in fashion, according to Lucien, who said her accent was still faintly from Toulouse. But life is cruel, and though French society may have outwardly destroyed the class system when they toppled the monarchy, it left in place a rigid caste system. To succeed in France, you need to have grown up in the right areas (often prestigious Parisian neighbourhoods) and to have attended the right schools and universities. Pauline had not. And the world she tried to break into had known it and closed ranks. Ironically, she had now become the system's most hard-line fanatic. Upholding the rules with a cruel and uncompromising resoluteness.

As such she was a woman who had a touch of the tragic in her deep green eyes. Physically you would say she possessed a faded beauty; what was left of it had been hidden under the heavily applied make-up. It was only in daylight that this was visible; the puffy drinker's face with the slightly blue skin around the nose, the trembling hands as she ran her finger down the list of reservations. Her best years were behind her, and she knew it. However, she never showed it, not directly. It was in her cruel perceptions of others that it showed.

At night, however, when the shadows of the restaurant were at their most marked, she had an allure. Pauline was an object of desire among the waiting staff, and her ability to play clients and waiters made her a true master of her craft. She knew every single gesture that would strike home, and they were always so slight: the touch of the hair, the fleeting glance, the smile or, when necessary, the raised voice, the defiant stance; the right word at just the right time to put anyone in their place. She was, in every sense of the expression, a true master. Her presence was a constant in the restaurant, even for the diners. It was as if she ran the place; as if the whole show was for her. And she treated it as such. How we all looked was her business. We were extras in her show.

You could say that she was perfectly suited to her environment, but whether she was a product of it or had just adapted was never clear. There was something in the bitterness with which she judged people that suggested a deep unhappiness. Lucien maintained that she'd joined the restaurant as the *patron*'s mistress but that he'd long ago got bored with her and, to make her happy, gave her this job. Other waiters even went as far as to say it was because she'd fallen pregnant with the *patron*'s child and her price for an abortion was a job for life. This malice was due no doubt in some part to the fact that she wielded a certain amount of power over them, both sexually and hierarchically. In this distinctly masculine world, Pauline, a woman, was most definitely at the top.

My own enquiries into Pauline got nowhere further. Like her true face that lay somewhere behind the make-up, so too hid the real Pauline. She was vague when I asked her how long she'd worked in the restaurant.

'Longer than I care to remember,' she said.

Lucien reckoned it was close to ten years, possibly twelve, which meant she arrived when she was sometime in her mid-twenties. As, though she looked older, Salvatore assured us she was only thirty-six. He'd seen her driving licence, he said, with one of his usual sly winks.

Pauline had said I couldn't wait tables yet, but the thing that stuck was when she said I could make tips. That I must make them want to give them to me.

The Rise of the Runner

In the dining room before dinner De Souza and Adrien are setting the tables. Industrially cleaned and ironed white tablecloths float down onto tables; plates, cutlery and glasses are positioned with precision. The two men work in silence. Years and years of working together; it's all gestures, automated.

De Souza and Adrien are different sides of the same coin. Even the way they speak has similarities and Adrien will be best man at De Souza's wedding. De Souza gives out an instant warmth, whether he's dealing with a diner or a waiter. Despite his short, squat physique and his bravado about boxing, it is generally understood that the Little Boxer couldn't hurt a fly. It's as if he talks about boxing to seem harder than he actually is. Whereas Adrien is one of those Parisian waiters that you encounter everywhere across the city, the kind that you feel instantly dislikes you, who is inconvenienced by the very fact you've even come into a restaurant, let alone that you are expecting to exchange money for food and, on top of that, that you expect him – a waiter! – to bring it to you. But, in that sense, he's the consummate professional; his time is precious, and he wants you to know it. And because of this, and because of the way in which he carries out his duties, you want him to like you; it's theatre and he's an actor, and as such he is insufferable.

When the *salle* has been set, the waiters are assembled in the corner for the briefing. Before the dinner service there's the usual nervous energy; however, unlike lunch, which tends to be stressful, the dinner services have a slightly more relaxed pace as the reservations are more spread out, although the work is just as demanding. Pauline turns up with the reservations book, and I feel a tinge of jealousy when the tables are given out. Being a waiter does have its advantages. Notably the tips, but also the respect. As a runner the waiters have next to none for me, nor do the management. However, this evening, I've decided to change that. My plan is to teach Renaud a lesson for stealing my tips from the Brazilian couple and also Jamaal for bad-mouthing me to the management, and in doing so remind the other waiters of the value of my role.

In the words of Joe Strummer: death or glory.

To get the ball rolling, and to up my resolve, I ask Renaud if he ever found out what happened to the tip that was left for me.

'What tip?' he asks. His round head and dark eyes looking to the others for a laugh. 'You a runner or a waiter? Hey?'

'A runner,' I reply. 'You also still owe me three euros from yesterday.'

'Et alors?'

I let it hang and don't reply.

A trickle of diners begin to arrive. There's something so animalistic about them from this side of it all. The way they all turn up at the same time looking for food. Like wildebeest at a drinking hole. From this side they all become one, one faceless mass of people. All that distinguishes them is the way that they treat you and the salaciousness of their conversation.

They say that the best-informed person in the city is the Parisian waiter. It wouldn't surprise me. An invisible presence that hovers at the shoulders of politicians, businessmen, lovers and celebrities as they discuss the most private or intimate of matters. The assumption that I don't speak English has led to me overhearing some incredible conversations among foreigners, as I meekly pick up plates. Everything from premature ejaculation to Premier League transfer negotiations.

Once the starters are out, a few of us are at the Pass. Salvatore is telling us that he knows that the minister for _____, whom he is currently serving, is actually gay; although, when pressed for details by the other waiters, he concedes that he believes it not simply from what he overheard, but also because the minister ordered a Caesar salad.

'Isn't Caesar salad Italian?' the Little Boxer asks with a laugh.

Jamaal comes over to me. '*Mon ami*,' he says with faux concern, 'go and get the drinks order for *cent quatre*. You work with me today, hey?'

I do what he says without question. It's my job. Back and forth between the kitchen and its malodorous residents, and the resplendent dining room with its perfumed guests. I'm the middleman, Hermes the Messenger with my winged, blister-giving leather shoes, slipping between the two worlds – the Underworld and the profane – as little a part of one as I am of the other.

I bide my time during the service, slowly but surely carrying out my duties ferrying cargo between the two worlds. When I notice that both Renaud's and Jamaal's *rangs* are starting to get busy I deliberately shift my efforts to the other waiters and their tables, and therefore begin to actively avoid taking Renaud's or Jamaal's plates from the Pass or clearing their tables. The effect on their services is gradual at first but soon ramps up. All it requires is for one table to be complaining about their food, while another is waiting to order, a third wants their table cleared, a fourth wants to order dessert, another has been trying to pay and another party can't be seated because the table hasn't been cleared... and meanwhile the orders for the tables that are waiting are having their plates pillaged by other waiters at the Pass, so by the time they're finally delivered items are missing, or cold, and need to be reordered, which means going back to the Pass and arguing with Nimsath, while more people get annoyed...

Renaud finds me behind the swinging door chatting with Lucien and, losing it, tells me that he's not going to make any tips tonight. He's almost frothing at the mouth.

'I know how you feel,' I assure him with a smile. 'The same happened to me with that Brazilian couple.'

Jamaal, too, is overwhelmed. He's so sweaty from running back and forth that the diners are visibly perturbed by him.

I double down on my efforts with the other waiters, making sure to keep busy when a manager comes and berates Renaud or Jamaal so that I can't be accused of not working. I pull off a blinding effort with the Untouchable and the Little Boxer who quickly leap to my defence when the Rat, at the behest of Renaud and Jamaal, tries to suggest I should be fired for not doing my job.

'I've never seen a better runner,' Adrien even says, before making a point of handing me a ten-euro note and thanking me for my work so far.

De Souza does the same. They're doing it for the work I've carried out, but also as a means of engaging my service for the rest of the evening. The role of the runner, it turns out, is a corrupt one. This is my source of prestige, I realize. If the waiters are bounty hunters, constantly chasing tips, then the runner is a mercenary, a gun for hire. His allegiances are to no one, only the person who pays him best. The waiters know that, if the runner is working with them, then he's not working with anyone else. And this appeals to their sense of competition and vanity. And of course it means more tips. *Other people's failure – your success.*

At a moment late in the service Jamaal cottons on to this and hands me a euro, begging that I help him with the *digestifs* for one of his tables. This, of course, is not enough money for any real commitment, so I ask for more, but I don't push it, because at exactly the same time Renaud is having a breakdown in the Pass because one of his tables just left without paying as they were so offended by the service. The *directeur*, his face almost violet with rage, is screaming that whatever they have not paid for will be taken out of Renaud's wages.

At the end of the evening there's no need to ask the waiters for the three euros. They all give more. It's like protection money. When a deal has been struck between us during a service I'll focus my efforts on helping them more than the others, as thanks I'll touch some of their tips, too. Before, I'd be lucky to go home at the end of the day with three euros in my pocket; now I've learned how to broker deals with the waiters. I reckon I can easily leave with around thirty euros in cash, probably more. And this will be the same every service as long as I don't push it, and I'm clever and don't get too greedy.

This is a development that has made the job a lot more interesting, providing Renaud and Jamaal don't get me sacked first, which having overheard them at the end of the service seems like their sole objective. I've noticed a change in the others, too: they see me as an equal, as one of them – no longer a plaything. That's what they were waiting for, perhaps, to see if I had enough grit to stick it out.

My pockets are stuffed with cash as I leave that evening. *Liberté, égalité, fraternité* – for the first time since being here I have them in my pocket.

I spend my ill-gotten gains, my short-term *liberté*, on a slap-up meal in a small Japanese restaurant off the Rue Sainte-Anne, in the Japanese Quarter. It's tiny, and I'm sitting at a bar overlooking the chefs sizzling gyozas or spooning soba noodles out of giant vats of boiling water. I'm crammed in between Japanese men. Other men who have finished a late shift somewhere. More sake and my mind drifts back to the restaurant. So, this is how the machine works; the slow and calculated accumulation of power, as you weaken those around you and rise to the surface. The restaurant perhaps isn't too different to the corporate world: unlike a septic tank, the real shits rise to the top.

For the time being, the runner might be at the bottom, but he, like the others, is an integral part of making the machine run. And just like the others, he's conniving his way to the top. And he'll line his pockets on the way as he does so. With this revelation, I order another sake.

THE SOMMELIER

With the advent of making tips I've stopped sleeping in hotel toilets during my rare breaks. I am still in the Hôtel du Simplon, and despite being at the restaurant for more than a month, I still haven't been paid. 'It's coming,' they keep saying. However, I can now afford the luxury of sitting in a café. The best place is an address that Lucien gave me, a small bistro on Rue du Mont-Thabor called Le Fer à Cheval, the Horseshoe, where, when I have some money in my pocket, I'm sure to be found. Le Fer à Cheval is the sort of place populated by other members of the Underworld: hotel valets, taxi drivers, labourers, street sweepers and the like. We all sit there together, but alone; avoiding each other's gaze, in the strange light reflected off the faded green walls. It's a narrow joint, with a small bar at the front manned by the elderly husband where a couple of the regulars stand drinking cassis or Pelforth beers with Picon. The decoration is spartan, the small booths with their Formica tables can only fit two grown men, and by the time I'm there, at the end of the afternoon, the elderly wife, who is in charge of a kitchen so small that she has to have one foot in the *salle* as she cooks, will have commandeered one of the tables to butcher whatever meat is to be served the next day. There's no music, just the sound of the cleaver coming down on the knuckles of meat and the occasional chatter from the bar. Fortunately for me there's always something left over from the lunch service, which only ever offers one option, and it's sure to be a French classic. *Coq au vin, canard confit, bœuf bourguignon, hachis parmentier à la viande de cheval, blanquette de veau*. Ironically, it's here that I learn about French cooking, not in the restaurant.

In short it is the ideal place to sit when you're hungry and can't face being with normal people in a normal bistro with all the stress from the waiters wanting you in and out as quickly as possible and expecting you to leave something for the poor service.

Which is why I am surprised when, looking up from my plate of *gigot d'agneau*, I see the old sommelier, Franjo, standing at the bar removing his jacket. I have never actually spoken to him. Since I arrived he's made it clear that he has no interest in speaking to me, and from what I've heard he is an incredibly pretentious man. I once asked him about wines when we were in the dining room, and he just wafted his hand in my direction and walked off.

'It's beneath his rank to speak to you,' Lucien explained. 'He doesn't want to be seen as a waiter. And he's right, he's not a waiter. He doesn't carry food.'

Knowing this, I hope he hasn't seen me in my booth. Yet I can't help but look at him. Here is one of the proudest men in the restaurant – a consummate professional, always impeccably dressed – in a bistro with aspirations as low as this one. The sommelier is standing at the bar with his jacket hanging over the back of the chair so that I can see the gold lapel badge – a bunch of grapes – twinkling like a medal. He looks a lot smaller here, fragile and somehow even older. He is obviously well past retirement age.

The sommelier has narrow shoulders that hunch forwards slightly, a mop of straight white hair, white bushy eyebrows, large glasses and small, slightly arthritic hands, which he moves slowly and with great care. The man in front of me is no longer the famous sommelier, he is like the rest of us in here. Working men. Only a lot older.

For the entire time I am there the sommelier and I don't say a word to one another. When I finally get up to leave, he simply nods, as if we didn't know each other, and takes my place. To my surprise, the elderly lady who is butchering a leg of lamb at one of the other Formica tables immediately stops and begins to make a huge fuss, though she is still brandishing the giant meat cleaver as she does so.

'Oh no, *monsieur* must not sit here. Look at all this mess. Maurice!'

she cries to her husband behind the bar, who is busy counting out my change with the dexterity of a statue. 'Maurice, *notre cher* sommelier... the table... it's not ready.'

'Please, Loïs,' Maurice, the owner, snaps in his deep voice from under his tobacco-stained moustache, 'leave the man be. That is his table. He does not mind.'

There is something regal about the way the sommelier sits there as the old lady fusses about him. He is like a visiting monarch, mute, his hands in his lap, his eyes cast downwards. Meanwhile Maurice, bent down behind the bar, is rummaging through the fridge, having stopped counting my change mid-transaction.

'*Ah, voilà,*' he says, as he reappears with a bottle of white wine.

A few other men enter and ask the owner for drinks as he is about to pour a small glass of wine for the sommelier. Visibly overwhelmed by the sudden spike in trade, he asks me to take the glass and bottle over to the sommelier's table while he counts out the rest of my change and serves the men coffees.

So, having dutifully avoided each other, I am now to serve the sommelier wine. Even in the restaurant I don't serve wine. I put the glass down in front of him and am about to pour when he puts a hand over the glass to stop me.

'You will at least show me what I'm to drink?'

I show him the bottle. He nods pretentiously. I begin pouring. He picks up the glass, looks at the wine, purses his lips, closes his eyes, then sips...

It is as if the whole room has gone silent. Standing to my side is the old lady, frozen, meat cleaver still in hand, as if witnessing a miracle; behind me the husband, also immobile, waiting for the sommelier's blessing of his wine choice, the other customers impatient for their coffees.

...Finally, he swallows. Then another dramatic pause is followed by a thoughtful rocking of the head and a pope-like gesture with his free hand. Then, a nod of approval. At that moment it feels as if everyone in the tiny bistro lets go of their breath. I turn to go.

'You can leave the bottle,' the sommelier says, before taking it in his hand and looking up at me. 'Do you know what it is?' For the first time I notice the slight accent when he speaks French. He has turned the bottle so as to obscure the label. 'You should. You work in the same restaurant as me.'

'No,' I reply, embarrassed. I can't say 'white wine' – the French already have a low enough opinion of the English.

'Gewürztraminer. Smell it.' He holds out the small glass.

As I smell the wine, which is thick and aromatic, the old lady arrives with a pungent cheese board. I place the glass back on the table next to the sommelier, who has already picked up his knife in his left hand.

'One must know wines,' he says. 'Like women. It's a matter of respect.'

'Yes,' I agree.

'To work in a restaurant, it is a necessity. To live correctly, indispensable.'

As I am collecting my change from the bar the sommelier says one last thing: 'The shape of the bottle.'

'Pardon?'

'The shape. It was the clue – long and thin. Then the wine, blonde in colour, like straw; it could only be a Frenchwoman with a bit of German in her.' He laughs at his joke. 'From Alsace, then.'

I realize then that, if I am going to have a shot at becoming a waiter I need to start seriously learning about wines. And that if I am going to do that, then it is from the sommelier that I must do so. I go back to his table and ask him if he will teach me about wines.

'It takes a lifetime to learn about wines,' he says.

I anticipated a pretentious response but this one surpasses my expectations.

'I want to become a waiter. I need you to teach me. Please, you're the expert.'

He considers this for some time.

'No.'

'Why?'

'I don't have the time. Besides, it cannot be taught. Not like that.'

'I won't take any of your time. I'll just listen. I'll even help you; I'll be your runner. No money involved. You'll have less to do.' The whole pitch sounds a touch desperate, which I am.

'Anyone would think you wanted my job.'

'No, no. Just to become a waiter.'

'Just a waiter… You don't give up, do you?'

'No.'

'Fine. I'll teach you,' he says. 'But be warned, if you don't do this properly, I'll stop. Wines are serious. We begin tomorrow. First, the wines on the main menu. Take a copy home. Learn it. If you don't know the basics, I can't help you.'

Before leaving work that evening I rip out the wine page from one of the menus and stuff it in my pocket. On the Métro home I study it, committing every name to memory. The next day, having found a small book entitled *The Wine Drinker's Manual* in one of the second-hand bookshops behind Odéon, I begin more serious study.

Drinking with Salvatore

It's late, after a dinner service, and Sal and I are in one of the small bars in a backstreet off the Avenue de l'Opéra. He's in a good mood, you can feel it; he's made decent money, that's why he's invited me along; he wants someone to drink with, someone to see him act the rich man. Every time we order he insists on paying.

I'm telling him about my troubles getting paid and getting a contract. I'm still stuck in the French administrative catch-22.

'I can't open a bank account because I don't have a work contract, and I can't get a work contract because I don't have a social security number...'

Sal asks that we speak in English, he wants to practise on me, he says. But it's probably because I'm making very little sense.

'You don't have a social security number. This is what you were saying, yes?'

'Yeah. I filled out the documents in December, but now I'm living in this other place – the Hôtel du Simplon – everything must have been sent to my old address.'

'Just do the papers again. And speak slower.'

'I would, but I need to get paid. Also, when can I go to the administration office and sort it out? I don't have long enough breaks.'

'You complain about French administration. I'm telling you, for an Italian, it's different. France shows us how a complicated administrative machine can *actually* work. OK, in Italy, maybe it's simpler. We just don't bother doing it – like taxes. But in France you must. You want my advice?'

'Sure.'

'Love story.'

'Love story?'

'The French, they complain all the time, but deep down they love a good love story. You tell the woman at the desk what you told me about your girl leaving and all that.'

We drink our beers, and Sal orders two more.

'I'm sorry, *Inglese*. You must forgive me for taking *demis* of beer. I know that in London to do such a thing would make me look European. But I can't bring myself to drink those huge glasses of warm beer. We take *demis* – the entire beer will always be cold for a start.'

'I think it's just that people don't want to queue at the bar all the time.'

'Don't get me wrong, I have nothing against gays. We Italians were already being gay while you Northern Europeans were still painting your faces blue and living in the forest. It seems you still don't even have table service there. Such an uncivilized people.'

'Would you ever want to live in London?'

'Never,' Sal says. 'Honestly, if I could be anywhere... it's back on my parents' farm. In Sicily. That's all I need. Not this.' He makes a gesture towards the window as if to suggest Paris. 'The problem is the money. Always the money. In Italy, no work. We young people must leave our beautiful country to go and work in other people's. Like yours. In return, you – the English and the Germans – you send us your old people. Why? This is not a fair exchange. What did we do to you? *Dai.* It's actually very hard to be an Italian these days. You see how much bad coffee we must drink, eh?'

'Your English is pretty good when you want.'

'Thank you, *Inglese*. It must be the beer. *Ey*, you like sambuca? I order.'

The woman behind the bar has no sambuca, she says, but proposes another *anis*. Sal looks at me as if this confirms everything that is difficult about being Italian. But he orders it anyway. As we drink, a sharp wind blows in from outside.

'Close the door properly!' the woman behind the bar shouts at two men who have just entered and sat down at one of the tables.

'Waiters,' Salvatore says with a mock *tut*.

'Sure?'

'Certain. We bet?'

'The next round.'

The two young men remove their jackets to reveal unbuttoned white shirts. They've got the same slight frame as most of us in the restaurant. Not an ounce of excess fat on either of them. Salvatore, on the other hand, is quite big for a waiter. However, because he's tall he seems to carry it well.

'How did you know for sure? That they were waiters?

'The shoes. Always look at the shoes. Show me a man's shoes, and I will tell you his nationality. French men, too pointed; Italian men, a little over-the-top, I guess; English, you have good shoes, I must say; the Germans, *mamma mia*, these are the worst – you see a man with bad shoes, German. You know it straight away…'

'You know,' he continues, 'when I was young, I used to think that I would be a professional free diver – that was all I believed, really. I was almost on the Italian team. For my whole adolescence, I thought only of this. I did not have a Plan B. I did not prepare for any other outcome. At school I did what was necessary, but very little at school is necessary when you will travel the world as a free diver. *Inglese*, why are you smiling?'

I can't stop thinking of Jean Reno's character Enzo in the film *Le Grand Bleu*.

'Enzo, *mio dio*. I have more hair at least.' Salvatore drinks some more of his beer and stays silent for a moment. Finally, he speaks: 'Free diving, I couldn't make a life of it. So, I start waiting. And then I do more waiting. I say to myself I will go to university. But then another job comes up. Then Paris. And then, well, you end up here, waiting. To be fair, I've had fun. I have fun! You work with interesting people. Travel the world. The money can be good. You don't work in an office all day. If you're lucky, you work in a place that serves decent food, although this is rare. I always find it funny that when people go food shopping, they are very interested in what they buy, you know, free-range meat or nice-looking vegetables. But in a restaurant, they don't care. They don't even ask what is in the dish. So of course restaurants, they're not going to serve the good stuff. Why do it? They'd make less money. Let them eat shit!'

We clink glasses.

'You still dive?'

'This year I promise myself that yes, I will. Fuck it.'

One of the two men at the table comes to the bar and orders two beers and buys a pack of smokes with a wad of crumpled notes. He too has that exhausted look in his eyes and the black fingernails.

'Good day?' Salvatore says to him as he glances with his blue eyes at the money in the waiter's hand.

'*Ouais, ça va.*'

'Where do you guys work?' Salvatore asks with his characteristic smile.

'Café de la Roche, up by the Opéra,' the waiter responds with evident pride. 'You?'

'Le Bistrot de la Seine,' Salvatore says flatly.

'Pay's good there, I hear.'

'*Ce n'est pas mal,*' Sal shrugs. 'But we work like dogs.'

'*Ey*, we all do.'

'Same shit, different restaurant.'

The waiter leaves with his beers.

'And you?' Sal asks. 'You want to be waiter, hey?'

'For the time being.'

'Time being? I don't know this expression.'

'Yeah, I want to be a waiter.'

'Well, first, and you know what I'm going to say...'

'The jacket.'

'*Esatto*, it's a crime. It makes me so very sad. It is like you have taken the bags the bread is delivered in and put them onto your back. Also, and don't take this personally...'

'Go on...'

'Your hair. Have you never seen a barber? You look like a man who carries the guitars for a band.'

Salvatore starts talking passionately about suits, particularly Italian ones, which according to him are the greatest in the world.

'...French fashion is for women; beautiful clothes for women, but not men,' he says with regret. 'You know what we waiters really are?'

'I thought you weren't a waiter?'

'I'm not. But I like to say that we are beautiful people, doing bad things for money. Like many people in this city, *d'ailleurs*.'

Salvatore orders more drinks, including a round for the waiters at the other table, who thank him with a nod of the head.

'The life of a waiter isn't so bad. Of course, you'll never be a rich man. Unless you open a restaurant. Maybe then you become rich. Especially if you pull the kind of tricks these places do. But, to become rich from other people's suffering, this is not how to live. A waiter works hard. A cook, too. Why pay him so little? In the big cities we've moved so far away from food. In Italy, we still have it. But here... You know today a tourist asked me if we served American food? American food? What is that? Why come to Paris for American food?'

I concede to Salvatore that I actually have very little idea what's on the menu apart from what I carry.

'Ah, well, if you want to be a waiter, you must know every single item on the menu. To describe how it tastes, how it's made...'

'How? We can't eat any of it.'

'Not important. You lie. That's your job, really.'

'To lie?'

'Sure. It makes me sad to say it. But your job – because we're not working in a fancy restaurant – is to make the diner *believe* they get special service.'

'Sounds simple.'

'It's not that simple. But, if you can make people feel that they have passed a memorable evening in your presence, that's special. That's maybe why I keep doing this.'

'That and the money.'

'*Inglese, dai.* You mock me. Even a communist must live.'

He orders more beers.

'You must know wines, too.'

I tell him about my conversation with Franjo, the sommelier.

'*Bene.*' Sal fishes his hand into his pocket and pulls out his *limo*, his corkscrew. 'You'll need one of these, then. Take it. I have many.'

I'm touched by Sal's generosity.

'You know in English we call this a "waiter's friend",' I tell him.

'A "waiter's friend" for a waiter's friend,' he says, placing his paw on my shoulder again, happy with the wordplay in English.

I'm happy, too – it feels like I finally have a friend in the restaurant.

'The *limo* is the most important tool for a waiter,' he continues.

Sal takes the *limo* and gives me a quick masterclass. The virtue of this tool, and why it is so prized by waiters, is that it can be manipulated with one hand, leaving the other free to hold the bottle, and thus avoiding having to place the bottle on the table. Although after the speed at which we've been knocking back beers, Sal's dexterity is notably more lethargic. Eventually he gives up and places the *limo* back on the bar.

'I want to get drunk,' he says. 'You join? I pay.'

We finish the next beers quickly. Sal orders more. After a day in the restaurant the effect is divine (helped in no small part, I imagine, by quite how dehydrated and exhausted we are after working non-stop and drinking almost exclusively coffee). As for eating, it's too late to find anywhere open, and Sal doesn't seem that interested anyway.

'What do you think about it?' he says later, as if he's been having the first part of the conversation alone in his head.

'About what?'

'Life.' He pauses and looks into his beer. 'When I dive, I don't think. Just breathing – nothing. But in Paris, when the work stops... I don't know. I think about it – a lot.'

'The meaning of life?' I can feel Salvatore slipping into melancholy. Not surprising for a guy who's only had a few hours' sleep, just come off a fourteen-hour day and is now back on the booze.

'*Si*, life.' He exhales. 'You want my advice, *Inglese*?'

'Sure.'

'Live where the tomatoes are good.'

'Live where the tomatoes are good?'

'I'm telling you. Follow that advice, you'll always be happy. You don't need anything else. Religion, philosophy, self-help books...'

'Women?'

His mood slides gracefully back into something more buoyant. The spectre of his melancholy may have been avoided. Dealing with him alone, having flipped, is not something I want.

'*Inglese*, please. The most beautiful people live where the tomatoes taste good. I have thought about this for much time. I am telling you. It is the only philosophy. *Vivi dove i pomodori sono buoni*. You think about it, seriously. And then we talk again. But you'll have no questions. Once you have learned this, you cannot go back. It is the ultimate truth.' He prods me. 'I, my friend, have just changed your life. You can thank me by buying the next round.'

'Why aren't you there, then?' I say it before my mind can stop me.

Salvatore's face clouds. 'Fear, perhaps. Money, certainly. I don't know. I ask myself more often these days...'

For the remainder of the night, we talk politics. Salvatore involves the other two waiters and soon has them interested after explaining some of his more extreme ideas for social change. On a whim Salvatore convinces us to go to a bar in the east of the city that he says is run by his 'comrades' and where the drinks are cheap. After shots of Génepi, and what feels like an eternity looking for a taxi (which Salvatore explains is due to the taxi drivers' union and government stake refusing to give out enough licences so that they always have too much work), we end up in a crowded bar not much wider than a train carriage. The air is heavy with smoke. At the back of the room a Russian dissident is eliciting cries of support from the drunk and enraptured students before him. Behind the bar, on the small steps up to what must be the storeroom, a group of tousle-haired musicians are playing. The song is raucous, and the whole place is soon clapping and cheering. People are speaking French, but also Russian, and other Slavic languages. In a lull the barman leans across to us and, having poured shots of vodka, shouts above the noise:

'They are gypsies! It's gypsy music! The last song. It was about a terrible massacre. Many of them died. Hundreds. Maybe thousands.'

The room is heaving, the air laden with sweat as the crowd weaves to the sound of the gypsy massacre. Salvatore, the Bear, and the other two waiters are sweaty, drunk and happy. Their white shirts cling to their backs, almost see-through. Conversations spill out onto the pavement where people seek refuge in the cold air and quiet. Salvatore manages to pick up two students who are enamoured by his stories of beating up fascists. Whether they're true or not is irrelevant, he is an excellent raconteur. One of the girls says she knows of an after-party in an office block that has been taken over by squatters. Salvatore loves this. Stopping the wheels of capitalism from grinding down the poor souls who must work in offices.

'We shall go immediately,' he says, 'in support of the movement. But first, shots.'

When the bar closes Sal stops in a small *épicerie* and loads up with alcohol. 'Fuel for the revolution,' he quips. 'And *birre di strada*. Highly important.'

Birre di strada, street beers, it turns out, are beers to be drunk between bars so as to avoid having to stop.

The office block has banners draped outside the windows. Inside it has been crudely transformed into a party, with shenanigans of truly debauched proportions taking place. The revolution is alive and well, it appears. Former office spaces have been turned into separate party areas. To move from what was probably the marketing department down to accounting is to travel sonically from bebop jazz to heavy house music. Half of the cast members appear to be in fancy dress, having arrived from another party. In the fire stairs a human-sized rabbit squats to unload his bowels. 'The shit they cut it with these days,' is all he says. In the large conference room, a small group have drawn a crude hammer and sickle in ketamine and are proceeding to inhale the full essence of the revolution while another revolutionary loads balloons full of laughing gas and hands them out.

'Come,' they shout, 'don't be afraid to get your nose dirty.'

In the spirit of sharing Salvatore has dished out what is left of Adrien's cocaine, which has made us a lot of friends very quickly, but now it has run out, and Salvatore is on a mission to find more. In what takes quite a desperate turn he stands outside the toilets and berates people who come out, offering them a cigarette in exchange for a line. The night moves on:

eventually people start to drift away. I remember Salvatore, wearing cheap sunglasses inside at this point, explaining to me with seriousness that sunglasses may only be worn inside by actors and Italian. We then speak about Marcello Mastroianni, before he disappears again looking for drugs.

During his quest for narcotics Sal has lost the two students, and we both realize with a certain amount of surprise that the evening has played a cruel trick of time against us. For it is already 5am.

'Well, in half an hour, we can take the Métro,' he says, as if it is a good thing.

The next morning before work, after two hours' sleep, I return to the administration office regarding my social security number. It's one of those typical places that they put up in abandoned offices with blue carpets, foam-panelled ceilings and harsh lighting. Not too different from the squat last night. There's quite a mix of us there, newly arrived in France, all clutching our tickets and our dossiers of paper, waiting to be called forward. No one is happy: we've all been here before and we know we'll all be back again, usually because of some obscure form we've forgotten to bring. At one of the desks a man is being asked to quieten down as he begins to shout. At another a woman is crying and pointing at her baby. I'm finally called forward to the desk with the dour woman who has just had the shouting man escorted out.

'*Oui?*' she says with a sigh.

I explain my situation, that I can't progress with obtaining my social security number as I never received the documents.

'They were sent to you,' she says. 'On this date.' She spins the screen around and points.

'But I don't live there anymore.'

She shrugs her shoulders as if this isn't her problem. Although as far as I can tell it is.

'What do I do?'

'You need to do the forms again. Or bring the letter that was sent to you.'

'I can't get the letter. It's at my old address.'

The woman shrugs again.

'I can't get this letter because... it's in the flat of my ex-girlfriend.' I continue, trying to channel as much of Salvatore as I can while also remembering the French words I looked up and jotted down before coming. 'You know how it is. She says she doesn't want to see me again. That it is over between us... It's hard for me. I really loved her. I think she already has a new boyfriend. I can't go back there. He lives there now.'

The dour woman leans forward and whispers to me, 'She's French? Your ex-girlfriend?'

I shrug my shoulders with all the Gallic indifference I can muster, and instantly feel more confident.

'French women can be difficult sometimes,' she continues.

'*C'est vrai,*' I say, with what I hope is a forlorn look.

'I understand. Listen, I'll print the document here, but don't tell my colleagues. We don't usually do this.'

When I arrive at the restaurant before the lunch service, I have the missing document in one pocket and my new *limo* in the other. There is no way I won't get a contract this time. I hand the *directeur* the document with a great sense of ceremony. He casts a disparaging look at it, places it on his table and then dismisses me. Before leaving I ask when I will be paid.

'Now we have this? Maybe in a few days. Maybe more. A week. I will tell you.'

A few days? I had calculated on being paid tomorrow. Another week on stolen bread rolls and coffee from the Tamils, and no matter how many tips I make I still can't get out of the Hôtel du Simplon.

Moreover, I am suffering from an incredibly acute hangover. The inside of my head is filled with some kind of heavy viscous liquid, like a poisonous lava lamp, which with every slight move sends sharp pains across my body. Particularly to my eyes, which feel as if they have been filled with hot sand, so difficult is it to see properly or to move them. I am doing anything in my power to avoid ocular movement. But worst of all is my mouth. To my knowledge, I didn't drink whisky last night. Yet the taste being created in the dark, sinister orifice in the front of my head is similar to whisky, though more acidic, and gelatinous. As if 4,000 Marlboro Reds had been smoked and extinguished on my tongue, creating some kind of primordial gunk that, possessed with its own thoughts, its own free will, has taken it upon itself to torment me and make me feel as if vomiting is the only way to exorcize the evil. The problem is that, apart from the liquids, nothing will come up. I haven't eaten in over twenty-four hours.

To expedite the removal of the beast, I resolve to sleep in the customer toilets. It is a high-risk strategy, but a necessity. It will also give me time to think, in blissful pre-natal darkness, of how the hell I'm going to get through the next week without my wage from last month.

Silence Pays

There's a knock on the back door of the Pass. It swings open with a gust of cold air. A delivery man throws down four enormous brown-paper bags. The dingy little Pass is filled momentarily with the smell of hope: warm bread – baguettes, croissants and *pains au chocolat*. Everyone has the same idea – just one for them, no one will know. We watch the bags out of the corner of our eyes, it's a stalemate. There are too many of us. No one will eat them now. There's no trust. Nimsath and Baloo appear and drag the bags back into the depths of the Pass.

'*Allez, un petit croissant,*' Salvatore tries.

'Forget about it,' Lucien says. 'Nimsath can't be corrupted.'

'*Pas de croissant,*' Nimsath intervenes. 'Ingleeshman, no girlfriend? Why Paris?'

'No girlfriend. I have my Tamil brothers,' I say.

With a smile the Tamils return to their task of sawing the baguettes into slices and filling the baskets with *viennoiseries*. There is no smell more comforting than that of warm bread, even in the Pass. Nimsath is in a talkative mood this morning.

'No French lady for Tamil man. For Ingleeshman...' he points towards the dining room, '...many women. No Brown skin, like Tamil,' he says in order to clarify. 'Ingleeshman can have all the French ladies.' He nods like a savant.

'*Ingleeshman. Prends,*' Baloo interrupts us.

Baskets of *viennoiseries* and fresh bread slide across the Pass with tickets on them. I take them up to the dining room. The smell enveloping me.

I can feel how warm they still are, how fresh. They're in my hands but I can't touch them. It's the Tantalus-like curse of the waiter. You're so close to things you so desperately want – namely to eat and sit down – but you cannot have them. You're punished with it all day: people sitting on their arses, eating. For the waiter there is nowhere to sit down unless you smoke and sit on the kerb. Or sleep on the floor of the toilets of five-star hotels...

When I return to the Pass, ready to enquire about getting paid, to force it, if necessary, I find Lucien and Salvatore shouting at Valentine.

'...I'm not even a waitress. I wasn't going to serve them. I don't serve tables. I'm a manager,' Valentine is saying.

'Do you hear yourself?' Sal shouts at her.

'I'm asking them to leave,' Lucien says.

'No.' Valentine grabs his arm. 'No. Just serve them.'

'Piece of shit fascists,' Sal says.

'You think that's normal? You hear what you are saying?' Lucien says to her.

'The *directeur* insists,' Valentine says timidly. 'Corentin called him.'

'He can do it himself then,' Sal says.

'None of us will, OK?' Lucien looks at all of us in the Pass.

I've absolutely no idea what they're talking about, but it is clear that Valentine is upset, which is unusual. Usually she has a quiet grace; each of her movements seems considered, like a dancer. And no matter what time it is, she always looks perfect. Never a hair out of place, always in the finest evening gown, and her make-up applied to perfection – even at 6am. As a manager Valentine is respected by the waiting staff. She is strict, but never cruel; she expects your best, and in return the waiters give it to her, for she is always reasonable. When Valentine is on duty, the likelihood of me having a split shift, and thus being able to go and meet the sommelier or even sleep in the hotel toilets, greatly increases.

Even the Tamils respect Valentine. Of course, she is undeniably beautiful: tall, dark and slender with almond-shaped eyes that always have a touch of sadness. And though the waiters occasionally flirt with her, they do so respectfully, unlike with Pauline and the hostesses, who are generally treated like fair game.

But, despite all that, this morning, Valentine looks shaken.

151

Lucien takes me aside and explains that after Valentine showed an elderly couple to their seats, they requested that they be served by someone else. Someone who is not black.

"'It's nothing personal,' they said. Can you believe that? We've got two Pétainists here. And she's saying we have to serve them. But we won't. What are they going to do? Fire us? Fine.'

I agree not to serve the racists. Sal and Lucien nod. Suddenly the printer on the wall chatters to life and spits out a ticket.

'*Deux cent dix,*' Nimsath says.

'Give me that,' Lucien takes it off him. 'Who put the order through?'

Nimsath begins putting the order together.

'Stop,' Salvatore shouts at the Tamils.

Nimsath carries on, his actions are automatic. Like a soldier following orders without questioning them.

'Don't do it, Nimsath.' Lucien says this firmly, a hint of a threat. 'You want to serve racists?'

'I want to keep my job.' Nimsath carries on. He might be interested in politics, in what's right, but like everyone here, he's more interested in keeping his job.

'Give me the ticket. Which piece of shit took their order?' Salvatore is looking for the name on the ticket but there is none.

'Which order?' The Rat's voice startles everyone in the Pass. 'If you're talking about the *deux cent dix*, I took it. This is a restaurant. People come to eat. Not to talk about politics with waiters. Nimsath, hurry up.'

'You know what they said to Valentine?' Salvatore says. He's much taller than the Rat and he towers over him. 'You call that politics?'

'I know what they apparently said,' the Rat replies obstinately.

'And you're going to serve them? You dirty little *lèche-cul*.' Salvatore is right up in the Rat's face.

'All of you, get out of here,' the Rat snaps. 'If you did your jobs properly, I wouldn't have to do them for you.'

Corentin steps out of Sal's space and busies himself at the Pass.

'We do our jobs properly,' Salvatore threatens him. 'That's how we sleep at night.'

The Rat spins around. 'You'll have a lot more time for sleeping if you don't get out of my way.'

Lucien pulls Salvatore away. 'Leave it.'

'Good. Back to work. Forget about this. Nimsath, where are the coffees?'

The Rat, with his thin face and tasteless earring, tries to hide his fear by repeatedly smoothing down the front of his grey jacket.

As I'm following the others out of the Pass the Rat shouts at me, '*L'Anglais*. I don't know where you're going. I'm taking these coffees out. When the omelettes arrive, you bring them. If you want to be a hero, now's not the time. You will do as I say, or you won't see this restaurant ever again. Valentine, back to the office.'

The Rat disappears with the two coffees and freshly squeezed orange juices. Valentine following meekly after him. Baloo, Nimsath and I are alone. Nimsath puts the basket of *viennoiseries* on the Pass.

'Are you sure?' I ask him.

'It's my job,' he says.

There's a buzz as the dolly lift arrives. Nimsath removes the two omelettes and places them in front of me.

'Now it's your job. Take it,' he says.

We all look at the two plates. The Tamils say nothing. I know that, if I take them, I'll lose the respect of Lucien and Salvatore, which I am slowly gaining. However, if I don't take them, then I'll probably lose my job. And probably won't even be paid. And I'm broke.

'He come back soon, Ingleeshman, go,' Nimsath says in English, referring to Corentin.

I'm frozen.

'Paris many racists. No change happen today.'

We hear the outer door bang open. The sound of the restaurant. It closes. The echo of leather footsteps.

'*Donne moi ça. Donne moi ça!*' It's the *directeur* carrying a motorcycle helmet. He's not wearing a suit and has clearly just rushed in as he is all red and out of breath. 'Take this. Take it now.' He pushes me down the corridor with the two omelettes and the basket of *viennoiseries*.

The Rat is just behind him. 'You're a runner,' he says. 'Is it too complicated for you to understand? You pick up plates, you take them to tables. You're not a revolutionary—'

'Shut up, Corentin,' the *directeur* snaps. '*Deux cent dix.*' He stops at the door and pushes me out. I can see the table, they're not far off. From a distance they look like anyone's grandparents. Sal and Lucien are watching me. Their eyes drilling into my soul; they have no respect for me anymore, I know it. I place the basket on the table in between them, the elderly woman peers up at me through her glasses.

'*Très bien.* And the jam?' she says.

'It's there. Already on the table,' the old man tells her.

'*Omelette mixte?*' I ask.

'*Pour moi,*' the man says.

I say nothing and head back to the Pass. Sal and Lucien are already there.

'You had no choice,' Lucien says.

'It's those bastards in that office. Not you,' Salvatore reassures me.

'I might not be around for much longer. The Rat said—'

'We'll speak to the *directeur.*'

More breakfasts appear on the Pass – eggs Benedict, smoked salmon blinis. Lucien and Salvatore disappear with them. Baloo is alone at the Pass.

'Ingleesh,' he says awkwardly. His eyes dart towards the stacked teacups at the back of the room. Hidden among them, still warm, a croissant. The taste of France. Impossible to eat without making a mess. I tear half off and stuff it in my mouth, the other half I offer back to him. He shakes his head and turns away, so I hide it back in the cups. As I chew I brush myself down.

'Tamil Tiger, Freedom Fighter,' he says.

'Tamil Tiger,' I say, spewing croissant particles in the air but managing to hold my fist up.

He smiles and does the same.

'Be careful, Ingleesh. That croissant has been touched by Brown hands.' He laughs. 'Like the omelette!'

The Rat storms in.

'You really are as stupid as you look, aren't you? You're a runner, why are you never running?'

Without a word as my mouth is still full of croissant I nod and scurry up the stairs. I push through the door and back into the hushed luxury of the *salle*. Valentine is out of sight. I meet Lucien and Salvatore at one of the stations and nod at the elderly couple.

'Do you think they know that the man who made their omelette came from Burkina Faso? And that the Tamils' Brown hands touched their croissants?' I say.

'You let them know?' Lucien says. 'It looks like they're almost finished.'

'It is *your job* to collect the finished plates, *Inglese*,' Sal adds. 'And, like I told you, I think it's important that diners have a connection with the kitchen...'

When I pick the plates up I pass the information on to the diners.

After the breakfast service I find Valentine sitting huddled in front of the small heater in the back office. She looks up and smiles. My dealings with the racist couple have done the rounds of the restaurant and I'm enjoying a fleeting moment of hero status. Lucien, much to my surprise, has even invited me for dinner after the service at his parents' restaurant. In the office I tell Valentine, in halting French, that since I've been working in the restaurant I've not been paid, that I don't have a contract and that I need one so I can find somewhere to live. As if believing it to be some kind of magic pass I show her the piece of paper I received with my national insurance number, the one I gave to the *directeur* five days ago.

I keep speaking, clumsily explaining why I need to be paid. Silently Valentine takes down a shoe box from one of the shelves and after a laboured search through the envelopes inside hands me one with a quiet '*Tiens.*' Inside the first is my payslip, upon which is written my old address, an arbitrary French national insurance number (0000000 000000 00000 XX), and then columns of acronyms and deductions before the final amount on the bottom right: €1,086.13, accompanied by a cheque.

It turns out it's been sitting there for the last three days, and no one has told me. How I will bank a French cheque is my next problem; also, it appears there is no contract. And, seeing as they've put a fictional national insurance number, absolutely no reason for the delay.

'I'm sure it's coming,' Valentine says about the contract.

'*Bello*. I can tell you have changed from here,' Sal says back at the Pass. 'Money, you see, it hurts me to say it, but it makes all the difference.' He leans down. 'A coffee for our runner, *ragazzi*!'

'*Corretto?*'

'And the grappa, Nimsath.'

The coffee, though no different, tastes less bitter.

'*Allora*, the first thing you buy?' Sal asks as he continues to file his nails.

'The suit. I'm getting it adjusted. Then cheap sunglasses, *ovviamente*.'

'*Bravo, bravo!*'

Renaud with his reptilian face and dandruff-flecked shoulders is counting his money from the service in the corner: 'Always get your cheque quickly, *l'Anglais*. They keep them on purpose. To make more interest in the bank.'

'They've got you now,' says Lucien, who is slowly polishing his *plateau* with olive oil – like a soldier who knows he's going to die. 'Anyway, hurry up, I'm hungry. I'll meet you outside.' He puts his *plateau* down, shakes forearms with the other waiters and leaves.

'Wait, I still have a last table,' I shout to him, but he's gone. I hope he waits; he's been talking all day about the food we'll eat, and now I'm starving.

'What about contracts, though?' I ask Sal and Renaud. 'How long until we get one?'

'Contracts?' Renaud laughs. 'We're waiters!'

'But!' Sal interrupts. 'You're now officially a Parisian waiter, *Inglese*.'

'Parisian, maybe. But a waiter, no,' Renaud simpers.

Sal corrects himself 'True. Officially a Parisian runner, *Inglese*.'

Exactly €1,086.13 of runner to be precise, after social charges have been paid but not attributed to me. That's just over 250 euros a week, often working seven days a week, for sometimes up to fourteen hours a day.

PART 4

LE PLAT PRINCIPAL

Dinner with Lucien

_____

The last diners leave at 11pm. Lucien is on the kerb waiting in the thin rain. After dreaming about it for the last few hours, we will finally eat at his parents' restaurant.

'*Putain. J'ai fumé cinq clopes*. What were you doing?' he says in French.

'Corentin. That fucking guy...'

'He's going up in the world, you know. Getting his own office and everything. Next stop, *directeur*!'

'Who'd want a sadist running a restaurant?'

'It's his obsession. And getting to the top means bending over and taking it. Doing the dirty work, being a real *salaud*. And when you take it like he does – and he really takes it from the *patron* – you've got to give it to others. Share it around. In his case, you.'

'*Une grande chaîne d'enculation.*'

'Exactly. You're at the bottom of the chain.'

We hurry down the steps and into the mouth of the Métro. There's that familiar blast of stale air, like the breath of a dying man. In the Métro there are three barriers in front of us. Sleek steel corridors with gates at the end at chest height that slam backwards into their frames with a bang every time someone passes through. In a glass booth next to the barriers sits a middle-aged man staring vacantly into the low-ceilinged, subterranean hallway.

'Wait,' I shout to Lucien as he advances towards the barriers. 'I don't have a ticket.'

'You're Parisian now,' he says in English. 'We don't buy Métro tickets.'

I throw a look at the man in the booth, who is staring down at a crossword.

'And him?'

'His job is to sell tickets, not enforce them. That's someone else's job.' Lucien places two hands on the gates and deftly sails right over. 'Besides, it's late. He just wants to get home, like us.'

I follow behind, suppressing the urge to run as soon as my feet hit the ground.

'But why doesn't he just do it? He's there anyway,' I ask, looking back to the man in the booth, who couldn't care less about what we've just done.

'Hah!' Lucien laughs. 'You Anglo-Saxons are all the same – always about money.' Without noting the irony of it being said by a waiter. 'Put it this way, it's not his job.'

Just like in the restaurant, everyone in Paris has a rank, a role.

'Besides, you see how many taxes you pay in France?' he continues when we're on the platform.

We look at my payslip. An A4 sheet. One number at the top, what I was paid; and then right at the bottom, after a dizzying number of acronyms, which even Lucien doesn't quite know what they mean, my net salary.

'...and that's just the social charges. No income tax. I think we can say that we already paid the Métro.'

There's a whirring sound and a gust of the Métro again, more concentrated here: brake dust, skin particles, dirt and whatever else makes up the most infamous of Parisian perfumes.

On the Grands Boulevards we sit drinking pints of Pelforth beer under the leaking awning of a busy café. We're on the other side, with the public, but I can never shake the feeling that we're impostors.

'This beer's disgusting.'

'Please, speak with me only in English today. I must practise,' he says.

'You waiters. You refuse to speak to diners in English, but as soon as we're out of the restaurant, you all want to speak English with me.'

'Who else speaks with you in English?'

'Sal.'

'He's good? Better than me?'

The waiter's sense of pride and competition has been tickled.

'He's all right, yeah. Anyway, tell me about this piss we're drinking.'

In laboured English Lucien says that he insists on drinking Pelforth because it is the only French beer any self-respecting labourer should drink. He speaks with pride about his membership of *la classe ouvrière*. How he comes from a long family line of waiters and restaurateurs.

Later we leave the Grands Boulevards, with their lights and cafés and theatres and streams of cars, and head back to where the city is asleep in the small backstreets. The shops are empty and small ateliers dead, the only lights the ones in the apartments up above us towards the sky. Occasionally we pass another figure on the pavement, hurrying somewhere unknown. It's in moments like these that Paris seems eternal.

At a small restaurant called La Résistance, all the lights are off. Lucien looks up at the windows above.

'Don't make any noise. My parents... they sleep upstairs,' he says.

We enter the building by a small side entrance. It's a low-ceilinged corridor at the end of which is an old door that leads into a courtyard. I follow Lucien's silhouette until it is completely absorbed by the night. There's a smell of bins, of slight damp. After some moments I see him again, opening the door into the courtyard. Off to the side is a door into the back of the restaurant kitchen. After a moment fumbling with the keys he has the door open and we're standing right in the kitchen. It's tiny. In the weak moonlight the steel surfaces shine blue and there's a homely smell of food.

'*Viens,*' he says.

I follow Lucien through the back of the restaurant towards the small bar. He turns a light on above the till, then looks for something in a drawer.

'*Voilà,*' he says as he lights a candle. 'Like the old days.'

He takes down two shallow wine glasses and sets them before us.

'You see ze place *en face*?' He points out of the window onto the street. 'During ze occupation ze Nazis published propaganda zere. What zay did not know was that, at night, *la résistance* were using zee same machines to print another newspaper called *Combat*. Perhaps you hear? Lots of big writers write for it... Camus, Sartre, Malraux. And it was in zis restaurant zat zey would meet to discuss zee *résistance*. Welcome to La Résistance.'

'The only resistance going on in Paris today is yours.'

''Ow do you mean?'

'Your resistance to making the *th* sound in English. It's incredible.'

'Like yours to the *ou* sound, hey? 'Ow about you repeat zis: *la mouette sur la bouée a commandé une bouteille de Brouilly.*'

'*Touché.*'

'Talking of wine...'

From his bag he extracts an almost full bottle with a cork forced in that he's most definitely taken from the restaurant, a Gigondas. He smiles at me.

'A table of bankers had at lunch,' he explains. 'It was their fourth. I slipped it down my trousers, took it down to the lockers – like zis, upside down so it don't fall. That's why the cork is so far in...'

He struggles for a moment with the cork, using his *limo*. It has a wooden handle, burnished from all the years of use. In a way it tells me everything about Lucien. There's a pop as the cork comes out.

'*Voilà.*'

He pours the wine and continues the story: 'Trying to get down the stairs to the prep kitchen... I was sure it would slip out... smash everywhere. The cooks were suspicious. A waiter going to the lockers during service, no, no, no, zay knew what was up. As soon as I am gone zay will look in the lockers for whatever I had taken. So... I hide it behind the lockers. Zat is why it's so dusty.'

'It does make it look more valuable.'

'Hah. The English. It's all about the labels for you. If it has a château on it, or some really French-sounding name, you assume it must be good. Just add some dust and we can sell it for even more! Perhaps this is a business idea? Selling wine to the English? You know all the French vineyards only send the bottles that are corked to England?'

'Sure.'

'Really! Because you English don't know zee difference. You have no great wines, and no great philosophers.'

We touch glasses in the darkness. They ring out like tiny bells in the night. The wine tastes warm and thick, with a hint of tobacco. After refilling our glasses Lucien takes the candle and disappears into the back of the restaurant. The restaurant is very small, it's a low-ceilinged room with old beams running across it. There are a handful of tables packed intimately into the cramped space; beyond the windows onto the street the pavement outside is so narrow that one could almost lean out and touch the cars parked bumper to bumper under the sulphuric orange streetlights. It is beginning to rain harder now. I won't be going home anytime soon.

Lucien returns carrying a tray laden with food: pâtés, cheese and a large terracotta pot. 'The cassoulet is cold, but it's good. My mother made this one,' he says. 'Wait, the bread!'

Bread, cheese and wine – the French holy trinity. We eat in near-silence, like a vigil. Even our cutlery hardly makes a sound. When the Gigondas is finished, Lucien helps himself to the open bottles behind the bar; when they're empty, he rummages around for another one, but fails to find anything.

'We drink Armagnac,' he announces, having pulled a bottle down from a shelf. 'Armagnac is to cognac what zee Rolling Stones are to zee Beatles. Not my words, unfortunately.'

I would learn that with Lucien you always ate well. It wasn't about sustenance, but about living.

'No one can take the pleasure of eating away from you,' he would say. 'Well, just avoid restaurants like where we work. Go to the bistros with the small daily menus. And order the cheaper cuts of meat. They have more flavour anyway.'

The idea that people in London ate sandwiches at their desks filled him with horror. 'You English, you really don't know how to live,' he would always say. 'But in Paris things aren't much better now. The number of restaurants I've worked in. The stuff they serve. Disgusting. You ask yourself if there are any chefs left in this city that cook. Most of it's bought ready-made. Industrialized duck confit, you imagine? Always look for the little *fait maison* sign on the door. Wait, this reminds me, *aligot*.'

'*Aligot?*'

'You've never tried *aligot*? *Fait maison, bien entendu.* My mother is from the Auvergne – in the centre of France, where *aligot* comes from. And she makes the best. Divine. Very simple, but hard to get right. Like the best things in life... Picture this: *purée de pommes de terres, ail et fromage... c'est tout. Mais c'est une merveille.* If you don't already believe in God, you will after my mother's *aligot*.' He smiles, fully aware of the torture he is inflicting on my cramping stomach.

'Go and get it. Quick!'

As we devour all the food in front of us, I tell Lucien about the Hôtel du Simplon and how I'm struggling to find somewhere to live.

'Of course it's hard. You're foreign, and a waiter.'

'A runner,' I correct him. 'Not yet a waiter.'

'Being a waiter isn't what is used to be. Sure, it's fun. You really want to be like De Souza, Adrien, Renaud... me?'

I say nothing, busy gorging myself on pâté. Lucien's face in the candlelight looks like a mask.

'*Putain.* You see me like them, don't you?'

'What? No. No!'

'You were meant to say, no, you're not like them.' He imitates a poor British accent.

'Aren't you?'

He pours us more Armagnac.

'All of us have something else. We wouldn't be waiters if we didn't think we were waiting to be somewhere else.' He takes a sip of the Armagnac. 'It's funny, in English you call our job waiting – it's accurate. We're all waiting for something.'

We raise our glasses and touch them together with a dull thud. The rain is now heavy on the windows. The restaurant is warm. Paris in the rain.

'What are you waiting for, then? If you're not a waiter?' I ask.

'An actor,' he says, his eyes darting to mine to judge my response. 'Or, at least, I'm *waiting* to be.'

It turns out that when Lucien was a lot younger, he appeared in a couple of television shows, and that, since leaving school at eighteen, he's been looking for acting jobs. He is now twenty-nine. If you ask what he does, he'll tell you he's a waiter, not an actor. Even if an actor is what he believes he is. However, waiting appears to be his longest role to date: eight years.

'What do they think of your acting? Your family.'

'Ah, that's a different story.'

As far as his family are aware, Lucien works as an actor. He left the family restaurant three years ago to join an avant-garde theatre company. After a couple of weeks, he realized they were never going to pay him, so to avoid the shame of returning home he found work at the Bistrot de la Seine. When his father suggests coming to see one of his shows Lucien tells him he won't enjoy it: 'It's very conceptual. Violent – you won't like it, Papa.' Since then, Lucien hasn't told anyone about his desire to become an actor. I'm the only one in the restaurant who knows, he tells me. And the reason he's told me is that he wants to perfect his English.

'All the other kids these days, they speak English. I mean real English, not restaurant English – "Are you ready to order, *madame*? Please, can I help you?"'

The kids he's referring to are the other students at his acting class. This is actually where he is on Sunday mornings, not church. It's also why he 'borrowed' my trench coat, it turns out. He needed it for a play they were doing, *En attendant Godot*.

'But seriously, if I don't get a proper role, I may as well give up. It's not going to happen. You know, all those other kids at the school, they've never been on TV. I have. But they feel sorry for me. Because I'm older, and I'm a waiter. I'd like to have spent the last years at acting school like them, sure; but who's going to pay? I had to work. In the end I worked so much, I never acted. Recently I've realized it's now or never. I don't want to miss my opportunity.'

Lucien takes a gulp of Armagnac and goes on to describe the Parisian world of acting with its agents and theatres and prestigious acting schools and families. 'It's all about the castings. That's the hard part. I'm sure that once they see me in a casting…'

Lucien concedes that he doesn't know how to get a casting. I tell him about one of my jobs as an extra in a film before I became a runner.

'I found it on Le Bon Coin,' I tell him, the website for small ads.

'Le Bon Coin? Interesting.'

As the hours creep into the early morning, we make what we consider to be a bullet-proof plan for becoming a French actor. Lucien says that his error has been spending too much time being a waiter; now he will reduce his hours and spend all his free time frequenting the cafés near the theatres where the agents are said to go before shows. He will also try and find out the bars that the actors frequent after shows. On top of that he will regularly check a host of websites and apply for any open-casting calls.

'I'll speak to the *directeur*. Tell him my ambition. See if they can be more flexible.'

Eventually he is less negative about his situation: 'You're right. I can't give up. I must continue. That's the whole point. If I don't, what have I got? I'm just another Renaud or Adrien or Jamaal. I don't mind telling you, I don't want to be a waiter anymore. The daily humiliation. Tell me another job where people think they can talk so badly to you? They go into a restaurant and suddenly they're little dictators. "Do this. Do that. I don't like this. Take it away." It's insufferable.'

'You can tell a lot about someone by the way they talk to a waiter,' I say.

'Yes. Someone should write a book about it.'

In a night of shared hopes, I decide to tell Lucien that I'd actually love to be a writer. But that I, too, have no idea how. In a sense we are in a similar predicament: nebulous ambitions, no concrete idea how to realize them.

'Well, at least now you can be a waiter. A real waiter.'

'Oh yeah?'

'Yeah. Because you're waiting for something else,' he says. 'Writer, I can see you as a writer. Of course, if you do write about me, you must change my name. I don't want it affecting my career.'

'I don't think it will have a negative effect on your waiting career.'

'*Bâtard*. I am a grand actor.' He stands up, raises his voice, and begins to bellow: '*Il pleure dans mon cœur / comme il pleut sur la ville. Quelle est cette langueur / qui pénètre mon cœur?*' before quietening down. 'Verlaine.'

Even though he is slightly drunk, and the light is low, there is a look of self-doubt that passes across his eyes, as if he knows, as I do, that the chances of him becoming an actor are slowly disappearing, if not already completely gone. It's a look I am starting to become familiar with in the restaurant, between Pauline, Salvatore and now Lucien. I can't decide if the restaurant is a waiting room, or purgatory. Perhaps both. Perhaps they're essentially the same thing. I wonder, also, if, to an outsider, I too have that look. The condemned man, life without parole.

'…I always thought that talking about it, about acting, only made it less likely. Maybe that's where I was wrong.'

'These things take time,' I assure him in that irritating way that people with no idea tend to do.

'Restaurant work is like prison,' he says, as if following my thoughts. 'A very high rate of reoffending. Either you never get out, or you're straight back in. The worst part is you don't know how long your sentence is. I just need my break, then I'm out. People still become actors in their thirties.' Mumbling to himself, he drains his glass.

On the next glass we raise a toast to being the best waiters in Paris.

'Know this, when the time comes. When I get the call-up. I'll disappear. A waiter's exit is almost as dramatic as an actor's.' He looks at me seriously, a touch of the thespian. 'Always… always leave them wanting more.'

Later, as we are standing at the door that opens from the kitchen into the courtyard, smoking and watching the heavy rain ricocheting off the cobblestones and shuttered windows, Lucien slurs, 'The American Church.' His large eyes no longer both look in the same direction and his head is lolling slightly. 'The American Church. S'perfect. They have… notice boards…places to rent. You must go. Catholics and Americans… together… think about it.' He taps his temple.

'What about my dossier? I have one payslip and no contract.'

'Don't worry about that. I know just the person.'

The rain is so heavy by the time we have finished the Armagnac and cigarettes that, with the Métro having closed long ago, we decide to sleep in the dining room and leave at first light. I am quite pleased not to go back to the Hôtel du Simplon, even if it means sleeping on a wooden bench and getting up in a few hours' time.

THE AMERICAN CHURCH

In France, for your life to be easy, you must be something, you must be defin-
able, they must be able to encadrer *you, to put you in a frame. In short, you*
are what you do. I am now a runner, so I am finally something definable; but
not the kind of something that anyone wants to rent to. This is the problem
I now face. Because, as a waiter, where you live is a temporary arrangement:
you're a nowhere person; an itinerant breed with a precarious job that moves
with the seasons. And, as such, you're the last person anyone wants to rent
to. Despite their reliance on them, Parisians have a low opinion of waiters,
especially when it comes to being their landlord.

It is just after 7am and Lucien and I are sitting huddled on the terrace of
a café near Arts et Métiers saying very little due to the searing *gueule de*
bois we both have. Fortunately, it is a Tuesday – we both have the day off.

'The last Armagnac. Why?' Lucien's voice is dry and weak.

'How do you manage to smoke this early?'

'It helps. Thins the blood. Gets the alcohol moving.'

We order coffee, croissants and *citron pressé*, squeezed lemon and
water, from a waiter who looks as hungover as we are, but who still manages to give us a disdainful look as if he is above serving the likes of us.

'*Putain de serveurs,*' Lucien says when he has gone. 'Who do they take
themselves for? He's like a cadaver that's been dug up and put in a suit.'

The disdainful waiter returns with our order. To my disappointment
it is Café Richard, the taste of which instantly transports me back to the
restaurant, as it's the same bitter stuff they serve there and which we,

as waiters, survive on.

'I need tea,' I say.

'Don't order tea. Seriously, a cup of hot water with a tea bag? You could buy a whole box of tea for the same price. Who orders tea in a café?'

'I know, but Café Richard?'

'You sound like Salvatore. There's nothing wrong with this coffee.'

And to prove the point, Lucien drinks his coffee, finishes mine and orders another. 'You know Balzac drank fifty cups a day. You want to be a writer? You're not drinking enough coffee. That's your problem,' he says.

The sky is lightening, the grainy light of Parisian mornings, the slow-moving river, the wet boulevard, figures hurrying along with rolled umbrellas and heads down, the plane trees along the Seine bending in the wind. Winter is ending and spring is just around the corner; you can feel it. The nights are no longer so cold. It is now possible to sit on the terraces.

At eight o'clock, having bought fresh croissants and orange juice, we head to an address Lucien has told me will 'solve all my administrative troubles'. We arrive at a small bedsit where a half-asleep guy opens the door.

'Lucien, what the hell?'

'I brought you breakfast, *cousin*. Jules, this is *l'Anglais*. *L'Anglais*, Jules.'

'Get your breath away from me,' he says as Lucien tries to give him a kiss on the cheek.

Lucien's cousin is a graphic designer, and in exchange for breakfast he agrees to forge me a contract and two previous payslips, including a new one for last month, so that it suggests I've been working at the restaurant for some time. It's a time-consuming process that requires zooming in and changing each digit pixel by pixel. As Jules works, Lucien kips on the sofa. But the results are incredible.

'Wait, before we go,' says Lucien, reclining on the sofa smoking, like some modern-day Roman emperor. 'Give him the total package. You'll love this, *l'Anglais*.'

'You got something with an ID photo?' Jules asks.

With my UK driving licence, Jules gets to work. Half an hour later I have been issued with a fake press card for an art magazine called

Was ist Kunst? and a fake student card for the Sorbonne.

'With the press card you will never have to pay for a museum again. And with the student card, cheap cinema tickets. Jules, *mon cher cousin*, I love you. I owe you.'

'How much do I owe you?' I ask.

'Nothing. A friend of Lucien's is a friend of mine. Besides, the idea that the state makes us pay to see artwork that rightfully belongs to us, the people, is an outrage. Go forth and become more cultured.'

'Yes, *cousin*! Our mission is to cultivate the English people. You see what we are doing? Bringing light to the barbarians. You know they eat factory-made sandwiches at their desks?'

'A second enlightenment,' he smiles. 'Right, I'm going back to bed.'

'A first, really. Anyway, we're going to the American Church.'

'I don't want to know,' Jules says.

The courtyard of the American Church is sheltered from the blustering wind and the noise of the cars thundering down the *quai* on their way to work. Lucien sits on a stone bench with his collar up, rolling cigarettes and thinking out loud about ways he could advance his acting career while I look over the notice boards.

'What about this? "*Chambre de bonne à louer pour étudiant(e). Crimée. 550€/mois.*" Where's that?'

'The 19th. What if we borrow a camera, you write a short film, I act and we send it to agents? Godard style. That way...'

'But it's for a student.'

'Just tell them you are. It's all acting. Besides, you have the card now.'

'What's a *chambre de bonne*?'

'A maid's room.'

Lucien explains. It turns out that there are *chambres de bonne* all over Paris. These tiny rooms popped up at the beginning of the nineteenth century and were conceived as places for the staff of the apartments below to sleep. They're hidden away in the roofs of the Haussmannian buildings, and usually accessed by a completely different staircase from the ones of the grand apartments below.

'...In reality nothing much has changed since the 19th century. The only difference now is that we no longer work in the apartments below. We work in restaurants.'

It is too early to call the number on the advert, so Lucien and I sit outside the church smoking and watching the river to pass the time. Occasionally barges nose their way up the river against the current. The water is heavy and brown from the rain.

'Imagine getting on one,' I say.

'Why?'

'Doesn't it intrigue you? To travel through France like that?'

'You know the source of the Seine is where some of the finest wines come from? La Côte d'Or. In Burgundy.'

My mind's eye transports me to the misty Burgundy countryside.

'I'm bored,' Lucien says. 'I'm not bothered about travelling through France, but back in time would be good...'

'To before the Armagnac?'

'Or, the nineteenth century.'

He lies down on the bench.

'Did you know that Parisians used to visit the morgue, for fun? Just to look at the bloated bodies they'd taken out of the Seine. Imagine doing that now. That would wake us up!'

'Looking like we do, they might not let us leave.'

Lucien ignores me; his train of thought has moved on. 'What about voice-over work? You laugh, but you can make a lot of money. Imagine the guy that did the voice of some new, unknown American actor; say Brad Pitt. Ever since then he's the voice of Brad Pitt. He has to be – it's what people in France think Brad Pitt sounds like. So, as long as Brad Pitt is acting, this guy has got work. And often, these voice-over guys will play several actors. I'm thinking, if I'm the voice of one of the actors in the next big TV series...'

At nine I call the number on the advertisement. It rings for some time, then there's a click and an old woman picks up.

'*Allô.*'

'*Bonjour, madame...*'

Dressed in our waiters' clothes and still with terrible hangovers we decide to spend the last of my tips for the week in a second-hand shop near Étienne Marcel Métro station on some fake reading glasses, a clean shirt, a tie and a scarf.

'You need to act more like a student,' Lucien is saying on the way to visit the *chambre de bonne*. 'You know how they are, all arrogant, like they think they've got it worked out. Even if they've never lifted a finger. I think I hate students as much as waiters – always complaining, and then standing outside libraries all day smoking and doing nothing.'

'You sound jealous.'

'Perhaps.'

'Did you go?' I ask.

'To university? No. No one in my family did. Jules taught himself. That's how we do it. You?'

'Yeah.'

A pause.

'And we're both waiters. Makes me laugh. Aren't you meant to be a waiter *while* you're at university, not after?'

'I'm glad someone finds it funny.'

After a quick detour via a perfume store to spray myself with samples and moisturize my face, which according to Lucien is of the utmost importance, I am ready.

'She cannot say no,' Lucien says, standing on the busy Avenue de Flandre, where the apartment is. I give him the plastic bag with my waiter's clothes in and tell him I'll meet him in the café near the canal.

'When you come back, I'll have some nice Parisian students for us to spend the day with.' He winks. 'But more importantly, pastis.'

'With eyes as red as yours they'll certainly be desperate. You look like a *clochard* with your shitty plastic bag of dirty clothes.'

'*Your* shitty plastic bag of dirty clothes,' he smiles. 'Good luck.'

A New Room with a View

A tiny woman opens the door and after a suspicious look down her nose invites me in. She lives in a small, well-appointed yet cold apartment on the sixth floor with a creaky floor. Madame Maury invites me to sit down in a musty-smelling room full of books and decorations such as ceramic dogs, tables covered with framed photos of ancestors, and at least two dozen small statues of the Virgin Mary. The room is cold, so I keep my coat on but open it enough for her to see the new tie.

'My great-great-grandfather fought with Napoleon – in Russia. That's him,' she says. 'An officer, not a soldier. What? You'll have to speak louder. My hearing.' As she listens she cups her ear and leans forwards with her eyes closed. 'As you can understand... I don't particularly like the English.'

In the deathly silence between bits of conversation a clock ticks somewhere.

'I'm Scottish,' I say.

'Is that right? Scotland... I don't mind the Scottish. They don't like the English either, do they?'

'No. And Mary Queen of Scots, her first language was French.'

'If you say so. What do you do?' she asks.

'I'm a student. Law.'

'At the Sorbonne? You'll have to speak up. My hearing.'

'Yes. The Sorbonne.'

'It's not very close to here. You know this area? It used to be very Jewish. Not the rich ones, mind,' she corrects herself.

Tick tock, tick tock.

'When do you want the room, then?'

'Today, if possible. Today,' I say, more loudy.

She considers this for a moment.

'Where are you now, then?'

I tell her I'm with an aunt, but that it is a temporary arrangement.

'The room is perfect for a student like you. The only thing I ask is that you pay in cash. You have a job? What? I see. Well, payment on the first day of the month. So, you take the room?'

'Can I see it?'

There's a silence. The ticking clock again. The cold. The musty smell. Finally, she heaves herself out of her chair and with trembling hands pulls a key out of her pocket. I follow her out the front door, which she locks behind her. Almost immediately next to it is a narrow door that looks like a cupboard but actually opens to reveal a tiny staircase. We follow the winding stairs up to a tiny corridor in the roof. We are directly above where we were sitting a few moments ago. Madame Maury unlocks the door, then stands back.

'*Je vous en prie,*' she says, gesturing to the door.

The room is tiny – there isn't enough room for two people to stand in it at the same time, which is why Madame Maury has remained outside. With the sloping walls of the roof, I can only stand upright in the middle. There's a horrible-looking single bed with a soiled mattress on one side of the room, from which, without getting up, one can reach the small table opposite with the sink and cooking rings. It gives a whole new meaning to 'breakfast in bed'.

'The shower is behind the door,' the little voice says from the corridor.

Behind a sliding door that is difficult to open is a miserable space to shower, with mould around the tiny window frame at head height. The room is more like the cabin in a turn-of-the-century boat.

Back in the hallway I tell the old lady I'll take it.

'*Bon,*' she says. 'But you pay me the first month's rent now, no funny business. The toilet is down there.' With a hand covered in sunspots she points at a door. 'But you don't need to see that. The rules are simple: no guests, and certainly no parties. And not that it will be a problem with you, but no smelly food. I rented to an Indian girl once.'

The timid old woman is gone, and there is suddenly something quite repugnant about Madame Maury. When I return with the money, which I've borrowed from Lucien, she takes it greedily from my hand, then sits at a small desk and begins to count while I remain standing. There's a smell of boiling vegetables coming from somewhere, which reminds me of the kitchens at the restaurant.

'I'm missing twenty.'

Madame Maury stays hunched over the desk, her hands still clutching the banknotes, staring at them.

'I'm sorry. I'll bring the rest later.'

'I don't like this one bit,' she sneers. 'The last girl, she was funny with money. Never paid on time. Then one day, just disappeared. That's why I want the money up front. You understand? You don't pay, I change the lock.'

The clock ticks, and Madame Maury looks at the banknotes, breathing heavily.

'*Bon*, when will you be coming back? I can't wait around all day for you. I'll give you the key when you give me the money. You've got the door codes.'

We agree that I'll be back at six.

I find Lucien asleep in a café on the Canal de l'Ourcq. We drink *démis* of Pelforth and pastis and soon feel much better. I'm consumed by a wave of euphoria. I finally have somewhere to live. Lucien and I part company at the Métro after he has withdrawn more money for me until I can cash my cheque. He's going to hang out in a bistro opposite the TF1 television offices on the outskirts of Paris before he starts the dinner service. 'Today is the first day of my future,' he says hopefully.

I'll see him tomorrow at 6am.

To celebrate my departure from the Hôtel du Simplon I invite Stéphane for a beer at the PMU betting bar on the corner. Feet among the discarded betting slips, surrounded by men clutching new ones as they watch the horse-racing on the screens around the bar, Stéphane tells me he's moving on, too. That his *affaires* are taking him to Germany, then possibly America.

Behind the little rectangular glasses, his vole-like face is completely sincere. We drink our beers, and I let Stéphane speak about where he will go after America. He says, quite casually, that he has a wife in Russia, and so he hopes his business will take him there. Beyond him in the window the men in the street are dismantling the market. I let it all wash over me, Stéphane, the bar, the taste of the cheap beer, the need to shower, Paris, the city, the horse-racing commentary on the TV.

'I wanted to give you something,' he says as he opens his battered black briefcase and feels around for something. 'Here.'

He hands me a small, wooden-handled Opinel knife. We shake hands in the doorway to the bar. I realize that I will never know what will become of Stéphane – unless he commits some atrocious crime one day. All I can hope is that he'll no longer be working casinos at night or whatever it is he does. I smile to myself as I walk away: the image of Stéphane, with his little square glasses and child's face all over the news, is too funny. I imagine myself being interviewed on France24, 'My time with the killer' on the ticker line below my face.

Before collecting my bags from the Simplon, I go and see Youssef. When I enter he's sitting at his desk, sewing.

'*Ah, bonjour, mon ami,*' he says. 'Please, take a seat.'

It's not long before he returns with two small glasses of fresh mint tea. Before I have a chance to open my mouth he is telling me about his wife leaving him again. I look out at the street. The dealers hanging around outside Le Seau, a young couple sitting on a scooter, idly smoking a joint.

'What happened to the woman with the little girl who used to live in the car across the road?' I ask.

'People from the *Mairie* came. And by the evening, well, they were gone. The car, too.'

Youssef serves us some more tea.

'I have a favour to ask, Youssef.'

'Tell me.'

'I'm leaving the hotel today. But before I go, I need you to finish what we started. I've been paid. I need you to adjust my jacket. I have the money now.'

Youssef laughs. The gold teeth at the back of his mouth twinkle.

'No, no, no. I've already told you. Your jacket is fine as it is,' he protests.

'You don't understand the waiter's style. We've been through this.'

'I will miss you. As a gift I'll do this for you straight away. I, Youssef, will ruin this perfectly good jacket. That's how much I like you. It will be ready in one hour.'

While Youssef works I go for a final stroll around the 18th arrondissement. I pass over the Rue Ordener into the 'Paris of the Bobos' and begin to climb the hill towards the Sacré-Coeur, the enormous white church at the top of Montmartre that overlooks the whole of Paris from the north. Fast, low clouds are running across the city on a blustery wind. The streets smell of the rain from earlier. From up here, the whole of Paris below, it's like being on the prow of an enormous boat that's surging forward. You can see all the landmarks: Les Invalides, where Napoleon is buried, the Centre Pompidou, the Eiffel Tower, the Tour Montparnasse, Notre-Dame, the main stations – Gare du Nord, Gare de l'Est, Montparnasse, Saint-Lazare – and, of course, there, somewhere in the middle of it all, Le Bistrot de la Seine. On days like this it can be almost overwhelming to think of all the secrets the city holds, present and past; all the lives that have passed through; everything that goes on behind the closed doors and façades of this metropolis.

When I return to pick up the jacket Youssef pulls the small curtain aside to reveal the long mirror. I look at myself. With the trousers fitted and now finally the jacket adjusted to be tightly fitted in all the right places – I am starting to look like a real waiter. Just like Adrien the Untouchable, I am even starting to get the gaunt face and sunken eyes from lack of sleep and sustenance.

That night, having moved into my new room, I go to one of the cinemas near Stalingrad and try out my new student card. This is exactly how I imagined living in Paris. They are showing *The Maltese Falcon*, during which I promptly fall asleep and wake once the credits are rolling. Back in my room, I notice the lights on in the *chambre de bonne* over the road and the flash of a head with a towel wrapped around it. In Paris, I have got used to the fact that we know our neighbours intimately. Despite the proximity of buildings across a street no one uses net curtains for privacy.

We live together. Our lives become a show for our neighbours. Perhaps, I think to myself, perhaps I will be living across from a beautiful French girl. The kind of girl who reads Sartre topless while smoking at her window. Like a true voyeur I wait in my room with the lights off: lo and behold the lady in question returns. Her back to me, she's looking in a mirror, a flick of the towel, then the head... then... the figure spins around to reveal... a chubby little man singing into a hairbrush. I open the window and hear Céline Dion, French Céline Dion, drifting across the small courtyard. Later on, I catch him trying to reposition the mirror so he can – as far as I can make out – take a photo of his anus using the camera on his phone.

The Upper Kitchen

It's lunch and we're short-staffed. An American woman stops me. Indignant that her *filet de bœuf* is not *à point* as requested, but most definitely *saignant*. The sliced-open, offending piece of meat's rose centre stares up at me like an old wound. What she has is what French chefs would consider 'medium', I say politely, and perhaps she should try it first. Using terms more suited to the Pass, the lady thrusts the plate into my hand and tells me to get out of her sight. As a waiter, you quickly get used to the fact that people believe they can talk to you like a lower species. With no *plateau* to hand I pray to God I'm not caught by a manager. Carrying dirty plates on one's hand is fine, but never something with food on. And when you do carry dirty plates you must carry as many as possible. It must look impressive. It's part of the show.

At the Pass the timing couldn't be worse. Almost all the waiters are there, and the atmosphere is toxic. Accusations flying, Nimsath shouting Tamil obscenities, and De Souza and Renaud in a stand-off officiated by Adrien. De Souza is saying something about Renaud stealing tips again. Nimsath flatly refuses to send the beef back. The other waiters agree and I'm pulled back from the Pass and thrust back towards the restaurant. I'll have to take it to the upper kitchen myself, I decide. I've never been there before. We're told to stay away. The caste system keeps us separate. It's from the upper kitchen that all the important parts of each dish come: the meats and the fish. Sent down in the service lifts to join the rest of the dish that comes up from the lower kitchen. Where the Tamils piece them together into orders.

I imagine the upper kitchen to be quite a glamorous place, considering its importance, full of highly skilled people doing important culinary work on gleaming metal worksurfaces using fancy equipment. However, at the top of the steps I find a cockpit-sized room with flaming hobs on all sides cooking on full gas. The roar is deafening, a constant blast of extractor fans, sizzling meat, metal crashing against metal and shouting. There's a tiny window above head height, which is closed. The intensity of the heat is indescribable. The black walls and ceiling are covered with huge globs of condensation. Manning the flames are five African men. Big men in sweat-drenched, soiled cook's clothes. The place feels more like an iron forgery in a remote Roman outpost than a Parisian kitchen. I watch as pieces of searing meat and sizzling fish are scooped from pans and tossed onto plates to be sent down in the lifts after a quick wipe with a dirty towel.

Presiding over this terrestrial inferno is the Chef. The only white man in the entire kitchen. A Corsican, and a giant of a man who wields a knife so large it probably once belonged to Hercules himself. With this he points, prods, slicks, licks and hits metal surfaces. He's a man full of frothing rage. Nothing is ever good enough. The little printer is constantly spitting out tickets which he rips off with such ferocity that it seems the machine will come off the wall. The orders he shouts violently into the ears of the cooks, as if he takes an intense pleasure from treating them with such disdain.

'*Deux poulets! Trois loups! Un filet – bien cuit!*' He leans right into their ears as he shouts: 'Did you fucking hear me?'

'*Oui, chef!*' they cry back in trance-like unison. Not even bothering to wipe the spit from their cheeks. Their sweaty faces glowing in the flames.

'*Bon, espèce de connard. Encore! Deux magrets! Un loup! Trois saumons! Deux veaux!*'

This is when he sees me.

'Get-the-fuck-out!'

I stand there like an idiot with the plate outstretched.

He charges me with the giant knife.

'Did you not understand me? *Va te faire foutre! Fils de pute!*'

Under pressure, my French fails me and I stutter. He pushes me to shout. Louder and louder. I feel like I'm in the basic training scenes of a Vietnam War movie.

'*Dégage!* This steak is medium. Your client is not special. She's a *pute*!'

He turns back to the cooks. For some reason, I stay where I am, on the threshold. Determined to get the meat cooked.

When he turns back and sees me still there with the plate of steak in my hand I glimpse the exact moment when he's consumed by rage: pure, total hatred. Within an instant he has me up against the wall with his free hand on my throat and the point of the giant knife near my eye.

'How dare you tell me how to cook!' he screams.

I can't breathe. His vice-like grip is crushing my trachea. Still holding my throat, he slams the knife down and pulls the plate from my hand. The steak slides into a pan with a piece of cooking lamb.

'Cremate it!' he shouts at the cook.

'*Oui, chef!*'

Panic overcomes me as I still can't breathe. I try in vain to remove his hand, which only angers him further, making him increase the pressure. His breath smells of cigarettes and cognac, and the wall smells of meat. Time has never passed so slowly. I'm about to black out when...

'*Cramé, chef!*' shouts the cook nearest to us. Burnt.

The chef at last takes his hand from my throat, picks up the piece of meat with his bare hand, holds it to my face so it touches my nose, then slams it down onto the plate, which nearly falls from my hand. I turn and hurry down the steps. At the bottom I collect myself. I'm struggling to breathe, to pull enough oxygen into my lungs. After a few moments I check my appearance and smooth my hair back. I use a serviette that has been left on the side to wipe down the plate and then my face, then make my way back along the narrow corridors and into the restaurant.

In the dining room nothing has changed. I've been gone hardly a couple of minutes. There's still the clattering of cutlery against plates, the hubbub of polite conversation and waiters flitting about like flies. I go straight to the table and put the meat down in front of the American lady. She doesn't look at me, or thank me. She simply prods it with her fork, declares it OK and proceeds to eat. I make a beeline for the Pass, ignoring every diner and waiter who tries to solicit my attention. I shout at Nimsath for water, which I cough back up as I drink. Yulia, one of the less glamorous hostesses, and therefore more humane and more inclined to speak to us, hurries into the Pass.

'What have you done?'

I turn. Panicked.

'What?'

'Your back!'

She spins me around and begins rubbing with a cloth. 'It's disgusting.'

The entire thing is covered in a layer of slime. The grease, sweat and condensation from the upper kitchen walls. My newly fitted jacket. Youssef's work. Ruined. And it's the middle of the service. If I don't have a jacket, I can't work in the *salle*; if I can't work, I'm sacked. I hurry back down to the locker room beyond the lower kitchen. The cooks ignore me. I look through the unlocked lockers, hoping to God that one of the waiters not working has left a jacket somewhere. There's nothing. Back upstairs and Yulia has gone, my offending jacket lies screwed up on the side. The swinging door bangs open; I look up, thinking it's the Rat. Fortunately, it's Yulia; she has a jacket.

'Here, try this.'

I slip it on. It's huge. It would even be too big for Salvatore.

'But it's clean,' Yulia says. 'Keep it, until you can get yours cleaned.'

'But I don't have a day off until next week.'

Lucien comes in and see me: 'Either you've shrunk, or the clothes have grown.'

When I tell him how it happened, he's adamant: 'What did I tell you? Hey? You never go into the upper kitchen. Ever.'

The Actress and the Gangster

_____

The restaurant, like the Métro – and just like the city – has two personalities. And, like Pauline, it is that of the night that is the more alluring. When the sun has set, the small courtyard is only discernible from the dining rooms by the faint outline painted by the orange lamps that ring its perimeter. At night there's an air of complicit secrecy about everything. The restaurant becomes a hive of whispered confidences. The _salles_ are so low-lit that the tables appear like islands floating in a dark stream. As a runner you navigate between the tables by candlelight, your vast tray passing over the heads of the customers silently, like a giant silver albatross.

At one of the tables a group of Parisian fashionistas from one of the big couture houses are guzzling champagne and bitching about celebrities and models. The more they drink, the louder they get. All dressed in the uniform of those who work in fashion: black. If I had the remotest interest in this world, I'd now be privy to a whole host of trade secrets. But the fashionistas don't notice me. I'm in the background, a shadow.

Occasionally I see the sommelier enter the scene, but for the most part he'll be sitting on boxes in the stairwell off the Pass, reading one of the sports papers that the boys leave, his bushy eyebrows furrowed as he reads in the weak light, the newspaper almost touching his nose. When he is summoned he will wait until he has finished the article he is reading, then slowly he will rise and, with tiny, slow, methodical steps, make his way through the narrow corridors and up into the _salle_ – his thick book of wines tucked under his arm, his comfortable shoes squeaking on the flagstones. He has the demeanour of a doctor on call as he speaks to the

184

tables. He is not rushed; they know that he is bestowing a great honour upon them by sharing his knowledge. It's like being in the presence of a learned monk as he shows you through his codices, most of which you don't understand.

The sommelier has just taken an order from a man sitting alone at a table for two, and as he walks away he makes a small gesture to me to follow. We go to the back of the restaurant and the small locked door that leads to the famous wine cellar. I'm assuming that this is when my training will really begin. Taking a set of keys from his pocket with shaking, delicate hands, he proceeds to unlock the door. I'm about to follow him down the steps when he suddenly turns and tells me with an air of great severity, 'Two wine glasses. The big ones, not the small. The ones for the *vins nobles*.' And then as an afterthought: 'They're for the gangster on one-ten. So make sure they're clean.' And with this he's gone and the door is closed in my face. I'm surprised someone as professional as the sommelier should have referred to a diner as a gangster and make a mental note to inquire further.

The other waiters say that there are so many fine wines in the cellar that they are insured separately from the restaurant. That it is so vast that the different aisles are named after the streets above and that when the Germans occupied Paris, the sommelier at the time bricked up the finest wines and champagne to stop them being drunk. The wine cellar is not for mortals, however – only four people have the key: the sommelier, the *directeur*, the *patron* and the manager who is on duty when the *directeur* isn't here. For the rest of us it is a mythical place, out of bounds. The majority of wine orders are dealt with by the Tamils. But not the fine wines – these are kept in the wine cellar, under lock and key. As far away from the waiters as possible.

Later, back in the *salle*, I hear the sommelier recommend a magnum of Côtes de Provence rosé to the table of fashionistas. I follow him back to the Pass, where he tells me to deal with it. He is going to lie back down.

'You don't want to serve it?'

'No. They ordered rosé. In winter. Côtes de Provence. A Minuty.'

'You told them to.'

'Even worse, they are indecisive.'

Of all the wines on the menu, the sommelier is most disparaging about the rosés. He believes them to be not real wines but fashion statements. No wonder he is tired all the time – Le Bistrot de la Seine serves gallons of rosé, especially in summer.

'If you must drink rosé, you drink Sancerre rosé. It is quite rare, only 8 per cent of all Sancerre wine produced is rosé. We have some bottles here, actually. But then why you "must" drink rosé is beyond me. There are red and white wines for every occasion,' the sommelier mutters half to me, half to himself. He slumps back down on the potato sacks and picks up the sports paper.

De Souza the Pretend Boxer and Adrien the Untouchable are working tonight and will occasionally sweep in to refill glasses like dancers in a well-rehearsed ballet. Watching them work together is a pleasure. The way they recognize regulars, have their drinks ready before they've ordered. The way they'll cover for one another during fag breaks. I watch a French model as she nods politely to an older man who seems to never stop speaking: in the flickering candlelight her eyes are dark and alluring; occasionally she smiles and takes a small bite of food before placing her cutlery down again. She's unlikely to finish it, but it's a fish dish, which means there will be nothing left for the waiters. We may be hungry, but a half-eaten *filet de bar avec sauce vierge* really is out of the question.

Adrien comes over: 'Mate, have you seen one-ten?'

'*Le Gangster?*'

'*Gangster? Quoi? Non.* Go and look.'

At table 110, a well-proportioned Spanish actress in a very low-cut black dress has just arrived and, with great fanfare, sat down with the man the sommelier says is a gangster. At the Pass Adrien and De Souza talk excitedly about her, like schoolboys.

'Christ, have you seen her yet?' Adrien asks me, rubbing his hands together in delight.

'Never. *Never*, seen anything like it.' De Souza scratches his head and fidgets on his feet. 'She's super-famous in Portugal and Spain, you know.'

'She's mine, De Souza. You're getting married. As your best man it is my duty...'

'Hey, hey. I'm not married yet.'

The Tamils listen to the waiters talking, but they might as well be talking about America it is so far away. You can really sense their frustration. They want nothing more than to walk out into the restaurant and see what is going on. But they can't. The waiters and hostesses are the white tip of the iceberg that have this privilege; the rest must remain hidden.

'Fuck it. I'm going back,' Adrien says and bounds up the steps with another basket of bread rolls.

'*Putain. Moi aussi.*' De Souza is quick to follow, having picked up a carafe of water.

I follow the two of them back into the dining room. Adrien takes a protracted route via the Spanish actress to his own tables. Later, when he is sure Adrien can see him, De Souza sidles up to the Gangster's table and, having given Adrien the quickest of glances – enough to tell him that he'll never stand where he is – leans down to the table and asks if he can pour her some more water. The two diners raise their heads momentarily, all lit from the single light source like a Caravaggio painting, then go back to their conversation and meal. De Souza slowly straightens his back, casts a final, lingering look down the dress of the Spanish actress and then retreats to where Adrien is stationed. Despite the darkness, you can see the grin on De Souza's face as he speaks to Adrien. Later on, he won't stop talking about black lace.

When the coffees are out I tell De Souza I'm going to smoke, but not before informing him that the Spanish actress is actually the girlfriend of a well-known gangster. Naturally he doesn't believe me, but does have some doubts as the man in question has a prominent scar on his hand and – as I point out – is wearing stone-washed denim trousers with black leather shoes.

'So what?' De Souza asks.

'Only a Russian would wear that ensemble. If you don't believe me, we ask Franjo.'

We go in search of the sommelier and find him asleep on sacks of potatoes with his jacket over him.

'Should we wake him?' De Souza asks.

'I'm awake,' the sommelier grunts. 'What?'

'Who's the Gangster?'

The sommelier speaks without opening his eyes.

'Gangster, pimp, call him what you like. He's a bad man.'

'How do you know?' De Souza asks.

'I speak Russian. That's how.'

I give De Souza a look that says 'I told you so' and we leave the sommelier. Apart from this vague information from Franjo we really don't know if this man is a gangster or not. However, De Souza looks fairly concerned for the rest of the evening and keeps his distance from the Spanish actress's cleavage, citing Franjo's 'time in Russian prisons' as a reason for his knowing who the man is. We do, however, 'neglect' to inform Adrien, who we are reasonably certain will have a 'mysterious accident' on his way home tonight, due to his evident ogling of the gangster's moll.

While De Souza and Adrien are dealing with their amorous difficulty, I have my own. At the entrance to the restaurant is a new hostess, standing looking bored over the reservations book. Wearing bright red lipstick, a small black dress and long stiletto heels she looks like she's just stepped out of an Yves Saint Laurent advert. I've said hello. She just looked at me (OK, through me) and smiled, with disinterest verging on pity. I don't know where they find these girls: terrifyingly beautiful and terrifyingly severe. It's beyond them to even register our presence, let alone communicate with us directly.

'Forget about them,' Lucien says, as if the hostesses are another species. 'No hearts.'

'Where do they come from?'

'Agencies. They're all wannabe models and actresses. That's why they're so miserable. That's also why they don't want to talk to you.'

This seems a bit disingenuous, but I let him have it. He's clearly not in the mood to indulge my fantasy. We smoke in silence. The small square looks majestic at night, with the buildings illuminated. We're outside of time here; we could easily be footmen, in the days when some noble lived here. I tell this to Lucien, who couldn't care less. He prefers to talk about how he didn't do enough covers today and how the service could have been better. The hostesses aren't really too different from the waiters, I tell him. We're essentially selected on looks because we're front of house. But Lucien disagrees. For him they only have to look pretty, whereas we actually have to work. So maybe they're right – the hostesses, that is: they are above us on the ladder.

'...*c'est n'importe quoi*. They don't even know the first thing about seating people correctly. They put all the good ones on De Souza's side tonight. Probably on purpose.'

Lucien is really talking about tips.

'Was too easy for him tonight,' he says, running his hand through his dark hair.

'It's not finished yet.'

He looks at his watch. 'Forget about it. Service is finishing.'

To change the subject I tell him of my plan to make a move with the new hostess.

'*Ça ne mange pas de pain,*' he says, which roughly translates as it doesn't cost anything. 'But I'm telling you now: you've no chance. No chance at all. Do you even know her name?'

'Solène. I heard Pauline say it.'

'Bravo. Next step marriage.'

The silhouette of Lucien walks back towards the restaurant. The service is almost over; he's right, we can feel it, the entire organism of the restaurant can: the orders have slowed to a trickle; the line chefs are beginning to clean up their stations; waiters are nipping off for fag breaks, flirting with their hunger instead of ignoring it; most of the hostesses have been relieved of their duty.

When you're genuinely hungry it's amazing what kind of food you think about. After a night of carrying plates of French cuisine I find myself dreaming of Marmite on buttered bread and pickled onion Monster Munch. However, the loud gaggle of the Parisian fashionistas pouring down the steps of the terrace pulls me from my carbohydrate daydream and I head back in.

With only a few tables left to clear, the mood at the Pass is relaxed. Everyone works quietly, in a daze, tired. We're all thinking of our beds, or perhaps dinner, maybe even both. Or, in my case, Solène, who turns out to have already finished her shift by the time I've finished smoking. From the lower kitchen I can hear the *plongeurs* at work. Plates clattering, pressure jets. There's that dry smell of soap and rotten food.

Franjo has disappeared from his boxes and gone home now. The Rat appears as I work.

'You smell of smoke. You've been smoking? You want to smoke, you ask me first. Clear?'

If I'm to ask him when I can smoke I'll never have a break.

Lucien hurries in and deposits an enormous tray of dirty glasses and plates.

The Rat tells Lucien he is going to smoke, and to watch over the dining room. When he's gone Lucien asks me how it's going with Solène. Eager to prove him wrong, prove that hostesses do talk to waiters and that they're not all cold and heartless, I say we had a very encouraging exchange and agreed to have drinks next week.

'*Ah oui?*' he says in a half-mocking tone.

'Yeah.'

'If that's the case, tell me. Does she know your name? Because she's still outside. I can go and ask her. That's what I thought. Stop standing there and go and clear the tables. I want to go and drink.' He winks.

I look at the plates he's deposited. On the top one is the remains of a fish: head, teeth, cheeks, dull black eyeballs.

'Corentin's gone to smoke, right?' I ask.

'Yeah.'

'Have you seen his new office?'

'I haven't yet had the honour.'

'Me neither. Perhaps we could leave him a moving-in gift?' I say, looking at the fish.

'You're crazy.'

'Why? We'll hide it. He won't know until it starts smelling in a few weeks.'

Lucien says he'll stand guard. But first we decide to see if we can find any raw eggs in the lower kitchen. This takes more time that planned, but we find them. As the last of the diners are finishing up, we hurry through the restaurant. The *plateau* of dead fish aloft, the raw eggs in our pockets.

'I'll stand here,' Lucien says.

The Rat's new office is smaller than the *directeur*'s. A void between voids. There's a small desk, a chair and then a tatty sofa. I put the tray on the desk; it's just about big enough. The only place I can find to hide the dead fish and eggs is under the sofa. As I'm putting the sofa back down, I hear the eggs crunch and then, to my horror, I hear footsteps coming down the corridor. With nowhere to go, I pick the tray up, pray to God it's Lucien and open the door.

'You! What are you doing here?'

Corentin pushes me back into his office and shuts the door. Furiously he begins looking through the pieces of paper scattered about his desk.

'What did you steal? Hey?'

I act stupid. Try to confirm his suspicions that I really am mentally deficient. Stammer something about the contract. About overtime. It works – he's incensed that I would even dare to mention these subjects, which he has already explained to me, and on top of that, during a service.

'Get out! Get out! Get out!'

He chases me up the tiny narrow corridor that exists between two walls.

Back in the dining room Lucien is nowhere to be seen. When I do catch up with him later he says he tried to warn me, but it was no use.

'What did you do to warn me?'

'I used the code word.'

'What code word?'

'"Solène." I thought if I whispered it, the winds of love would transport it to you.'

'You're a real shit. He almost caught me.'

Learning About Wine

My meetings with Franjo the sommelier at the small café have become more frequent, to the extent that he now invites me to sit with him while we eat so that we can talk about wines. Originally I wanted to learn about wines to become a waiter, but now the subject fascinates me (*one must know about wines, to live it is indispensable...*); so, too, does the person telling me about them, Franjo.

We sit opposite one another in the small booth, Franjo always facing the door and the bar as he 'doesn't like to look over his shoulder', he says. In truth he says very little about himself. However, when he talks about wine, he can talk for hours. Recently we've moved on to the wines of Burgundy, 'the wines of the dukes', as the sommelier calls them.

'...The sixty or so kilometres south of Dijon produce some of, if not most of, the finest wines in the world. There's no question. Of course, Chablis is a Burgundy, but it is in an isolated area, between Dijon and Paris. This you know, I assume. Tell me, what is the main red grape variety in Burgundy?'

'Pinot noir?'

'Good, but don't forget that Beaujolais is made from Gamay. In my opinion, neither variety does as well anywhere else in the world. They lose their finesse when planted in warmer climates...'

The sommelier has very little time for New World wines. 'It's like literature,' he says. 'You'll never read everything; just concentrate on appreciating the classics.'

We finish the last of our glasses of Nuits-Saint-Georges. There are, of course, other advantages when learning about wines: firstly the sommelier seems to have a fixed, and very low, price per glass at the café; and secondly I go back to the restaurant with a nice buzz after my break as we've usually drunk quite a few glasses. All in the name of education, of course.

'This one is *juste un vin du village*,' he says of the Nuits-Saint-Georges, 'but a Grand Cru or Premier Cru really is something.' He loses his train of thought and stares out the window. 'I think that's enough for today. But you're getting there. That's most of the main regions – apart from champagne, of course. We'll save that for graduation.' He picks up a fork and begins eating the plate of sauerkraut in front of him. The sommelier eats incredibly slowly, I've noticed.

Despite his rough exterior the sommelier has turned out to be quite friendly, but he has never said anything personal. The stories that the other waiters tell about him – for example that he has spent most of his life in Russian prisons, having been involved with a militant group, or that he was once a hitman – are plainly not true. But I decide to ask him what the badge on his lapel means.

'*Mon dieu!* It means I'm a sommelier. If you don't know that—'

'No. The other one.'

'You had me worried for a second.'

He stops eating and without looking down touches the small brass badge on his lapel next to the golden bunch of grapes. It's a flag, green with a white square in the top corner within which is a green star. 'Esperanto.' He carries on eating, but I can tell by the way his eyebrows are concentrated that he is going to speak more. 'When I was at university... I ran the club. You know, back then, we really felt that this was the future: a universal language.'

I wait for more, but the conversation goes dead. Franjo is preoccupied with his lunch. Occasionally the owner comes over to check everything is OK, which the sommelier assures him it is. He refills our glasses. Outside there is a thin, penetrating rain.

'The wine is always good here. Never pretentious.' He takes another sip of the Nuits-Saint-Georges and savours it.

'You use it often?'

'*Quoi?*'

'Esperanto.'

'Ah, that. Sometimes. People don't believe in it like we did then. It's a loss. Sometimes people recognize the badge, but very few now. Imagine, imagine if there was a universal language in today's world – it would be so much easier for everyone. You English wouldn't have so many advantages for a start.'

It seems an enormous effort for the sommelier to speak when it's not about wine: perhaps this is why he says so little in the restaurant.

Later, the old lady clears our plates. '*Fromage?*'

'*Un petit peu,*' he says.

She shuffles back to the kitchen, and we hear the slamming of fridge doors and clanking of plates.

'You're not French,' I try.

'No. Croatian. How many sommeliers in Paris can say that? I think I'm the only one. Or, at least, I was.'

'Were you always a sommelier?'

'Oh no. No, no, no,' he sighs. 'Enough talking, I'm tired.'

I notice the time and realize I'm late for my next shift. There are so many more questions I have for Franjo, but I'll have to wait until our next meeting.

Back at the Pass, before the second shift begins, there is chaos as the *patron* has just come by unannounced and exploded in fury having seen that one section of the dining room has already been set up for the dinner service. Adrien and Valentine often do this, as it allows us to get ahead: laying the tables for dinner is incredibly time-consuming due to the number of things that need to be changed and added compared to the breakfast and lunch services. My lateness is duly noted, and I'm verbally assaulted by Adrien the Untouchable, Nimsath the Tiger and Salvatore the Bear, in a heady mixture of languages. With each of them mixing English, French, Tamil and Sicilian, and numerous gestures thrown in from each culture too.

I smile. This is effectively how all of us get along in the restaurant, short sharp sentences of a bastardized language – a modern-day Esperanto.

The Rat storms in and, grabbing me by the collar, berates me in straight French. It's too fast and furious for me to follow completely and, caught in the moment as I am, I'm unable to argue back. This is the problem with 'restaurant Esperanto' – only the underlings speak it. In the royal court, the true diplomatic language of power is French, which means the advantage rests with the management, as they have the voice, in more senses than one. We in the kitchens cannot argue back, we don't have *la langue*, as the French say, which means both language and tongue.

However, between us, though crude, and probably nonsensical to outsiders, the way we communicate – liberated as it is from any kind of rules and regulations – unites us.

THE PATRON'S OLIVES

Lucien and I are deep below the restaurant, in a small, damp storeroom that smells of mould and ammonia.

'The rats, you soon get used to them,' Lucien is saying. 'If everyone in Paris worried about rats – they'd never eat anywhere!'

'There's only one rat that bothers me.'

As he looks through the shelves I turn the carcass of the rat over with my shoe on the dusty stone floor. It is rigid and hollow and almost completely flat. In the evenings, when the service has quieted down and the kitchens have stopped, I often catch them scurrying along the walls, like shadows. But, now, seeing one up close gives me a real idea of their proportions.

'Next time you're in the dining room during the dinner service, look,' Lucien continues, slightly out of breath. 'Big as cats sometimes, I swear. But the clients, they never see them. At my parents' restaurant we used to set traps. You should have seen the size of the rats we caught.'

In the corner of the room is a pile of dried rat droppings, which is where the foul stench is coming from.

'*C'est bon,*' he finally cries, 'I've found them. Wait...'

Lucien is standing on the second shelf, his body completely engulfed between the fourth and fifth. We've been sent on a mission of critical importance. It's *l'heure de l'apéritif*, the *patron* is here entertaining guests and, crucially, there are no more olives – anywhere, in the entire restaurant. The mission was considered so important that it could not be entrusted to the Tamils, the *directeur* told us.

'There are definitely olives down there. There must be.' He was in a state of high anxiety as he briefed us. 'Those idiots just don't know what they are looking for. Get them. The *patron* has asked for them twice, he will not ask a third time.' The *directeur* looked set to explode. Already his top lip glistened with sweat and his fat cheeks burned red – symptoms that appeared only during a particularly busy dinner service or Sunday lunch.

The *patron* is a small, gnome-like man who occasionally comes to the restaurant unannounced, and in so doing sets the management into a state of extreme panic. He owns the Bistrot de la Seine and a number of other similar places across Paris, although the Bistrot is the jewel in the crown. As far as I can tell he only comes into the restaurant to complain about things, ask for things to be changed or threaten to fire people. He's got rich selling the illusion of fine food, simply by serving below-average food in stylish surroundings.

With today's arrival of the *patron* and some friends for an unexpected aperitif, even the *directeur* had come in – to ensure that everything went perfectly – for he was not meant to be here, he reminded us. He wasn't even wearing his suit, although it did look as if he had hastily removed make-up from his face before arriving. De Souza was sent to fetch and polish the expensive glasses; the Tamils were preparing generous servings of drinks as the machine spat out their orders with ***VIP VIP VIP*** written on the tickets; on the small speakerphone in the upper kitchen the chef was shouting for the best cuts of meat to be brought up to him in case the party stayed for dinner. The Rat, meanwhile, was down in the *cave* looking for the finer wines and cursing Franjo the sommelier as he was still on his break and didn't have a phone. It was a surprise attack. During this time, the *patron* was sitting with his female friends, perhaps oblivious, until for some unknown reason he'd stormed into the Pass crying to high heaven about the lack of olives. It was a disgrace, he was hosting an *apéro* and there were no olives. The *patron* has been known to sack people on the spot; the Tamils and waiters just stood there hoping that the earth would swallow them up. The *directeur* appeared soon afterwards, slightly out of breath, unsure what had happened but agreeing with the owner when he said to him, '*C'est n'importe quoi!*'

After criticizing how the *directeur* was dressed the *patron* finally left and went back to his table, at which point the *directeur*, trying to mask how terrified he actually was, asked, 'What did he want?'

Chaos ensued as the Tamils began emptying out their cupboards – there were no more olives. The delivery was due today, but hadn't come. Nimsath and the *directeur* argued as to whose fault it was. Baloo was sent down to the storerooms but came back saying there was nothing.

'What do you mean?' the *directeur* was shouting.

This is when Lucien and I enter the scene.

Presently, as Lucien manoeuvres the enormous plastic vat of olives from the back of the shelf, boxes and tins began to fall off from the front.

'Wait,' I say, as I hurry to pick them up.

But he can't hear me. I am crouching down picking up the fallen boxes when a heavy object lands on my back with a dull thud and almost pushes me to the floor. To stop myself falling I put my hand on the dusty stones just next to where the dead rat is. I turn around to see the giant vat of olives on its side, the lid off, the olives all over the floor, half the brine they were soaked in on my jacket, the rest oozing into the cracks of the floor as if a dam has just burst and is turning the centuries of dust that lie there into a kind of clay that it pushes before the surging wave of brine.

'Fuck.'

'*Putain.*'

Lucien and I look at each other in disbelief.

'Is there another one?'

Lucien climbs back onto the shelves.

'*Non.*'

'We need to pick them up,' I say. 'Then clean them.'

'The restaurant can finally be proud of you,' he says with a smirk.

'It's what the *patron* would want. We're saving money.'

'We shouldn't waste them, no. Bad for the bottom line.'

With our bare hands we begin to pick up as many of the olives as possible. Each one is covered in a light dusting of what can only be described as filth. We fling them into the plastic vat. I can feel the brine soaking into my shirt. The smell is revolting and stings the small cuts in my hands from earlier in the morning when I cut them polishing the knives.

When most of the olives are in the vat we pick it up and carry it upstairs to the lower kitchen, which is busy with dinner preparation. Men shouting, slicing, dicing, grilling. We try to use one of the deep metal sinks, but the cooks begin to yell, waving various kitchen implements in the air in a terrifying act of solidarity. They don't want to be involved in whatever is going on, one of them says.

'Your problem. Not ours.' He makes a menacing clicking noise with his tongue. There is no choice but to go back down to the cellars. We find another plastic box in the storeroom and, using a small tap coming out of the wall that looks as if it hasn't been turned on for some time, we fill the box with orange-tinged water and pour the olives in. While I wash the olives and place them back in the vat, Lucien goes to find olive oil. He comes back slightly out of breath with two of the pourers from the dinner service.

'That's not going to be enough!' I say. 'We need to disguise the taste!'

'It's all there is,' he replies. 'Hurry, the *directeur* is looking for us.'

We frantically wash the olives and put them back into the vat, and every so often Lucien pours a good glug of the table olive oil onto them. The *directeur* appears a few moments later. When he sees us, I could swear that his face goes completely white. He begins screaming, cursing. His fists clench as obscenities pour out of his face, which turns a worryingly deep shade of red. When he is done he demands rapeseed oil from the cooks and tells us to ensure the olives are properly washed.

'If he notices, you're gone. Both of you. Use that oil when you run out of the other.'

The *directeur* takes two short breaths and then hurries upstairs like a terrified courtier. However, he is soon back.

'And separate them. He doesn't like to see them together.'

'What?'

'The olives. Black and green. Never together!'

And for a second time he disappears.

'Does the *directeur* wear make-up?' I ask.

'That's a story for another time,' Lucien says.

When we bring the vat of olives up to the Pass the Tamils get to work putting them in small porcelain bowls. The *directeur* comes in to oversee this and drink a Diet Coke from the bottle with a straw.

'Black in one bowl, green in the other. Let me see, let me see.'

Lucien and I then load up trays with drinks orders and olives and without a word head into the restaurant with the *directeur* hot on our heels. The way everyone watches us, it feels like the final walk from Death Row.

The *patron* has commandeered the large table in the windows overlooking the square. He sits at the head, like a toad, with his usual look of discontent. He is with a group of fawning women who are half his age and twice his height and laugh exaggeratedly at anything he says. He is in his element, snapping at waiters, pointing with his half-closed arthritic hands or using them to push his long grey hair back. The Rat stands in the corner, trying to read the *patron*'s next complaint through lip-reading or body language; he then relays these messages to Adrien: 'Ice, get him ice', for example.

As we walk across the dining room, I can feel the *directeur* watching us from the crack in the swinging door. It is dusk and the candles have been lit on each table. No matter how hard I stare at the olives it is impossible to tell if they are still dusty. When we arrive at the table, the loudest of the women, who looks something like a younger Pauline but with a harder face, makes a huge commotion by trying to begin a round of applause at the appearance of the olives. The *patron* quickly hushes her with a swipe of a closed hand through the air in her general direction. She falls silent, picks up her wine glass, sits back in her chair, looks out of the window, then downs the whole thing in one go.

'We need more wine,' she says moodily, still looking out of the window.

'Another bottle,' the *patron* croaks at Lucien.

'*Oui, monsieur.*'

'And where's the sommelier?'

'On his break.'

'Find him.'

Already from the shadows there is a stirring of movement as the Rat briefs Adrien and hands him the large set of keys for the cellar, clearly unable to tear himself away from the potential car crash that is about to happen. Once we have placed the olives on the table the group fall upon them like starving animals. Lucien and I retreat into the shadows to await our fate. In the half-light we can see them all chewing the olives; one of the girls discreetly removes something from her mouth – it is hard to tell if it is the stone or something else. The girl with the harsh face at the end of the table says something indecipherable to the *patron*, who abruptly gets up and, with his phone clutched in his hand, heads straight towards Lucien and me. It is only now that I notice he is wearing leather trousers and a scarf that reaches almost to the floor.

'Where's the wine? Why are you just standing there? Do I pay you to do nothing?' He spits the olive stone into this hand and stands there. 'And these tables, why are they like this? They should be tables of two, not four. Cretins.'

He summons the *directeur*, who emerges from the darkness in an instant like some kind of enslaved genie, and rallies off a volley of commands. The *directeur* is practically bowing like a disgraced Japanese politician as he leaves. The Rat appears with the wine and shoos Adrien away. He will serve the *patron* himself, he says. Lucien and I get to work rearranging the tables, then retreat back to the Pass. Pauline is there with Salvatore.

'Who's the woman at the end of the table?' I ask.

'*Sa pute.*' His whore, is all she says before going up towards the swinging door and spying on the table.

'Ah, women,' Salvatore says.

It turns out that Pauline isn't too wide of the mark, as the woman in question is indeed the *patron*'s mistress. The biggest headache for the restaurant, particularly Pauline, is ensuring that the wife and mistress never cross paths, as both come here regularly to dine, alone or with friends.

Just like the green and black olives, the *patron* prefers that the two ladies are kept well apart.

A Taste of Restaurant Life

The restaurant, much like the city, runs on appearances. The difference between what you see and what you don't is as vast as an ocean. The restaurant, in reality, is a conman.

I feel a rising resentment of the restaurant's approach to gastronomy. Yet, I increasingly admire the waiters. The pride in what they do. Their no-nonsense work ethic. The Sisyphean nature of the job: redemption through repetition. The camaraderie. The competition. Their relationship with money and the ephemeral. The way they feel part of a great lineage, of something distinctly French. That they, unlike the rest of the citizens of the city, know something special. A secret order of magicians, perhaps. Just a lot less glamorous.

Because, if a waiter is doing his job correctly, he will be manipulating your perception of reality. He is, to all intents and purposes, an illusionist and his job is to deceive you. He wants you to believe that all is calm and luxurious, because on the other side of the wall, beyond that door, is hell. He is, in effect, the living example of the façade.

The management are always in a high state of anxiety because, for the restaurant to fulfil its role and provide the illusion of luxury that everyone in the dining room expects, the innards must come out. Out of the darkness, across the thin divide and into the world of the living. This puts the restaurant at its most exposed. Everything else happens out of sight: it suffices just to allude to 'the chef' and the diner will paint the picture themselves, which doubtless will not include a dozen emaciated immigrants being barked at by stressed Tamils or a scimitar-wielding Corsican.

The waiters are the weak point in this chain, emissaries from the Underworld sent out like yo-yos on the understanding that they will return, and in the meantime play their role and perpetuate the illusion. But a waiter isn't a soldier – as we know, he's a bounty hunter, and the restaurant pays him enough to ensure he can live his itinerant existence, but never enough for him to escape definitively. So, he steals and cheats and charms his way to whatever he can get, and this is why you pay him a tip. It's a tax, given on the understanding that he will perform his role to the best of his abilities as an actor, bounty hunter, stage manager, bully and everything else you want him to be so that your food arrives just as you'd expected it. You are paying him so that you get better service than the other tables. So, don't think the world behind that door has nothing to do with you. Just like us, you are complicit.

Running a restaurant is an exercise in driving down costs while serving the outcome with a straight face – and in Paris, just as in other cities, towns and villages, this is being entrusted to a group of delinquents. Men who for whatever reason have fallen into the waiting game. The only way to manage such a situation is to strip each person's role down to its constituent parts. Like engineers on a secret project, no one ever has the whole picture. In the prep kitchen there are men who are assigned specific dishes; just as on a production line, they will spend their day boiling eggs or toasting bread, while *plongeurs* wash, cooks are tasked with specific meats, the waiter serves. (There's a man in the lower kitchen whose job on weekends is to parboil eggs, hundreds of them, and lay them on ice so that they can be dropped back into the hot water for a second once another eggs Benedict is ordered.) However, the waiter is unique, because he must also have contact with the clientele and, of course, the other important thing: the money.

As the service unfolds the waiter's wallet begins to bulge with takings, each order has been logged and will be checked off at the end of the day, but until that point the money is his. A man you pay the minimum wage (the amount that someone has deemed the absolute legal minimum necessary to live in this city) has all the business's money. The waiters are treated with suspicion by every other employee for exactly this reason, but every station has its kick-back – you rarely see a cook go hungry, despite the management's best efforts, whereas the waiters must eat what has been rejected by the diners, like vultures.

I have been in the restaurant a few months now and I have no desire to leave. Not yet, perhaps never. I am strangely drawn to the world of the waiters; there is something ancient about it: waiting in Paris, with all the rituals – it intrigues me. And I am slowly being let in, becoming one of them, part of the brotherhood. I want to become a waiter, to have their respect, and my own. The prospect of an unpaid London internship (if I was lucky), tasteless supermarket sandwiches in front of a computer for lunch and a return to sofa-hopping wouldn't be a patch on living in Paris. Even when you're exhausted, broke and hungry, there's still an indefinable magic about the place. And no matter how much your feet hurt after a never-ending shift, how physically dead you feel as you walk up the Avenue de l'Opéra at night, or across the Seine under the shadow of Notre-Dame, inside, you can't help but feel intensely alive. Because you're in it, you're in the film. You're not watching, you've got a walk-on, speaking part. And everything feels possible. Besides, when you're in Paris you couldn't care less about anywhere else. Your world shrinks; it's the centre of the universe. There is nowhere else.

Having understood how to operate as a runner, and therefore get a cut of the waiters' tips, I now find that I always have cash, even if it is a lot less than the waiters have. Dirty old bills stuffed in our wallets. If we spend them on food, of course it is always in the cheap local bistros where a *faux-filet frites* costs nine euros and a carafe of the house wine five. This is the waiter's way. 'Eat where they can tell you where the food comes from and that they cooked it themselves' is his hard-learned motto. 'That and "Paying for the view" is a completely unacceptable approach to eating.'

Drinking takes place in dive bars or PMU bars after services, when, unable to sleep despite the physical fatigue, we consume rounds of drinks to calm the nerves. A waiter appears to have no real social life. You are condemned to work society's social hours and as such your world becomes the restaurant and the people in it. Adrien says that if he ever has enough time to take a girl out for a drink it is for two pints of La Chouffe, which has the equivalent strength of four, and that is it.

'After four we're both interested,' he says dryly.

The money, of course, disappears as quickly as it comes in, and there is never anything to show for it apart from the occasional haircut, fags or hangover. Of course, we all kick ourselves for spending it when we hit a dry patch and don't make any good tips for a while, yet this seems to be the reason to spend it freely when we have it.

The waiter, despite his lowly status, is unique. As the penultimate link in the chain that connects you, the diner, to the paperless immigrant scrubbing plates, the waiter is forced into an unbearable position. A position from which only physical action can offer a redemptive escape. He has no choice but to finish the job that was started by the others somewhere below ground. To continue the reaction and play his part in the game. Up and out of the infernos, only to return again.

I think about all this as I stand in the street smoking before a dinner service on a Friday night. Green-and-white buses move laboriously through the evening traffic, lights reflected in their opaque windows. They stop regularly, disgorging their human cargo into the river of silhouettes that move quickly in the darkness towards unknown destinations. There's that buzz of the weekend, the stench of free time. Occasionally you see a face, before it turns and fades into the evening. Each expression a glimpse into France; if only you can seize it for long enough – if only you can see enough of them.

Paris is not France; yet all of France can be found in Paris. It is the monumental city. The centre of the wheel. Imagined by great men and hewn by the currents of history like cliffs on a battered coastline. In Paris the street names are the same as those in every French village: Boulevard Ney, Avenue Foch, ...de Gaulle, ...Jules Joffrin, ...Gambetta, ...Victor Hugo, ...Voltaire and so on. Today's greats will have a public swimming pool or library named after them.

In Paris the grandeur of the monumental punctuates the intimate. Edifices to God, wars or thinkers, vast squares and parks. All of this overlooks the narrow streets of *boulangeries*, pharmacies, Thai massage parlours, rubbish, *tabacs*, graffiti, estate agents, dog shit and phone shops – the thread that ties together the twenty *quartiers* of the city. It is in these places that the people work. The people whose lives are played out below the indifferent regard of the city's monuments. Paris cares little for them, for she has seen them all before and will see many more afterwards. Indifferent because the city knows she will remain, even if just in the imagination. You feel it as you walk around. There are few other cities that offer such great panoramas as you go to work. It is both epic in its proportions and intimate. Even visitors to the city feel it; you can tell by the way they dress. How many other cities inspire people to dress well?

Right at the centre of this giant wheel that is Paris is the Bistrot de la Seine. A microcosm of the city, of the country as it is today. Replete with a defined social hierarchy cemented neatly in place by the physical layout of the restaurant. On the surface all is light, but the deeper one travels, the darker things become.

PART 5
LE FROMAGE

Spring Arrives

A deep-blue sky hangs over the city, the sun low and heavy, throwing thick light down the boulevards. It glistens on the surfaces of cars, tarmac and windows. Everywhere is light; the first days of spring. In the early morning I stand at my open window and drink coffee, looking out over the slanting roofs of all the small buildings crammed in behind the grandiose façades on the road. The air is cool and full of promise. It smells sweet. From the street below, the sound of ceramic cups on saucers and voices, snatched parts of conversations float upwards. There are thousands of dark, hard buds on the branches of the poplar trees in the avenues now. On the wooden floor of my room my feet are tough with solidified blisters.

The morning walk along the canal, a private moment to enjoy the city – the city that, in a matter of weeks, has suddenly exploded into life. Hemingway was right – Paris in spring, each day has no limits.

Adrien, De Souza and Salvatore are putting the final touches for breakfast to the main terrace which has now opened up – effectively tripling the capacity of the restaurant. The long terrace runs along the front of the restaurant, behind a stone balustrade overlooking a small, almost forgotten square below. Perfectly symmetrical tables, either side of a long walkway of stone slabs worn smooth and shiny from centuries of hurried courtiers' footsteps. Below the main terrace, in the corner of the quiet square, is a second, much smaller terrace, used only for drinks. As in the dining room, the *rangs* are distributed across its length, with the most important tables towards the centre.

We work in the cool morning air under the high vaulted ceiling held aloft by stone columns the diameter of oak trees. We're now in competition with the starlings, which dart about, diving down to the tables to pick at the remains of a breakfast, before we've even had the chance to clear it up and potentially eat it. As we drink coffee the sun creeps higher into the deep blue until finally its unrelenting light falls upon the terrace and the cool air begins to dissipate. Tourists are milling about the square below us. Pigeons being shooed away as they walk.

'There's no other city with as many beautiful women per square metre,' I tell the boys, knowing they revel in this kind of conversation.

'It's true,' says Adrien. 'But they're *chiantes*.' Pains in the arse.

'And Milano?' De Souza says.

'Forget about it. Too uptight. The girls in Rome are the finest, if you are talking about Italians,' Sal, the resident expert, says, sipping his espresso from a ceramic cup. 'But Sicilians...'

'Truffaut said it's in Montpellier, not Paris, that you find the prettiest girls,' Lucien interrupts, slightly out of breath, having just arrived two hours late for his service.

'Ah, our resident actor!' De Souza mocks him. 'Nice of you to join us.'

'Sure, fine, but what does Truffaut know?' Adrien asks, as he finishes gelling his hair. 'It's Provence. For sure. Here's why: first, they have that nice look, typically French – dark hair, olive skin, dark eyes. The accent is nice, too – and they're not *chiantes* like Parisian girls. You don't want a Parisian girl, *l'Anglais*. A nice Provençal girl and you're good. Go and live in Avignon or Aix. Forget about Paris.'

The other waiters agree. In France it is encouraged to be patriotic, but when it comes to women, wine and cheese, it is the region that is important.

'The tomatoes are good there, too.' Sal winks at me.

'But also, the English. Like Lady Dee.'

They're talking about Lady Diana, the late Princess of Wales, which naturally evolves into a conversation about the Royal Family. The French interest in the Royal Family genuinely knows no limits.

In the celebrated journals that he kept for forty-five years, Edmond de Goncourt wrote that 'when intelligent men drink and dine together, the subject of conversation is always women and love'. Working in the restaurant makes me wonder if in fact you just need to be *around* diners and only drinking cheap coffee. Perhaps the constant talk of women is provoked by the intensely masculine world of waiting, by the absence of females. There are of course plenty of female waiters across the city, but here in the Bistrot we're stuck in a different era. And no one can tell me why. *C'est comme ça,* they say.

'...Provence. That's where I'll open it,' Adrien is saying. The classic waiter's dream: open his own restaurant. '...a small place on a busy square. Me and my wife...'

'You're married?' I ask, surprised, as he's never mentioned it.

'No. No. Why do you sound so surprised, anyway? Besides, how am I gonna meet a girl working here? I'll meet her when I get there. No time for love right now.'

'Maybe at my wedding, Big Man. Best Man and all,' De Souza smiles.

The other waiters bristle at the mention of the wedding. Everyone is talking about it as we all want to go. However, no one has been invited yet. For me, an invitation to De Souza's wedding really would mean I'd been accepted by the waiters. For the others it would reassure them they're on the inside too. But it will be hard for so many staff to take the same day off, so the likelihood of getting there is slim.

We're all showing an inordinate interest in the planning of De Souza's wedding when Pauline hurries into the Pass, asking where Guillaume is. Guillaume is a new waiter who started a few weeks ago. Sal noticeably absents himself from the Pass as Pauline is speaking, which doesn't go unnoticed by Lucien. Something tells me he's up to something, now that Sal is ditching Pauline.

'Guillaume didn't come in?' Lucien asks.

'A bit like you this morning,' Adrien adds.

'A few minutes late, Adrien. It happens.'

'Few minutes? A few hours. I'll let it go this time. But do that again, you're sacked. That's three times in the last two weeks.'

When Adrien has gone Lucien says, 'Eh, *l'Anglais*. Have I got a

few things to tell you! But later, later. When the others aren't around.'
His excitement is palpable.

The *directeur* marches in: '*Il y a du monde déjà...*'
Breakfast is to be served.

It's All An Act

Immediately after the breakfast service a strange calm descends upon the restaurant, like a ceasefire. Cooks take turns to smoke in the hole-in-the-floor toilet – they're not allowed out above ground, that's where the waiters smoke, leaning against walls or cars in the small back roads across the city; eyeing up the elegant women hurrying on their way to and from work, their heels echoing off the pavement in the warm air. Smoking works in shifts, but here it's organized by our own hierarchy – with Adrien the Untouchable giving the nod – each man stepping out alone in his bow tie and jacket, conscious that the next man is waiting for his return. When you smoke, you smoke alone; you don't belong to the restaurant while you are outside of it. You belong to the city.

On the terrace the remains of breakfast, scattered tables of quiet people drinking coffee and reading papers. I watch and wait; waiting to go and smoke and sit down and be on my own. The empty tables are bare; we won't begin to lay them for lunch until eleven. Adrien appears at my shoulder, a smell of cigarette smoke. He reminds me of a crow in his black suit.

'*Tu peux y aller,*' he whispers, letting me know it's my turn.

Later at the Pass the Rat tells me to go and polish the glasses for the lunch service. He's also trying to tell the Tamils that there's a politician on table 104 and that everything must be perfect. He does this because there are different levels of 'perfect' in the restaurant. I listen to the conversation sitting on my upturned bucket in one of the lower cellars where I'm polishing.

'*Toujours parfait.*' Always perfect, the Tamils snap at the Rat.

The Rat threatens them, telling them that if there are any of their usual mistakes there will be hell to pay, that he'll be watching every single thing that comes out of that door. The Rat leaves, muttering something about the restaurant going downhill, and moments later Adrien arrives.

'*C'est qui?*' Nimsath is getting annoyed at Adrien. '*Punday* politician.'

'Some *punday* politician. I don't care. Just give me the coffees.'

'It's coming!'

Moments later I hear the Rat come back: 'Where's the politician's breakfast?'

'It's coming, Corentin. *Putain, fous-moi la paix,*' Adrien flings back at him.

'Good, good. Let me see that, Nimsath. One less croissant in the basket; he's a socialist after all. No, no. It's fine, I'll eat it. *Liberté, égalité, fraternité,*' the Rat says dully through mouthfuls of croissant.

In the restaurant fraternity is all we have, just – someone higher up the food chain has taken away the other two.

'Politician leaves big tips?' Nimsath chides Adrien when the Rat has gone.

'Not if he doesn't get his breakfast. Hurry the hell up.'

'*Punday* politician. *Punday pourboires.*' Nimsath shouts something incomprehensible into the intercom. From where I am I hear the reaction downstairs in the lower kitchen. They've finished the breakfast service and are starting to prep for lunch. They don't respond to Nimsath, just curse him between themselves, a wave of anger, as each person delegates down the chain.

I've been cleaning some time when Lucien comes into the cellar I'm working in.

'What's this news, then?' I ask.

'Wait. First, what do you make of Guillaume not showing?' He leans against a wall. 'They're saying he's got a job in a hotel…'

Lucien laughs at this. A job in a hotel is looked down upon by the men who consider themselves real waiters. There are no tips in hotels, he says; people just sign to the room. For a second, I let myself believe that, if it is true and Guillaume didn't turn up for work today, maybe, just maybe,

I'll finally get the call-up. Maybe there's a chance I'll be made a waiter.

Lucien leans in: 'But that's *n'importe quoi*. You know why? Because he did a runner. He's on the run. I'm telling you.'

Adrien goes past. 'Bullshit. What do you know, Lucien?'

'I know. At the end of his shift last night, he just disappeared, right?'

'We all do,' Adrien adds dryly. 'A bit like you this morning.'

'For the head waiter you're not very well informed. Guillaume stole from the restaurant. Never gave his money in to Corentin. That's why he's trying to brown-nose the politician. Last night, Guillaume just disappeared in the middle of the service. Ask Sal.'

Lucien says he's got it all worked out. His eyes glimmer as he tells the story: 'It's easy. All day we take money...' – he slips his waiter's wallet out of his jacket – '...this thing here. How much do you think it holds? Once I had *deux mille balles* in here.' Two thousand.

'Give it up. He didn't steal.' Adrien is adamant, though there's a touch of uncertainty in his voice. 'He's been a waiter for years. Where's he going to work now? His name will be ruined in Paris.'

'He was always talking about London, and New York. Bitching about Paris.'

'I can't stand people who *crachent dans la soupe*,' Adrien says.

'Exactly. But if you want to go there, how do you do it? You're not going to earn the plane fare here. Are you? I tell you. You steal and get the hell out. He had courage; you've got to respect that, Adrien.'

'Yeah, and now who pays the price? You and me, that's who. If he had any respect for us, he would have done it on a Monday night. Now we've got Saturday lunch and we're a waiter down...'

'It has to be on a Friday. That's what I told him. It's when you take the most cash; all the drinks...'

'Bullshit. You knew, Lucien. You and your *putain d'histoires*.'

Some other waiters arrive and a couple of minutes pass in which Guillaume's name is dragged through the mud and he's accused of every sin under the sun. Whether it's true or not is irrelevant to me. The fact that they are sharing this with me assures me that, in some way, I'm in the gang.

'*Alors, il t'a laissé combien?*' So, how much did he leave you? Lucien eventually asks Adrien to get rid of him.

'Who? The politician? Nothing,' Adrien says, leaving.

Lucien rolls his eyes when he's gone.

'Obviously you know how Adrien makes his money, *l'Anglais*?' Lucien asks with a conspiratorial air.

'I have an idea, yeah.'

'If you think a restaurant runs on food...'

'How does he get away with it?'

'Why do you think he's the Untouchable? They're all in on it.'

The Untouchable, of course.

'You going to tell me this news or not?'

Lucien turns a bucket over and joins me polishing. 'You know those bastards, the managers, wouldn't give me time off this morning?'

'Where were you?'

He leans in. 'Listen, you may not be seeing much more of me around here.'

'You're going to do a runner like Guillaume, too?'

'No, no, no. I was at... well, I was at a casting.' He jumps up, but whispers. 'It was a call-back, in fact. Big film. If I get it, *mon ami... putain! Je suis parfait pour le rôle, quoi?* Don't tell the others. Shhh shhh.'

Adrien returns: 'Why you so excited?'

'Me? Nothing...'

'You can't stop grinning.'

Lucien can't help but tell Adrien about the casting.

'Ha. You, a big actor? Forget about it.'

'You could learn a thing or two,' Lucien says as Adrien leaves. 'All of this won't be important soon.' He throws a handful of cutlery into the bucket with a splash. 'This shit job, these dirty clothes. My parents will see me in magazines. I'm finally doing it.' As he talks it's infectious.

'What will you do with all the money?'

'From the film? Probably buy an apartment, Rive Gauche. After the next film I'll buy my parents' restaurant from them.'

Jamaal squeezes past us on his way down to the locker room.

'*As-Salaam-Alaikum, mes frères.*' He rubs his nose on the back of his hand, then wipes it on his trousers.

'*Wa-Alaikum-Salaam,*' Lucien replies.

'It true? About Guillaume?' Jamaal asks, his crossed eyes searching ours.

'*Ouais,*' Lucien says.

'*Espèce de merde.* Today will be a shit show because of him. I hope he gets what he deserves.' He clears his nose and swallows. 'Damn hay fever, too. No break.'

I join in with Jamaal and Lucien, giving my two cents about Guillaume because I know it's expected of me. In all honesty I hardly remember the guy, but I know how hard a service is with the right number of staff, which is to say the strict minimum, so even one man down will make the suffering greater.

By now the prep kitchen below is in full swing. The hissing, clattering and shouting float up the stone steps with the weird, nauseating smell of shallots being fried off, pasta being blanched in giant pots constantly on the boil, and floors being cleaned with bleach. From above we can hear the slamming shut of the metal fridge doors and cries of words we recognize: 'Coca', 'Perrier', 'rosé', between long bouts of Tamil as they do the inventory before the service. Lucien and I finish polishing the glasses, then head back up to the Pass to prepare. When the *rangs* are given out I wait eagerly for mine, but it doesn't happen. I'm still running. It's now getting ridiculous.

Salvatore finally arrives, and Lucien disappears to smoke in the sun in order to 'help his tan'.

'*Guillaume, quel connard,*' I say.

'*Ouais, grave,*' he replies.

'How much did he take, then?'

'*Quoi?*'

'Guillaume, you were there last night. He stole a load of money. Ran off to New York.'

'What the hell you talking about?'

'Lucien...'

'Mister Hollywood? That guy's full of shit.'

A New Rank: The Drinks Terrace

It's 10.30am and I'm on the terrace, eyes closed. The morning sun is pleasant on my face and its warm fingers of light are now strong enough to penetrate my fitted suit through to my skin. It feels glorious. Down by my side hangs the enormous silver *plateau*. From the small square below, I imagine I must look like some kind of sculpture, shield gleaming. Groups of tourists are waiting for the little museum on the opposite side of the square to open. Occasionally one of the African street vendors, his arms laden with cheap trinkets, will appear from the eaves of the arcade and run over to them. 'Nice Paris memories,' he will say, waving his arms like some strange bird of paradise.

On the terrace business meetings take place over coffee – hushed conversations, expensive suits, firm handshakes and back-slapping. De Souza is putting the final glasses in his station for the lunch service. The metal shutter that connects the Pass to the terrace is now open, and behind the tall screen that shields this area from the diners I can hear Lucien chatting with Nimsath about the film he'll be in. I feel relaxed. Starlings chirp in the high eaves somewhere and occasionally dive down to retrieve crumbs that have been left on tables before the pigeons have had time to waddle over. Beyond the square the rumble of traffic can be heard – the harsh acceleration of the scooters and cars, like wasps, as they race for each traffic light on the boulevard behind.

'*Il est où, Guillaume?*'

The *directeur* is right next to me, having materialized out of thin air.

'I don't know. He didn't come in this morning,' I say, enjoying being an insider.

The *directeur* thinks about this for a minute, looking down below the terrace at the tourists, then back up to the sky.

'*L'Anglais, viens,*' he says.

We walk down the steps and into the square. The *directeur* points to a pile of stacked chairs and tables.

'Lay these out. I want perfect lines, five of them, seven wide. Two chairs to a table. Only ever two chairs to a table. Understand?'

'*Oui.*' I begin to make off.

'*Pas encore. Viens.*' We head back up onto the terrace. Lucien is now at the service station, refilling the perfectly folded white serviettes.

'You know how this works.' The *directeur* points to the small computer by the service station. 'It's easy. Drinks are here, snacks and food here. When you have removed their starters, you hit "*réclame*", so that the kitchens begin the main courses. Actually, you don't need that now. You will only serve drinks here. We'll see about starters. Your *rang* is now the drinks terrace,' he says, handing me a till key. 'Don't mess it up.'

Guillaume hasn't come in; perhaps he is ill, perhaps he was never going to, but – hallelujah! – I think I'm now a waiter! I couldn't care less about Guillaume; I'm glad he didn't come in for whatever reason. Indeed, I hope he never comes back.

'You have the drinks terrace. A waiter serves food,' Lucien says grimly, having noticed my contentment.

'*Merci*, Mister Hollywood.'

'*Eh, ta gueule avec Mister Hollywood.* But, do you want to know how to make more tips?' He slides over to me.

Lucien explains that people never leave much in the way of tips for drinks. 'You will be running around all day for the occasional ten centimes or euro, and they throw it there like you are a dog and should be happy with it. What can you buy with ten centimes? Tell me.' He pauses. 'Nothing. So, you must take some orders, how to say...directly.'

He is suddenly very serious.

'Listen, someone orders an espresso. Don't go to the computer. Go straight to the Pass. See if there's an espresso there – if yes, you take it.'

'But the Tamils...'

'They will be too busy with the lunch service. No one cares about coffee; coffee costs nothing. We charge 300 per cent more than it costs us. But if the Tamils start to shout – you shout back louder; you tell them you are missing an espresso, that they fucked up. This is the game; don't feel bad. People always take the drinks incorrectly. And the Tamils can't follow every coffee order. So, they make you another one. Now, when you give the customer the coffee you tell him the price directly – "One euro fifty", like this. And then you wait, like you are busy, and he is wasting your time with such a small order. See?' Lucien has his fists on his hips, his big potato-like nose turned slightly upwards, and he is sighing as he looks around. 'You see how I look, *l'Anglais*?' The client will then pay to get rid of you, and when he does, you put the money straight into your pocket. *Facile, hein?*

I agree; it does sound easy.

'Everybody does it. You have a lot to learn, *l'Anglais*. Don't be so worried. You want to be a waiter. Now is your chance. Start playing the game.'

I've not even finished laying out the tables when people begin gravitating towards the drinks terrace. It's the ideal location, small and south-facing, with a view over the little square. On top of that, it's part of the imposing restaurant on the terrace above, so people feel they're getting something of quality, which they most certainly are not. My very first customers are a middle-aged French couple. They order a *jus d'orange pressé*, *café allongé*, Perrier *menthe*. They leave me a twenty-centimes tip. I clear their glasses away, wipe down the table and stand alert by my rank. The tables don't have numbers, so I number them in my head: one to forty. With a quick calculation I realize that at any one time there could be up to eighty people sitting there. I put the idea out of my mind – it seems ridiculous that so many people would congregate in the same place for an overpriced coffee.

But they do. Tourists are drawn to places that are busy: the more of their kind they see, the more they feel reassured. And so it is that the lower terrace becomes my domain. A place that never stops during the entire day. Fortunately, it is fairly close to the Pass, since the *plateau*, when laden with bottles, teapots and full glasses, is probably heavier than when it has food. And then I need to thread my way through the tightly arranged tables, offloading the drinks orders correctly without spilling those on my *plateau*, while also fielding orders from tourists impatient to get back to queuing somewhere. Mercifully, the last few months' training has prepared me. And then there is my suit, which, despite how nice the cut is now, remains black and, as such, continues to absorb every last drop of the spring sun, not only retaining the heat throughout the day but increasing like an oven turned to maximum.

As the first day on the drinks terrace draws to a close there is a thin trace of light across the sky to the west. The Eiffel Tower bathed in violet air. The drinks terrace is quiet, just a few couples drinking champagne. From below the eaves the elderly saxophonist butchers 'Non, je ne regrette rien', which feels apt. I have time to nip off into the shadows for a quick smoke – I am incredibly autonomous now. Not once all day has a manager come to see me, so not only am I making my own tips, but I am free to smoke as and when I want – which, granted, is only now in the evening because it's been so busy, but still, freedom feels good. I really do have no regrets.

I stand there watching it all, in my finely cut suit, and I know that I am on the up. Spring in one of the most beautiful cities in the world, and with money in my pocket – suddenly everything seems possible. Behind me up on the terrace the waiters work quietly, and I let myself think that soon enough I'll be up there with them. I have, to all intents and purposes, completely forgotten about the outside world: the world of careers, futures and money.

This is now my world: the bistro, the waiters – coffee, cigarettes and cash.

Breakfast In America

At rush hour the boulevard is busy with the white and yellow headlights of cars heading westwards towards the setting sun. When the traffic lights go red the headlights dip abruptly and dark streams of pedestrians pour across the road in both directions. The sky is getting lighter in the evenings, spring is well and truly upon us.

It's seven o'clock, and the drinks terrace is quietening down as people go off for dinner. There's an amazing calm in the square, the peace of centuries.

When I return from my cigarette break an elderly American couple have installed themselves at one of the tables. The man is smartly dressed in a light suit with a cream roll-neck jumper, reading yesterday's *Wall Street Journal*. His wife is wrapped in cashmere with heavy gold jewellery dripping from any part of her body it will hang. Tippers, my mind says.

'I love Parisian coffee,' she says to me in English as I approach.

'*Petit déjeuner?*' The gentleman looks at me and raises his eyebrows as a way of communicating everything else he can't yet say in French.

'Sorry?' I say in English. Happy to talk with other English-speakers.

'*Nous voudrions un petit déjeuner,*' he says again in slow and careful French.

'Breakfast?' I say again in English. 'It's almost dinner.' My accent is unmistakably British.

'Don't give up,' his wife says without moving her lips, like a ventriloquist.

'*Petit déjeuner?*' I say, this time in French.

'Tell him we've just got off a flight. From California. It's still breakfast in LA. Tell him, darling.'

The husband orders two continental breakfasts, in French. I acquiesce and speak in French, or as I imagine a French person would speak English. I tell them that breakfast may be a little difficult as the kitchens are preparing for dinner.

'And croissants. Do you think they do wheat-free? How do you say wheat-free?' the wife nags.

'You're not wheat-free, Candice. You had crackers on the plane,' the husband snaps as he hands me the two drinks menus.

'But how do you say it? You don't know, do you?'

I don't know either, so keep my mouth shut.

Logically I begin my quest for croissants at the Pass. Nimsath refuses to believe that they are not for me, but eventually relents and hands me the basket with the day's remaining croissants. They're a little hard, so I look around the lower kitchen to see if someone can heat them up and make them a bit softer. The noise here is deafeningly loud and it's already hot and humid as the kitchen winds up for the dinner service. On one side the *plongeurs* are hosing and scrubbing. Cooking utensils and steel trays, pots and pans are violently sprayed with high-pressure water in giant metal sinks from hoses suspended above them. The noise of metal crashing against metal is violent and unabating. Then the sound of the knives; hundreds of them being poured into the plastic boxes, creating an effect like sharp metallic thunder – it rolls across the room, reverberating off the condensation-covered walls and piercing your ears.

On the other side of the room the men are screaming and shouting at each other as they prep food for dinner. I only understand some of what they say, but it's clear they have no interest in heating croissants. One man guts fish and slides the entrails into a bin – the wet bodies lie together on ice, silvery green scales and large empty eyes glistening under the bright lights; another is peeling vegetables into a bin already overflowing with skins; unintelligible shouting comes from a small radio on the wall; it's momentarily muted by the sound of a man tenderizing meat; violently he slams it before holding down a button on the radio and screaming back in patois. Around them moves another older man in rubber sandals pushing a rigid rubber mop. His hair is short and grey. He pushes the hot soapy water across the floor, occasionally using his bare hands to slop the soapy sludge that blocks the drains into the bin. On the hot and humid air there is the faint smell of cigarette smoke, too. I try repeatedly to find someone to reheat the croissants for me until eventually a young man with what seems like an exaggerated East London accent takes them out of my hand and goes over to one of the ovens.

'You British, yeah?' he says.

He introduces himself as Femi. It seems completely incongruous to hear his accent down here. He has a slight frame with large bloodshot eyes and moves quickly.

'Don't get many waiters down here. Know what I mean, bruv? Why's that?'

Femi says he spent a lot of his teenage years in the UK, before being deported. Before I've got time to ask him why, he's telling me that he used to be a waiter and that he shouldn't be down here in the kitchens and could I please speak to someone about getting him out? He says he's tried but the managers don't believe him. I assure him that I will do my best and he gives me the warm croissants.

'They're a bit hard. Since we started getting the frozen industrial ones a few weeks ago the quality's gone down. You can heat up the proper ones. Not these ones. They go all dry. Haven't got enough butter in them. Real croissants, you should see how much butter they put in!'

'Cheers. Oh, how do you say wheat-free? I can't get an answer from any of the waiters upstairs,' I ask.

'Good question, bruv. It's funny, I actually have to ask this all the time as my Ma, she ain't able to eat wheat or dairy. You should see the waiters' faces when I say it. It's like they short-circuited or something. So, I just tell them, she can't eat *blé*, wheat, she's "*sans blé*", you know what I mean? Like working down here.' Seeing my blank look, he continues, '*Sans blé*... It's a joke, *blé*, it's slang for money. Anyway, I found out recently it's actually *sans-gluten* and *sans produits laitiers*. But none of them understand that. So she just orders chicken salad, innit.'

'Incredible. I asked five different waiters upstairs and not one of them knew.'

'It's cuz they French, bruv. Look.'

All around us the men are cooking everything from vegetables to meats in bubbling, browning, oozing butter. I shake Femi's hand and thank him. As I'm leaving he keeps talking, trying to stop me from going. There's a desperation in his voice. And I feel guilty as I know there's no one I can speak to who will listen to me about Femi's plight. I'm too low down for anyone to listen. But I assure him, once again, that I will at least try. By now most of the other men are staring at me. One begins to shout at Femi, something incomprehensible that causes him to go back to his station where he's slicing leeks.

'Tell them. You can vouch for me, yeah. That I speak proper English and that I'm a proper waiter, bruv. It's a mistake I'm down here...' Femi's voice fades out as I climb the stone steps up to the Pass, where I pick up the coffees and pressed orange juices, then, having exited via the swinging door and traversed the dining room as Lucien and Adrien are setting it up (I tell them about *sans-gluten* but they ignore me), I hurry along the terrace and down to the drinks terrace to the American couple.

'Our first proper French breakfast in Paris, honey,' the wife says with genuine happiness.

This Parisian breakfast, from me, the English waiter who took the order, to the Tamil Tiger who made the coffee and pressed the orange juice and the West African expelled from the UK who heated the factory-made croissants...

'Do you want some butter with that croissant, darling?' the husband asks, smiling at me.

'Gawd, no. I'm trying to cut down on butter.'

'*Café au lait*, that's it – right?' He turns to me. 'I'm trying to work on my pronunciation.'

'*Parfait,*' I say.

'Thanks – sorry. *Merci.*'

'*De rien,*' I reply.

For the remainder of their meal we continue to make small talk with me speaking English in a French accent or correcting their French with my British-sounding French. It pays off, I'm playing my role, as Lucien would say. When the couple eventually leave, they thank me profusely and give me my largest tip to date: forty euros. Forty euros in crisp new banknotes. It seems criminal to take so much, but they insist. The kick I get from it is incredible and what's more I can already feel it burning a hole in my pocket; it opens up worlds of possibilities: of meals and drinks and cinemas, the theatre even. I want more of this, the short-term freedom these crisp notes in my pocket contain. And all because I pretended to be French. Lucien was right: it is all about acting. Pretending to be French with tourists soon becomes a regular habit. And an economically fruitful one at that.

The Changing of the Guard

In Paris there is a constant rotation of thin-looking, poorly dressed men and women of various ages who traipse the city with CVs clutched in their hands – these are the out-of-work waiters. A breed I am familiar with from back in January.

Yesterday it was Salvatore. The Sicilian Bear was suddenly gone. He simply didn't turn up. The waiters were noticeably less critical of his absence than they had been of other waiters' disappearances, but he was cursed nonetheless. I think we all felt in some way that he'd betrayed us. For he was a friend to all of us – in as much as one can be when you work in a restaurant; or perhaps I'd misread the situation. Pauline looked the glummest, having come into the Pass on various pretences throughout the service in the hope that he may have turned up late. She'd tried calling him, she said, but the number no longer existed. I had an image of him, just as he'd described, freediving in that mysterious hole in the desert in Egypt, disappearing into the deepening blue. Although the likelihood was that he'd gone to his friend's restaurant in Avola. The Rat made a point of saying it didn't matter: 'He'll be replaced before the end of the day. We need better waiters anyway. People we can trust. A waiter that size must have been stealing.'

It is now early June, and with spring turning to summer it is the time of the year when the 'seasonal waiters' begin to show up from the mountain resorts as the city's terraces start filling up and become crowded with revellers.

'Seasonal waiters are one thing. In a month or so the students looking for summer jobs will turn up,' Lucien says. 'Then you'll see. Things always get worse. Forget about proper service. You'll be dreaming of winter again soon.'

Back in January, when I was looking for a job, I could never work out why waiters in restaurants treated me with such disdain. Now I see more clearly. A waiter's understanding is this: the more potential people the restaurant has to replace you with, the more likely they are to sack you. There is nothing a waiter despises more than an out-of-work waiter. You represent everything they dislike about themselves: the precarity of their situation, the fact that, at any moment, they, too, could be like you. And your mere presence has made that more likely. Therefore, they do whatever they can to prevent new waiters being hired.

Within five months I have gone from being one of those unfortunates traipsing the streets of the city to one of the people I'd previously hated: a member of the dreaded fraternity of Parisian waiters, intent on preventing anyone from taking my job. I don't want to return to being a runner, I want to become a waiter. And I know all too well that any new recruits lessen my chances. This is all that matters to me. Preventing other waiters from arriving and pushing me down the food chain.

It is interesting to note that the most opportune time for job-seeking is just after the lunch service – the 3–4pm window – as the more experienced waiters often come around then. And that's exactly how it happens with one of the new guys. What remains of the lunch crew is at the Pass. The Untouchable and Lucien are still bitching about the Bear, while Renaud and Jamaal are on the verge of a nervous breakdown because of how the hostesses seated people during the service.

'Those whores do it on purpose,' Renaud is saying.

He keeps poking his head out of the Pass to see if there is a hostess around that he can broadside. But they've long since gone. Their job is short and brutal, and as soon as they can they are out of their high heels and short skirts, as far away as possible from the filth of the restaurant and back to the successful Paris of the Left Bank and 16th arrondissement. Away from people like Jamaal and Renaud.

'You? They gave me a table of French tourists,' Jamaal says, his temples glistening with sweat and his shirt untucked at the front.

'The worst,' Renaud agrees.

'You guys are just sore because the hostesses find you so physically offensive,' Lucien says. Despite being friends with Sal, Lucien is clearly feeling buoyed by his departure, as the route – according to him – is now clear for him to make a move with Pauline. The reason it hasn't happened in previous years is that he's never tried, he says. But now it will help his acting, he tells me, because he is going to use his relationship with Pauline to get better tables, and therefore save more tips for a flight to LA. Paris is dead to him if he doesn't get a part soon, and he's recently decided that he needs to go to America to get an agent.

'In America anyone can become rich, and people respect you for it. Not here. You see how they tax the rich?'

'Shut up, Mister Hollywood,' Renaud chides Lucien. His new nickname has quickly done the rounds, a small leaving gift from Sal, perhaps. 'What would you know about being rich?'

'Here you go, Renaud.' Lucien signs a slip of paper and hands it to him. 'What's this?'

'My autograph. You can sell it when I'm famous. Maybe buy yourself a decent suit. Or a shower.'

'Fuck you, Lucien. You'll never be an actor.'

Jamaal laughs and baits Lucien some more. Since Lucien has started talking in the restaurant about his plan of becoming an actor, he's also become more disparaging about waiting. This doesn't go down well with the waiters, who've given him a number of nicknames including Mister Hollywood and Petit César, after the annual César French film awards.

'*Petit César*, if you become an actor, I'll win the Loto,' Renaud says.

'Yeah, and I'll be a striker for PSG,' Jamaal adds.

'Let's not exaggerate,' Adrien says and whips Jamaal's belly with a serviette that he's dipped in water.

Renaud, meanwhile, spits on Lucien's autograph and throws it in the bin. 'That's what I think of your acting career,' he says.

'*Ey*, don't you ever spit in my restaurant,' Adrien protests.

'His restaurant,' Renaud mutters to Jamaal. 'You hear that?'

To see Jamaal and Renaud together is to see the worst of what your idea of a French waiter is. Jamaal is just plain lazy, but Renaud, with his permanently smug expression, spherical head and dark beady eyes is nasty and the way he talks about women pure misogyny. If your tips go missing, it is certain that he was around at the time. Waiters have some sense of pride, so they don't rush in and scoop up their tips as the diners are getting up. Instead they play it cool, acting as if they don't need the money. They'll pick up some plates and glasses and take them back to the Pass, leaving the tips and the table unguarded, as I had done with the Brazilians. When I was a runner, I was often accused of stealing people's tips, as I was constantly clearing tables. But no one accused me more than Renaud, who clearly made a living from this weak spot in the waiters' system. Recently, however, he appears to have taken a couple of tips that were left on Adrien's tables. Or, at least, that is the word among the waiters. Stealing another waiter's winnings is not the done thing, and the gossip is that he is interested in Adrien's place. The management care little for this kind of political rumbling. Renaud is a career waiter who can turn tables around quickly, that's what counts. Whether the waiters make tips or not is of little importance. And if Adrien isn't doing his job properly, the Rat tells us, then he can, of course, be replaced. This is a change in the party line – suddenly the Untouchable is looking on shaky ground. It appears that Renaud and Jamaal have been spreading rumours to management, this time about Adrien. And with the Rat eager to climb higher up the greasy drainpipe they've found a useful ally. Getting rid of Adrien suits him as, before becoming a manager, Corentin was a waiter under Adrien – the Untouchable had little respect for him and often treated him like a child.

It is at this point that a slim figure in a loose suit bounds up the steps and makes his way towards the entrance of the restaurant.

'*Ey, oh!*' Adrien cries.

The waiters have assembled behind him.

'The kitchen's closed,' Adrien shouts.

But the man ignores him and disappears through the heavy double doors.

'Another waiter,' Jamaal says. '*C'est sûr.*'

'He looked like a real piece of work, that one,' Renaud adds.

'That means he'll get the job then.' Adrien looks at Renaud as he says this.

'Fuck you,' Renaud replies. 'How much are you paying those whores on the door to give you the big tippers, *ey*? Why don't you share?'

'Something you could never afford, *pauvre con*.' Adrien makes an obscene gesture with his tongue.

'I wouldn't touch them anyway.'

'Hah, you think they'd touch you?'

'You've got your coke,' Renaud threatens Adrien. 'Leave what's left to the rest of us.'

'What you talking about? Maybe we should talk about you stealing other people's tips, hey? Talking shit to the management about me?'

Renaud collects up his drinks order, which has just arrived on the Pass, and hurriedly places it on his *plateau*.

'I'm no thief, but you're definitely a dealer. No spitting in the restaurant? But pushing coke's all right? We all know you'd have gone a long time ago if you weren't protected. You sell to the managers. *C'est simple.*'

He picks up his *plateau* on one hand and, turning to Adrien, says, 'You don't deserve to work here, and you know it. No one here respects you. You should be ashamed to call yourself head waiter.'

As Renaud turns to go Adrien sticks his foot out and trips him, sending him tumbling to the floor, accompanied by the horrifying sound of smashing glasses, and the hollow metallic ring of the *plateau* on the flagstones.

Renaud jumps back up and spits on Adrien's jacket, at which Adrien grabs Renaud's shirt and tries to push him to the floor. The fight is scrappy and messy, and initially we let it continue for our own reasons. Renaud is a thief – I have personal experience of that – and deserves what is coming to him as far as I am concerned. And by mentioning Adrien's dealing in public, he has broken a taboo. He may be a dealer, sure, but he is one of the waiters, the head waiter, and he looks out for us. Adrien eventually swings Renaud against a cupboard and a stack of ceramic cups falls and shatters with a deafening noise. By now Adrien is on top of Renaud with his forearm on his throat, demanding that he beg for mercy.

'*Merde, Corentin,*' De Souza hisses as he skids into the Pass area. Adrien is helped quickly up as Renaud remains on the floor out of breath, looking at all of us like traitors.

'What the hell's going on!' The Rat is standing in the doorway.

By the waiters' reactions and body language it is clear that Renaud is about to be hung out to dry.

'Nothing,' Adrien says. 'Just Renaud—'

'He slipped,' De Souza says. 'You OK, Renaud?'

The Rat looks at us all, then at Renaud, who does nothing to help himself apart from staring angrily at Adrien with a look that suggests he wants him dead. The Rat then pulls Renaud by his shoulder and tries pushing him out of the Pass. Renaud turns to De Souza and says, 'Sticking up for your boyfriend like that, very cute. Maybe he'll teach you to punch, too.' And then to Corentin: 'A drug dealer for a head waiter. No wonder there are problems! Someone should sort this restaurant out.'

'Get out,' Corentin hisses at Renaud, whose humiliation is now complete, for the Rat is much younger than he is. 'This is a restaurant.' He turns to the rest of us. 'It's shameful. I could hear you from my office. All of you, get out of here. And just so you know, I'll be making some big changes around here. The *patron* asked me to. This place won't sink because of you low-lifes.' He has a small and sinister smile on his face as he walks off up the terrace.

Being a waiter is like being in a gang, a mafia. There are ancient rituals and unspoken rules and everything exists under an uneasy truce. Of course, if someone felt cheated on, or hard done by, they would break the peace and all-out war would ensue – this happened almost every service. A waiter would break ranks, and new lines would be drawn based on old alliances. The fall of a waiter is something that other waiters watch with a sense of detachment, even pleasure, for every waiter believes that the others are made of money, and any misfortune that comes their way is considered deserved for their duplicitous behaviour. The fight between Adrien and Renaud looks set to continue, for Renaud is not a man to back down, and nor is Adrien. I have chosen my camp. I am firmly on the Untouchable's side. We just have to hope that the Rat's words are nothing more than empty threats. However, there is no doubting his rise in the ranks. He even has a shiny new suit to prove it.

Things are changing in the restaurant, whether we like it or not, and this is putting people on edge. But the biggest change is yet to come.

THE NEW SALVATORE

The disappearance of Salvatore has left everyone in a bit of a bad mood. It is a mixture of resentment and jealousy; resentment because his absence means more work, and jealousy because he's disappeared just before the busy season, and, as such, has somehow escaped the trap – and the waiters can't understand how or why. Most figure he's got a new job down on the Côte d'Azur or in Sicily; it is the only thing that makes sense to them. No one mentions his diving – I think I am the only person he ever told.

I am sad that Salvatore has left because I liked him, yet, true to the French system, his demise is good for me. I am suddenly on the inside, no longer the new guy. It is as if the other waiters have completely forgotten that I only joined a few months ago, and they are finally starting to see me as one of their own. Of course, Sal's parting is also a gift to me professionally, as there is no reason why I should not now be made a full waiter. I even have a film-style sequence in my head in which I come into work with the waiters lined up on both sides of the terrace clapping; as I walk between them, hostesses throw petals at me and cheer, honouring my ascension to the pantheon of *les serveurs*.

Unsurprisingly, Sal's name is dragged through the dirt for a couple of days, and I join in. I need to make sure I am more of a waiter than the rest of them. The only thing that preoccupies the crew now is who is going to replace me as runner. How they'll test him, see if he is made of the right stuff. When Adrien announces there will be not one replacement for Salvatore, but two, I feel that waiterhood is all but a given. I can already see myself playing the same cruel tricks on the new runner that the boys played on me. This all lasts until the afternoon when I hear that they've hired two new waiters, instead of promoting me. How the hell have I been passed over, once again?

I sense the hand of Corentin. Possibly in retribution for the crisis that followed the discovery of the source of the gag-inducing stench that pervaded his miserable little office: a rotting pile of eggs and seafood. When he found it he became apoplectic with rage. He had no idea who was responsible, but it was clearly an affront to his authority, and he would not stand for it. The *directeur*, to his credit, was not too fussed: most likely as it reassured him that the staff were on his side, not Corentin's and his power grab.

When I hear the news about the second new waiter from Adrien I go to see Valentine and the *directeur*. They tell me the usual, that it will happen soon enough; they just need the right person for the drinks terrace. With two new hires they probably won't need more waiters until summer is in full swing.

With dreams of waiterhood on hold again, I cling desperately to the hope that the new guys don't fit in better than I am beginning to. The added hours brought on by Sal's departure are hard, but in the back of my mind I am adding up the overtime; banking freedom. And with the weather being so fine, thoughts have turned to what I will do. Perhaps a week in the Loire? By the Mediterranean? The Alps? France is full of possibilities. Screw the restaurant. I consider going elsewhere, but the problem is, until I become a waiter, leaving and going elsewhere isn't really possible. Besides, I am close. And I want to be a waiter here. I want to beat this old institution at its own game. A foreigner as waiter: I know how much it would rile a few of them.

'Where are they, hey?' Renaud is at the Pass, shaking dandruff out of his hair.

'Late for the first shift – bad sign,' Jamaal replies.

Fortunately for me the first New Guy's arrival is about as spectacular and misjudged as I could have hoped for. Everyone is going through their last touches before the lunch service when a man in a horrifically baggy suit jumps out from behind the screen and proceeds to 'machine-gun' us with his folded-up umbrella, replete with sound effects and the throwing of a pin-pulled grenade. It is the man we saw stealing into the restaurant the other day.

Adrien's laconic '*Tu fais quoi, là?*' – What are you doing there? – soon wipes the smile off his face and he introduces himself, in heavily accented French, as Piotr. He has closely cropped hair, grey eyes and a small mouth. There is something birdlike in his face. Although he looks desperately thin, his neck seems to be the same size as his head and is clearly constricted quite significantly by his shirt, which acts more like a garotte than a collar. His face has the pallor of someone who has just emerged from a year in a cave, but his neck, thanks to the garrotte, is bright red, almost purple in places. What is most striking, however, is the old scar that runs down the left side of his face.

No sooner has Piotr introduced himself, a little too eagerly, than the waiters are all filing out of the Pass. Even I didn't have such a cold welcome. Piotr meanwhile is eager to tell me that he is Polish, that he owns a restaurant back in Gdansk and that he is in Paris purely for research. He has lots of experience, he assures me, in his almost comically Eastern European-accented French. Not that mine is much better.

'Where did the others go?' Piotr asks, reminding me that we need to be in the dining room for the briefing.

After a moment waiting around, the *directeur* appears from the back office, followed by his usual retinue of hostesses, and Corentin, skulking a little further behind than usual. There is also someone else, a new girl, whom everyone notices. I say 'girl'; she is more of a celestial vision – I, like the other waiters, assume she is a replacement for Solène, who departed a few days ago (much to the delight of Lucien, who loves to point out that she didn't say goodbye to me).

The *directeur* starts his usual pre-service discourse – minus input from Corentin, who appears to be in open mutiny by standing at a distance with his arms folded like a petulant child. The *directeur* in turn rises to this, emboldened perhaps by the discovery of the practical joke that has been played on Corentin, and is reciting something – in my mind at least – akin to Henry V's Agincourt speech. *We happy few, we band of brothers...*

Unfortunately, he's made an incredible oratorical faux pas by bringing along such a visual distraction. All the waiters can think of is not the honour of spilling blood together, but the new hostess. She really is quite something, like all your dreams of France in one: tall, with long, hazelnut-coloured hair and bright blue eyes.

At the end of the *directeur*'s Agincourt speech Pauline opens the reservations book and distributes the ranks. Part of me holds out for one, seeing as the second new waiter hasn't turned up, but I am not surprised to be allocated the drinks terrace.

The biggest shock comes when the VIP zone is awarded to a certain Camille. There is confusion, then consternation among the waiters, as it is confirmed that the new hostess is not a hostess at all but, in fact, the new Salvatore.

Piotr gives me a dig in the ribs and mutters, '*Pas mal, hein?*' And I can't help but smile at Lucien, who is looking at me in disbelief.

The arrival of Camille is like an explosion that has just severely shaken the foundations of the restaurant. It is quite amusing. For the waiters there is almost too much change happening at once. How will they compete for tips with a girl? And a pretty one at that? It isn't possible. It isn't fair. What does this mean for the men's chat that takes place at the Pass? The innuendo? The flirting? The shoddy practices?

'First an English guy that can't speak French. Now a hostess as a waiter,' Jamaal says, using the masculine for waiter, *un serveur*.

Their fear, in a sense, is understandable. The precarity of their job, the threat of losing it to another waiter is omnipresent. Hiring a woman as a waiter, in their eyes, effectively doubles the number of people who could take their jobs.

Of course, some people take it in their stride. Lucien jokes that, with her dark hair and blue eyes, Camille could even be Salvatore in disguise.

'Sure. Sal's been away, lost a load of weight and returned as *un avion de chasse*,' Adrien says, using a common French expression for a pretty girl, a fighter jet.

Renaud is the most annoyed: 'The restaurant is fully booked, and this *pute* – who has never worked here – and probably never done a day of work in her life, has been given the VIP zone. This place is finished. I'm telling you.'

'Oi, I've got a daughter, all right?' De Souza snaps.

'Your daughter, sure.'

'I'm tired of it. Why can't she be a waiter? This isn't the Stone Age.'

'You're tired because you work like a dog for your wedding.'

'*Et alors?*'

'I'm not criticizing. We're all working like dogs. But the wedding, that's your choice. And why's Adrien not made you joint head waiter? Not cut you in? You've been here long enough. And he's got his side business. Doesn't have a family to supp—'

'Shut up.'

There are grunts of agreement – with Renaud or De Souza, I don't know. Renaud looks smug, De Souza perturbed. Later we all loiter at the Pass carrying out fictional jobs incredibly slowly so that we can introduce ourselves to Camille. The general and unspoken consensus seems to be that she is fair game. Does she have any idea what she is getting into? If I'd had a tough ride…

'Maybe you can tell her your name.' Lucien is clearly trying to sabotage my chances early.

'Even you don't know my real name.'

'*L'Anglais.* I'll make sure to tell her,' Adrien says.

'Also, that he's not actually a waiter,' Lucien puts in.

'What are you?' Jamaal adds spitefully.

'An intern. Is that worse than a wannabe actor?' Renaud says.

With everyone feeling that their jobs are suddenly at risk, it is amazing to see how quickly they gang up on people. Even Adrien and Renaud appear to be able to put aside their differences if it means strengthening their positions.

Fortunately, Camille – with what is probably a heightened sense of intuition, or indeed just common sense – never comes to the Pass before the service. And so never lets them play their cruel games.

'She thinks she's better than us or something?' Renaud fumes.

'Let it go,' says Piotr who, despite having just arrived and being viewed by and large as a joke, has clearly got the measure of Renaud and instantly become a little more popular, especially with me.

As far as I can make out from the drinks terrace, Camille doesn't talk with the other waiters at all. Instead, she stands at her *rang*, letting the diners' gaze wash over her. She is professional, distant and in a different league from the waiters, which no doubt incenses them further.

Naturally, like the others, I also spend an inordinate amount of time hanging around the Pass towards the end of the service, but again, Camille never comes. She leaves straight after lunch. Pauline comes in, however, clearly sensing that her time at the top is perhaps numbered as, next to Camille, she doesn't really have the same allure as before.

'Before you know it, they'll be wearing trousers and voting!' I say, as a joke.

'She's with Corentin, you know,' Pauline tells us, as casually as she can manage.

Renaud and Jamaal love this and egg Pauline on, despite everyone knowing that Corentin is gay. The conclusion among them therefore is that, to all intents and purposes, Camille is a bitch and a whore, and Renaud should ensure that this is well known and circulate it to other waiters so that they don't fall into her trap. She is spying for Corentin, too, to get us sacked, he declares, citing as proof the Rat's threat that there will be changes around here.

Naturally this doesn't go completely to plan, as the waiters give into their more basic instincts and relish the new-found female attention that the arrival of Camille has precipitated. She acts, among other things, as a kind of bridge between the waiters and the hostesses. And for the first time since I arrived, we are all talking.

Over the coming weeks I come to know more about her. She is from Nice, she says. And, interestingly, she isn't a model or remotely interested in fashion. She is a *pigiste*, a freelance journalist, although struggling to make a living. She's taken this waiting job on as she is behind on her rent. Camille speaks fluent English, which is a relief: I am no longer stuck behind the mask of an imbecile. She's also been to university. I learn that she is passionate about journalism, but politics is what really motivates her. She refuses to write for certain papers and will only write about what interests her, which tends to be social issues. Hence the lack of money. An idealist. She is faintly flirty, but only marginally more than she is with the diners, and this is probably just a reflection of the effort I am making. Which in turn reflects how dire my romantic life has become. Like that of most waiters. The only time I'm in a bar is in a dirty suit, exhausted, long after all the other punters have gone home. If the management are all screwing one another, as is considered common knowledge, the hostesses certainly aren't letting the waiters near them. Although perhaps that will change, too? No. Something tells me that is a step too far. Despite the easing of relations, the hostesses remain super-humans. They are not ordinary girls. They have a physical perfection which suggests the hand of the gods at some point in their conception. Not to worry, I will focus on Camille.

It isn't long before Camille lets slip, a little too casually, that she has a boyfriend who has some achingly cool job. They met on a political march. I can't bring myself to tell her that I am not really a waiter, that I too want to write – being a glorified runner with nothing published to my name makes the mere idea of suggesting it make me sound like a fantasist. So instead we speak about more inane subjects, although a particular favourite is the new waiter, Piotr, who intrigues all of us.

'You know his father was an aristocrat,' Camille tells me one day during a lull in service. 'He was telling me how he used to go shooting on Tito's private estates as a kid.'

'Really? He told me he had a restaurant in Gdansk,' I say.

'No? Well, he told me he grew up in a Bavarian castle! A bastard child or something. The cook's son. He even tried to tell me that his family's "special recipe" was roasted marmot.'

'Marmot? Can you eat them?'

'Apparently you can. He said it's OK.' Camille grimaces. 'Just a bit chewy.'

The Doctor's Orders

An overcast late-spring afternoon, and after a quiet lunch service on the terrace I'm dispatched by Valentine for a break. Oddly, as I've become more aware of being allowed breaks, I'm given them more often, though not all the time.

As I leave the Pass I can see that the sommelier isn't occupying his usual place on the sacks of deliveries, so I make a beeline for the café, hoping to find him. I'd like to finish learning about wines with Franjo, but more than that I enjoy his company. He's taciturn, but when he does speak, his mind moves slowly, surely and lucidly; a fertile stream of information sprung from a deep and mysterious source that has travelled and is well read. After the intensity of the restaurant and its immediate stress, it's a welcome respite. To sit and talk with Franjo is to be reminded of how rich the world is.

In the Fer à Cheval I am now greeted like a regular, handshakes across the bar, a kind-hearted '*Comment vas-tu, mon grand?*' from Maurice, the owner; fussing from his wife, Loïs. It sounds sad, because the restaurant plays the same cheap trick on regular diners, but there really is no better feeling than being recognized when you go into an establishment. It ensures you keep coming back. It's also a kind of bellwether of your standing in society; at least, that's how you perceive it. Indeed, 'entering a restaurant' really is an art in itself. The confidence, the charm, the way the new arrivals move across the space – there's a real elegance to someone who knows how to do it.

Happily, the sommelier is also in the café at what has, since our regular wine lessons, become our 'usual table'. He's there with his big white bushy eyebrows furrowed in concentration behind the giant old glasses. Our conversation over lunch meanders around wines, like the great rivers of France and her vineyards, but I'm eager to go upriver, to the source, to know more about Franjo's story.

'The last time we were here you said you were from Croatia.'

'Well, now it's called that. When I left it had a different name...'

'You go back often?'

'Not once.' He removes his glasses and pinches the top of his nose. 'When I left – and this was a long, long time ago – I lost everything,' he says, completely matter-of-factly.

'But you said you went to university.'

'Not just any university – the best medical school in the country. In Belgrade. I'd almost finished my studies to become a doctor. Two more years. I wanted to be a surgeon. Remember, at the time, Yugoslavia was a very different place.'

Maurice comes over, removes our plates and puts down two short champagne flutes. Franjo smiles.

'Today, we drink champagne, *l'Anglais*. A celebration. Your education, the basics at least, are complete.'

Maurice returns with a bottle. It's a Deutz *blanc de blancs*. One hundred per cent chardonnay. The cork pops, the pale golden liquid pours forth from the squat bottle with the long slender neck and then froths excitedly as it hits the glasses. The sommelier returns to his story:

'Then one night, very late, my friends came to my flat and told me that I had to leave; it was too dangerous to stay.' He raises his glass. '*Zivjeli*.'

'*Santé*.' The champagne is cool, crisp, ethereal.

'Where was I?'

'Your friends told you to leave...'

'Ah yes. We went immediately to tell my family, who were also in Belgrade at the time. I still remember how my mother cried all night and my father said nothing, just smoked his pipe. We passed the entire night together in the living room with the lights off. My father convinced there would be a knock on the door. Originally I was going to go and hide in the countryside, back in Croatia; but when my parents found out that two of my friends from university had gone missing two weeks before, they insisted that I leave Yugoslavia at once. It was decided I'd go to Germany on the first train. Germany made sense: we learned a bit of German back then because of the old Austro-Hungarian Empire, so I'd be able to get by all right.

'Before dawn I said goodbye to my parents and a friend took me to the station in their car. Unfortunately the train to Germany had been cancelled. We never knew why. Of all mornings! So, while we were at the station, we decided that I would go to Paris.'

'Why?'

'It was the only train leaving that morning that would take me out of Yugoslavia.' He sips his champagne. 'You should have seen me when I arrived here, I couldn't speak a single word. I learned one thing on the train, "*Voulez-vous coucher avec moi?*" I had no idea what it meant!'

We drink more of the champagne in silence.

'What kind of stuff did you do? I heard from Salvatore you were in a Russian jail.'

'Hah! Russian jail. No, no Russian jail.'

'So?'

'Wait. First the champagne. It deserves more attention from us, surely?' Maurice returns and refills the glasses. 'So?'

'Very aromatic. Perfect harmony.'

'Go on.' Franjo closes his eyes.

'It's bright. And mineral. There are citrus aromas...'

'Yes, grapefruit. Green. And the butter, can you taste it?'

He is right: there is butter in there, too. He opens his eyes, looks at me and smiles.

'Typical of a classic chardonnay.'

As Franjo continues to talk, we drink the champagne. A toast to the present and to the past.

'...You know what it's like when you're a student. I was involved in certain groups. It was fine at first, harmless; but then my friends began to disappear, people got hurt, things escalated... Secret police...' He tails off.

There is a shuffling behind us, and Loïs appears with the sommelier's cheese board. She knows how short the breaks we waiters get are, so the courses come out quickly.

'*Alors, aujourd'hui* we have Saint-Nectaire, Brie and a little bit of goat's cheese. Perhaps *monsieur* would like some wine?'

The sommelier looks at his cheese and considers this for a moment. 'Not today, *madame*,' he says. 'Today something stronger.'

Loïs shouts to her husband at the bar to ask what is available that is stronger. Despite there only being four bottles on the shelf, Maurice turns around and, having lifted his glasses to his eyes, gives a dramatic reading of the labels and their provenance.

'I'll take the Armagnac,' the sommelier says. 'Two.' He gives me a youthful smile.

Franjo begins to eat his cheese in a very precise manner. Cutting off small slices and placing them in his mouth. Occasionally he sips some of the Armagnac. He says nothing again, but I sense he is deep in thought. Finally, as if the conversation has continued in his head without me, he speaks.

'*Oui, donc...* I decided I needed to learn French and then take up my studies at the Sorbonne and finish my training to be a surgeon. But...' He takes a large sip of the Armagnac. '...of course, at this time, they wouldn't recognize my studies from Belgrade. The Sorbonne did eventually say they'd accept me, but that I must start my studies again. Can you imagine? Five years I had lost.'

He finishes the plate of cheese and pushes it away. He takes off his big square glasses and rubs the bridge of his nose.

'I couldn't. I didn't have the money; my parents had given everything for my studies. And to spend another five years learning what I already knew... No, it was not possible. I was completely lost. I knew nobody, I spoke no French and I'd lost everything I'd worked for. I couldn't go back to my friends, my family. I didn't even know what had happened to some of them. I had to be careful, even in Paris – the police still had informants everywhere. You never knew what would happen to you. It was a lonely time.'

Almost reflexively he looks to the door. He taps the Esperanto flag badge on his lapel.

'Eventually I found the local Esperanto club. And there, finally, I could speak to people. You can't imagine how it felt. After all those weeks struggling to understand anything. I couldn't even understand street signs! But it was at the Esperanto club that I met a young man, a Basque, who had spent the last year working on a vineyard. In Bordeaux. I knew a bit about wines, but when he said he could sort me out with a job I said yes. A vineyard seemed the ideal place to hide. You think waiting is hard! Try picking grapes. Eventually they took me on as a farmhand. In the evenings I worked as a waiter for some extra cash, and then eventually, after many more waiting jobs, well, I became a sommelier, because I knew about wines. It's still a shame that we don't have Esperanto. It felt so hopeful... Anyway, enough of this, it's just an old story. What about you, *l'Anglais*, what brought you here?'

'It's not quite so interesting. A girl, originally. Although she's gone.'

'And you're still here.'

'Still here.'

'Why?'

'I like it here.'

'And why be a waiter?'

'I don't really know what else I can do,' I laugh. 'No one else will have me apart from you guys.'

It is true. Sitting here with the sommelier, sharing our lives like this, I have the feeling of a family. Or a house for orphaned boys and lost souls. A place of shelter, a waiting room. One that some will stay in for their whole lives, while others may leave straight away.

Loïs shuffles over, clears the cheese plate and refills our glasses.

'*Oh là là*, I will need to sleep this afternoon. Join me for a coffee.'

When we have finished the coffees the sommelier gets up to leave.

'Same time tomorrow?' I ask.

'Of course. But, *l'Anglais*, you know everything about the wine menu now. You don't need me. Go and become a waiter. But promise me one thing.'

'What?'

'Don't stay too long. This isn't your destiny. Me, I'm old – too old for this job. It tires me. I work because my wife is ill. Because I have to. If things had been different... well, they would have been... different.'

He laughs, an avuncular chuckle that seems to spring from the very depths of his belly and fill the room. It is an enormous laugh for such a small man. But it is a laugh that tells you that, whatever happens, everything will be all right.

The Great Flood

It rains solidly for the next three days. I am demoted back to runner as the drinks terrace is closed and the dining rooms are overflowing with people. As a result, all free time has gone and I am working without a break from opening until close, my tips from the American couple still burning a hole in my pocket. By dawn on the fourth day, after a night of heavy rain, the weather appears to have eased, but the wind is still blowing hard. It is a cold, damp wind that splashes rain on the windows of my garret and makes them rattle.

I roll out of bed exhausted. As I walk back down the corridor from the shared toilet the linoleum flooring squeaks behind me, as if I am being followed by my own ghost. Through the small porthole window in the roof, dawn is breaking across the city: it is just after five, and the road, the city and my entire building are silent. Even the young couple in the apartment next door with the baby who never sleeps are asleep. I turn the radio on and roll the tuning wheel until I get a news station. The new president, François Hollande, is promising change. The Seine has also blown its banks. I decide to go to work via the canal, although it is hard to get near as that has completely flooded, too.

It's just after six and in front of the restaurant there's a small con-gregation of what seem like quite agitated people. It's hard to tell who they are from a distance, as they're all wrapped up in coats that are being buffeted by the wind and rain. Upon closer inspection they turn out to be employees of the restaurant. There's an incredible mix. Young men with slick haircuts from the prep kitchens, including Femi; the Tamils;

the burly cooks with the cut-up hands from the upper kitchen. I can see Renaud with his dark eyes and round head, looking miserable as usual. Jamaal talking in Arabic with one of the men from the lower kitchen while gesturing angrily. With them standing all together like this on the deserted terrace it's as if the restaurant has vomited up its innards. The reason for the commotion is that the front door is locked and there's a note: '*Fermeture exceptionnelle.*'

Rumours abound: some of the men think the restaurant is being permanently shut. Jamaal is telling them that inspectors must have come around and closed the place down – he's not surprised, he says; if he was running the place, it wouldn't have happened. Renaud, the Serpent, keeps telling the cooks that the place has gone bust and they won't be paid for the last month's work. For some reason they believe him and become angry and panicked. He assures them he knows, that he heard the *directeur* and the *patron* talking the other night when he was closing up. He smiles, a sadistic smile. 'You can never trust these types of people,' he tells them. 'Manager, owners, the rich. They're all the same.'

Salvatore always said that Renaud had 'a face you want to punch'. He's such a miserable, dishonest-looking person and his presence is only ever negative, so I have to agree. And since his run-in with Adrien, he's only become more and more conniving.

The men bang on the door looking for answers. From the darkness inside, Valentine materializes and opens the door with her keys. There's a clamour and a surge forwards as people try to get to the locker room to take back the belongings they believe they will lose – dirty old shoes, soiled chef's whites, tobacco. The assorted paraphernalia that restaurant workers can call their own.

Valentine stands firm, the door half ajar with her foot wedged behind it. She stays calm, angelic almost, and in her quiet voice, barely audible above the wind, tells us that the kitchens have flooded. The men erupt in shouts and surge forwards again, but never across the threshold. Despite her being alone, Valentine's dignity seems to keep the wave of angry testosterone at bay.

One of the men from the lower kitchen shouts something, and the others erupt in anger. Valentine keeps her foot behind the door. Without answering any questions, she repeats more firmly, 'You can go home. Please, go home.' And then she heaves the door shut, bolts it and disappears back into the darkness.

The group erupts into discussion, most of which I can't follow, but the general gist is that either the restaurant is shutting down, they are hiring new people, or it will be closed for some time because of the damage from the flooding, and we should all start looking for jobs immediately. I find Jamaal among the mêlée.

'Ça va, mon frère?,' he says. 'The restaurant will be closed for at least a week. Maybe two. It's happened before.'

The other men overhear him, and the look in their eyes suggests that each of them is doing the same calculation: how much will I have at the end of the month, and will it be enough to pay the rent? I am doing the same myself. We won't be paid for not working. Have I lost my overtime? Also, if I lose this job, will I be able to get another? Will I be able to go straight into work as a waiter, or will I have to start again from the bottom?

'Me, I'm going to the hammam,' Jamaal announces.

'Hammam?'

'Not the one at the Mosque de Paris. Another,' he says, as if I even knew there was one at the Mosque de Paris.

'What's special about it?'

'It's up by Barbès. Best hammam in Paris. Can get rid of the stench of anything.' He gestures to the lower kitchen guys to suggest he means them, too. 'Even the stink of the restaurant. I'll give you the address.'

Before he does he's assailed by two friends from the kitchens. Not being able to speak Arabic, I have no idea what they're talking about. After some time, like many of the others, I begin to drift away from the restaurant and leave the men arguing in the wind. It's starting to rain again, so I go into the Fer à Cheval. Franjo isn't there – it's too early – but Félix the night porter is.

Food, Glorious Food

Félix is standing at the bar staring into space. Beside him another fairly elderly Black man is also drinking a small beer. They're together but alone, for neither speaks to the other. The small café is busy at this time, but it's a different busy from during the day. It's like the changing of the troops on the frontline at Verdun, with the fast-eyed reinforcements passing the returning soldiers with the thousand-yard stares. For the men starting their day there's an urgency; they huddle at the end of the bar nearest the door and talk loudly to one another over the hissing of the coffee machine, or gesture with their half-eaten croissants, the crumbs all down their chins and overalls. There's a smell of damp clothes from the rain, the windows are misted.

I stand next to Félix, further into the café with the men who have finished night shifts, and order a coffee. He doesn't notice me. He looks empty. I see that beside his beer is a small thimble of *eau de vie*. Félix smells unmistakably of the kitchens; that strange damp smell tinged with cleaning products and acrid body odour. It's a smell that we all take home with us each night; one that permeates our clothes, our pores, our bed sheets. It's a smell that makes you want to gag when you don't smell of it; it's like death, only the living can feel it. I resolve to go to the hammam when I get the address from Jamaal. See if it's as magic as he promises.

My coffee arrives. Without turning to me Félix pats my forearm.

'*Salut, l'Anglais.*'

We sip our drinks; there's an intense lethargy in his actions. The man to his left says something that I don't catch to which Félix responds with a slow nod and a mumbled, '*En effet, oui.*'

'I've never said *bonjour* to you,' I say to him. 'It's always *bonsoir*.'

His stoic face momentarily breaks into a smile. '*C'est vrai, c'est vrai*.'

The man is exhausted.

'What happened last night?'

He takes a long pull of his beer before responding: 'Lots of water. *Beaucoup*.' His voice has a low sing-song quality to it.

'It's bad?'

Félix takes a step back from the bar and points to just above his knee: 'To here. Everything is soaked. But what do I know?'

The door opens and two road sweepers enter in their glistening green waterproofs. The rivulets of water are still running off them when they reach the bar and the warm welcome of their friends. The coffee machine starts up its grinding and hissing, and the men exchange stories of the flooding. Félix, meanwhile, finishes his thimble of alcohol and, without being asked, the proprietor refills it. It's cognac. The noise in the room settles down to the clinking of crockery, spoons and chatter.

'How long will the restaurant be closed for?' I ask.

Félix thinks about this as he considers his cognac.

'Who knows? Depends. What do I know? Me?' He shoots a glance at the steamed windows. 'But it's getting worse again.'

I buy another cognac for the two men.

We remain together at the bar in silence. Sometimes I think that Félix is the wisest man in the restaurant, for he always claims to know nothing, but probably knows everything. Eventually he finishes the last of his beer and throws down the cognac.

'*Bon*,' he says to no one in particular. '*Je m'en vais. Salut, les gars*.'

He pats me and the other guy on the shoulder and wearily shuffles out into the rain. A little later the café window begins to pulsate with the orange lights of a bin lorry. The four bin men enter and leave the truck blocking the road. They're all served coffee without delay with shots of Cointreau or Calvados. '*Un peu de force*,' one says happily, before he pours it down his throat. '*Prenez des croissants*,' Loïs fusses them. Meanwhile one of them gets up and goes to the back of the café, towards the small cockpit kitchen. He returns hauling two great black bin bags. The bin men talk loudly to everyone, fielding questions and dispatching rumours.

'*Mais non, c'est n'importe quoi. On y était ce matin.*' That's bullshit, we were there this morning.

'*Complètement fermé, je te dis. Les deux quais en plus.*' Completely closed, I'm telling you. Both quays, too.

'You should see Maison d'Alfort. *Oh putain.*'

'It's up to his chest,' one of the other men at the bar says. 'I heard it on the radio.'

'*À peu près, oui.*'

I ask the barman what they're talking about. He says that when the Seine floods, its height is measured not in metres, but how by high up it reaches on a certain statue, *Le Zouave*, which is under the Pont d'Alma.

Suddenly a car horn from the street, followed by three others. The noise echoes off the buildings, even in the rain. The bin men slowly but surely drain their drinks. There are shouts from the streets from the drivers stuck in the cars. The bin men leave with the rubbish bags. We hear them shouting at the drivers. In an instant they're gone, the orange pulsing, the car horns. Everything is back to normal again in the little bistro. The bin men haven't paid for their drinks, but that is normal – in Paris they never do.

I order a *pain au chocolat*. It's now 7am and I realize that the closing of the restaurant heralds me some freedom, so I ask for a *demi* of Pelforth, too. The day is full of possibilities. For a day, Paris is mine, and I have money in my pocket – forty crisp euros from the Americans, plus the rest. I could find an internet café and apply for more jobs, I think, but the thought depresses me. Fortunately, before I can slip into some kind of existential crisis about my future, Lucien turns up with what looks and smells like a severe hangover.

'You look like shit.'

'I feel like shit.'

Over cognacs we decide to look at the flooded Seine and then walk around the Rive Gauche.

'Everything is more beautiful on the Rive Gauche. The buildings, the people, even the rain will be.'

'Hangovers, too?'

'That's the magic of Paris,' he says. 'She is so beautiful, we put up with the bad stuff.'

It turns out that last night Lucien ended up with a bunch of broke actors in a small bar in the 9th. In order to win their favour, he proceeded to spend all his money buying them drinks. Now he's broke, and the worst part is, he was so drunk when they parted ways that he'd noted their numbers down wrong.

'I thought, it's fine, I'll make some tips today. I even put on my clean shirt!'

'What's the news on the film, then?'

'No news. Let's not talk about it. Talking about it will jinx it.'

When he finds out about the American tip he insists that we treat ourselves to a three-course lunch in a bistro near Saint-Germain called Au Pied de Fouet. Lucien reminds me that tips are, quite literally, for drinking. And this place hasn't raised its prices since the 1950s. So we should be able to fill our boots.

'It's the waiter's code of honour.'

'What is?'

'To help another waiter when he's down.'

'You're not down, you're hungover. What else does the code of honour say?'

'It's simple really. You must make sure you spend all of your tips. But not on just anything.'

'No?'

'Of course not! Tips are for the ephemeral, the finer pleasures in life. Remember, there are no pockets in shrouds.'

'You can't take it with you.'

'Exactly.'

In the restaurant we eat *gésiers confits en salade* and a *potage maison de saison* as a starter, followed by a *cuisse de canard* accompanied by a carafe of the house wine. For the cheese board we take a viscous wedge of Brie de Meaux, which, when we break the chalky rind, oozes slowly over the plate.

'You know, Brie was one of Charlemagne's favourite cheeses,' Lucien says as he eats. 'It's true. He stopped in Meaux after a campaign once, I forget when; anyway, he loved it so much that he requested it be delivered to his castle in Aachen.'

'You're not as stupid as you look,' I say.

'Thanks. For that comment you can pay for the dessert.'

'I thought I was paying for everything.'

'You are.'

'What shall we have then?'

'When there's *tarte Tatin*, that's the only thing you have.'

The waiter quips that we eat like people who have just got out of prison, to which I tell him I have. For this he gives me a large glass of *vieille prune* and also coffee on the house. 'Is that where you learned French?' he asks. 'You speak French with an Indian accent.'

I can't remember the last time I ate so much, and for the next hour we have to walk around in the rain praying to God we aren't going to vomit, talking about French cinema to take our mind off the pain. Over more drinks Lucien becomes convinced that I could write him a one-man show, in English, that would get us both noticed and therefore out of the waiting world. He has an idea, it is about a boy going blind. And is sure, according to Lucien, to allow him to really demonstrate his talent.

'I have an expressive face,' he keeps saying. 'I imagine the *salle* slowly getting darker and darker.

'And attaching me to your play after I've appeared in this Hollywood movie—'

'What's the latest with that?'

Lucien ignores me.

We have another espresso and Calvados in a café opposite a theatre on the off chance of spotting an actor or agent but there are none, so we go back to walking.

'You know you keep scratching your wrists?' Lucien says.

I hadn't noticed. But it is true they are covered in small red marks. Perhaps a rash from some cleaning product in the kitchen? Stress?

'No, no reaction. Those are *punaises des lits*,' Lucien says.

'What?'

'*Punaises des lits*. You know. Little animals. Live in your bed. Eat you when you sleep. You're fucked. There's no way to get rid of them.'

What follows is an in-depth conversation about bed bugs. Lucien, like many people in Paris it appears, is a specialist.

'The problem is that the landlady will say it was your fault. Say that you brought them.'

'I bet they were there before. That's why the last girl left so soon.'

'Maybe, but she doesn't sound like the kind of woman who's going to pay to get rid of them.'

Bed bugs, it turns out, are incredibly difficult to get rid of. They're not just in the mattress, they're in the walls, the furniture. Lucien's advice: get out of there. And wash or burn all your clothes before putting them in the new place. In the meantime, I am dinner for the bed bugs.

Paris is a city made for walking, it's truly inspiring. As we pad up and down the boulevards of Saint-Germain, along to Odéon then all the way to the Latin Quarter via the back roads, it feels like anything is possible. Lucien speaks about Camille: 'No one that pretty is ever single. You should know that' is his opinion. 'And no one that beautiful would touch a waiter.' Then he speaks unceasingly about our pending writer–actor partnership and paints a life of pleasure.

'First, we have minor success with a small French film. But you know, the kind that gets picked up. Before we know it, we are on the awards circuit. You've become the darling of French cinema. And because you are English, they will love your little accent *britannique*, huh. So, you spend your time between Paris and Cannes. And before you know it, I come to you with a film I'm working on – Hollywood film. The script isn't working; there's a big shoot waiting to happen, but we don't have the story. From a villa on Capri you rewrite it in one week. Then, well, my performance, it wins maybe an Oscar, and you can get one for best screenplay.'

'Just like that?'

'I'm serious. This is how it happens. I see you as a writer.'

'Then it doesn't matter if we get sacked from the Bistrot?'

'Not at all. I'll phone Corentin up later and ask him to sack us now. To save him time. They'll be trading off our fame in no time.'

'Maybe they'll put our photos on the menus?'

'Yes and name a salad after you.'

'What would you get? A side dish?'

'Please, I'm the famous one. They'll have something special.'

'*Poulet special frites...*'

'Don't talk about food actually, it's too soon.'

When enough time has passed and we are sure we aren't going to vomit as a result of our gluttony, we come across a small cinema that is playing a Jean-Pierre Melville double bill (*L'Armée des ombres* and *Le Cercle rouge*) and go in.

When we come out it is dark, but the rain has stopped. The tips are long gone, but I still have some money left in my account and we resolve to spend it all before the night is out, as I won't have a day off until next month anyway. Back on the Rive Droite, just south of the Marais, we drop into the Louis-Philippe, where we eat *onglet à l'échalotte*, drink a bottle of Brouilly and finish with a cheese board and *mousse au chocolat*. Lucien speaks about the intrigue at the restaurant; apparently Corentin has openly boasted to the waiters that he will be named *directeur* within the month and will finally make the changes he wants; as a result the atmosphere has grown even more sour.

'It's because a new investor is involved, which in restaurants means first saving money on the food – next on the staff,' Lucien says.

'So cheaper food?'

'Kind of. Cooking fresh food costs more than getting it ready-made. They've already been working towards this. No more fresh bread anymore, you noticed? Cheaper coffee, too, if you can believe it. Before there were food deliveries most days, now we're getting them a couple of times a week, maximum. The *directeur* is a dick, sure, but you know he likes food, at least a bit. Corentin, no. He just wants to please the bosses. They get rich, he thinks he will too.'

'That guy hates food about as much as he resents the diners. You think they'll sack people?'

'You don't sack waiters. You just cut their hours until they walk out. Same for the cooks, I guess.'

'Lucky we have your acting career to fall back on.'

That night must be one of the first since I arrived in Paris that I've gone to bed having eaten three full meals. And true to my word, and the waiter's code of honour, I have spent all of my tips and much more. Being back to zero means I need tips. But what I really need is to finally become a waiter and quick, before Corentin has a chance to get rid of me. And, with summer around the corner, the money will be really flowing.

I need to find a way to circumvent Corentin. Get myself noticed. And do it before he becomes boss. As I lie there, waiting for the bed bugs to come out and begin feasting on me, I have an idea.

RED SOCKS

The days are long and warm and summer is upon us. It is July and the thick air now quivers in the boulevards under the unrelenting regard of the Parisian sun. And with the arrival of the long days come the student waiters: young cocky types who stay separate from the real professionals – of whom I am now considered a part. Our suits are sharper and our haircuts slicker; we are cynical yet professional and have no time for beginners. We think, of course, that we are better than these students, and that by acting accordingly we will make them respect us, but, in reality, they probably pity us, just as six months ago I myself pitied the waiters – with their menial jobs and many delusions.

Currently the new waiters are unaware that I only run the drinks terrace; however, it will be no time before they come to know my true lowly status. Getting promoted now seems more important than ever. I've been on a concentrated campaign to become a waiter since I arrived, yet, despite regularly dropping hints to Adrien, Pauline and Valentine, I am consistently held back. Every morning when Pauline reads out the *rangs* I hold my breath, certain that my time will come. But it never does. The *directeur*, in his cramped office that feels like a forward-command tent during a siege, is unequivocal: 'You're a runner. Not a waiter. And English,' he adds, spitefully.

Being English I am considered an inferior race when it comes to anything that involves food, wine or literature. The idea that the English make any other cheese beyond Cheddar is laughable. When they ask who the famous writers or philosophers of England are, you draw a similarly blank look, one that verges on pity.

The only areas where the French concede superiority to 'Anglo-Saxon culture', as they refer to it, are music and the notion of the *le dandy*: a romantic ideal of an Englishman that sits somewhere between Oscar Wilde and David Bowie. I know this, because the *directeur* has said as much to me. He is, he said, a connoisseur of fashion and, even if he pitied me for having to live life as an Englishman, he did concede he likes their style. It is why he employed me. Since the beginning, Corentin has been against my being hired, but the *directeur* clearly had a soft spot somewhere. And seeing as they are now at one another's throats since Corentin has made his intentions clear about taking the *directeur*'s job, what I need to do, I reason, is to make my promotion to waiter appear, to the *directeur* at least, as a critical blow against Corentin. A way to reassert his power.

I decide I should get a little creative with the uniform. All the waiters wear black and white, but each has their 'thing'. Those little touches they were so keen to show me when I arrived. Now it is my turn. With the whiff of discontent, or perhaps revolution, in the air of the restaurant, I reason that it is time to push the boat out. Conversations with Camille have assured me that it is in fact the *directeur*, and not Corentin, who hired her, and that, if anything, Corentin had been against it. The *directeur*, it appears, is our Great Modernizer, and as such is not only drawing the ire of people like Corentin (our reactionary tyrant-in-waiting), but possibly also the *patron*. The *directeur*'s sense of pride tells me he is in for the long haul, that he'd rather go out in a blaze of glory than back down. At least, this is what I tell myself as I confidently stroll along the terrace this morning. Flashes of revolutionary red heralding my arrival as my fitted trouser rises seamlessly up my calf with each step. A look that is complemented by a red silk pocket square. It is audacious, a break with tradition, a bold attempt to step out of monochrome and into something more individual.

It doesn't take long for the beady-eyed Corentin to notice, and within minutes he is at my side doing that shouted-whisper that people in restaurant managerial positions are really good at. His face bruising with marks of red.

'Get out of here. Get out!'

Some other stooge, probably Renaud, has even summoned the *directeur*. By this point most of the waiting staff are behind the screen at the Pass, watching.

'What's going on?' the *directeur* bellows as he arrives.

'This. This is what's going on.' Corentin tugs viciously at my trousers and then tears out my pocket square and hands it to the *directeur*.

He considers it for a moment. In my arrogance I haven't brought a spare pair of black socks, and the trousers have been adjusted so short that working without socks is out of the question. Eventually the *directeur* speaks: 'Chic. Very chic. But only you may wear them. It's very English.'

When he leaves, Corentin is so angry he has to leave, too.

That service I am not promoted to waiter, but I have helped the *directeur* score a small victory against the usurper. That evening, in order to build on the momentum, I decide to go and see him myself, to inform him also that, unbeknown to him, I now know about wines. This is a step too far. The fleeting respect I felt for him this morning is not mutual.

'Hah! The idea. Just the idea! An English person knowing anything about wines. Sure, when chickens have teeth…'

The telephone on the desk rings and the *directeur* jumps to attention. '*Oui, monsieur. Bien sur, monsieur…*' It is clearly the *patron*. You can tell from the flutter of fear, the hesitation, in the *directeur*'s voice. Here is a man who, despite his pretension, is not so much different from the rest of us – a cog in the machine, slowly being worn down. The *patron* leans on the *directeur*, and the *directeur* leans on us. The carrot the *directeur* is constantly chasing is a post at a more prestigious restaurant. There are, of course, perks to his job, beyond acting like the *patron* when he entertains his own guests, for he also has an unbridled reign over the entire restaurant and can be as sadistic as he pleases. He just has to keep an eye on his insubordinates, lest they get any ideas of replacing him, as is the case now. His contempt for the waiting staff and adoration for the wealthy make him a fairly distasteful character, but it is a trait he shares with most of the management.

Nothing pleases these people more, on the surface at least, than providing special treatment to special people. But my theory is that it isn't even slightly genuine, they aren't actually trying to provide the best service. They are just there to propagate the myth of luxury. What they say to one another in this little back room, when the service is over and the coke is out, is anyone's guess, but we hear enough of the snide remarks about guests and the pity they have for them to have a decent enough idea. Couple that with the fact that you never see any of the management eating anything that is on the menu. These are the frustrations of being so close to wealth, yet not having it.

The *directeur*'s quirk is that he has a unique taste for women's shoes. And his collection of high heels is testament to this. As I wait in the office, I have the chance to look at the dozens of pairs in different sizes, scattered about below the shelves, cast off by hostesses at the end of a shift. His kick is to get the hostesses to spend all night in the highest possible shoes, in the greatest amount of discomfort. It is no surprise that the waiters assume he also wears them when the door is closed.

'What woman has size-46 feet?' Lucien always says. 'And he wears make-up.'

The *directeur* puts the phone down and jumps up, mumbling something about a guest of the *patron* coming. He is in a great state of panic. There is no sommelier today, and where is Camille? When he realizes I am still standing there he shoos me out. 'Get out. You waste of space. *Crétin.*'

It isn't too bad staying on the drinks terrace, but the real prize is up above, on the great stage of the main terrace, and it is really getting me frustrated. During summer it feels like the epicentre of Paris, with queues forming up long before the service and, much to Lucien's delight, a whole host of Hollywood celebrities among the diners. Lucien is amassing quite a collection of autographs, by making celebrities sign the wrong credit-card bill the first time and then pocketing it. This he manages by switching his tables with Camille and halving all his tips with her. In the long run, I think his hope is to get noticed by one of them.

The only person who doesn't seem bothered about the restaurant and its influx of celebrities is Piotr, our resident figure of ridicule, who contents himself with working his way up from the outer tables and buying the favour of the other waiters with his constant supply of foreign cigarettes or unfiltered soft-pack Gitanes. These at first make your head turn and leave loose tobacco in your mouth, but you soon get used to them: it seems appropriate to be smoking them, as they were the cigarette of choice of Serge Gainsbourg and Alain Delon.

During that summer we must be the best-looking waiters in Paris, such is our obsession with our appearance and the competition between waiters. Haircuts become something you get every two weeks, and people's defining 'thing' remains as prevalent as ever as we engage in constant one-upmanship. My red socks and accompanying pocket square have elevated my status among the waiters to something verging on myth: 'Only *l'Anglais* can wear colour,' they inform new recruits. To go around the back of the Bistrot de la Seine outside of service hours is to stumble across a scene from a *film noir* with someone well-dressed sitting on the curb, looking surly and smoking constantly.

In the evenings at the Pass the waiters swap stories or gossip about the tables they are serving. The funniest of late is of Adrien having to usher a well-known comedian out of the kitchens because he had got lost on his way to the toilets. Renaud is adamant that he was buying coke from Adrien, and, despite Adrien's protestations, the rumour will not die; much to the Untouchable's embarrassment, Corentin even takes him aside to find out if it is true. Since the fight between Adrien and Renaud the old waiters have split neatly into two camps. Renaud and Jamaal are often seen together and tend to avoid the rest of us, spending most of their time trying to corrupt the new waiters with propaganda. Jamaal is also doing his best to brown-nose the management, which mainly involves taking credit where credit isn't due and agreeing with them publicly on matters of service and cleanliness. This is a direct affront to Adrien's position, and he doesn't take kindly to it. Renaud and Jamaal are plotting something, but we don't know what it is. My bet is that they are the Laurel and Hardy equivalent of *agents provocateurs*, part of the apparatus of Corentin's government-in-waiting.

Despite these machinations behind the scenes, overall the mood is fairly buoyant, although Lucien has become more and more cynical of late, as there is still no news about his casting, and as a result he is fixating slightly too much on Pauline. He feels that all of his misfortune is the result of France and the way it favours the elite, and he maintains that going to LA will finally earn him respect for the talent that he is. Because he didn't attend one of the French acting schools, he has little chance of making it as an actor in France, he says.

'They're taking their time,' he says about the casting. 'How do they know I haven't already got another job? Hey? It's been how many weeks now?'

Meanwhile, much to Camille's and my own amusement, the enigma of Piotr continues to intrigue. He has told some of the student waiters that he is in fact a Russian actor researching Parisian restaurants for a role he is set to play. It doesn't take long for Lucien to get wind of this and, despite his cynicism, he can't help but believe it, in part, as he thinks it might help him with his own career, so desperate is he.

'They'll need a real French waiter if it's a film set in Paris, that's for sure. Russia, why didn't I think about that? I'll speak to Franjo about learning Russian from him.'

'I think you're right,' Camille says to Lucien. 'I watch a lot of Russian cinema, and his face does seem familiar.'

'Me too,' Lucien replies. 'Me too.'

GRADUATION

Among the restaurant's regular clientele there is an Australian couple. He is a mine-owner, with an immense fortune, or so the restaurant believes.

'He comes to the restaurant with his wife every summer when he's in Paris for business,' Pauline tells me. She has come with one of the student runners to relieve me of my duty on the drinks terrace. I have a terrible feeling that I am going back to being a runner, despite her insistence that it is just that the *directeur* wants my help with '*le milliardaire australien*' – the Australian Billionaire – as Camille, who speaks excellent English and usually works the VIP area, is currently off on her break.

The Australian Billionaire turns out to be a very regular Australian man, and though I doubt there are many outwardly recognizable features of an Australian billionaire, one can't help but get the impression that the restaurant has made some kind of mistake, or that the guy is simply taking the restaurant for a ride. A casual glance at his Swatch watch, trousers with thigh pockets and tatty shoes should surely have told Pauline enough, but so certain are they that it seems these sartorial transgressions only serve as further confirmation that he is indeed a billionaire – a billionaire would clearly dress down.

'Even the Italian industrialists wear Swatch watches,' Pauline says, as if it is common knowledge.

I hand the couple their menus and stand back. The *directeur*, who is pretending to act busy at the lectern, beckons me over. The Australian Mine-Owner and his wife are not drinkers, he says. She may occasionally take a glass of Côtes de Provence rosé, and he a small glass of the Côte de Beaune, but they rarely touch it. Could I please tell Nimsath to prepare these immediately? I disappear to the Pass and inform Nimsath of the order. Naturally he refuses to take it as it hasn't come on a ticket via the till. The rosé isn't a problem, but the Côte de Beaune is and, as far as he is concerned, I am ordering directly so that I can pocket the money for the two drinks myself, which to a certain extent he tolerates, but not this time. I assure him I am now working the VIP zone but he only laughs and says, 'Engleeshman runner. No VIP.'

On my way back, I see the *directeur* bent double by the Australian Billionaire, as if in a protracted bowing gesture; catching me out of the corner of his eye, he makes an urgent hand gesture, wafting air around his behind and beckoning me over. The Mine-Owner, who is quietly spoken and has an impenetrable accent, is trying to explain to the *directeur* that he and his wife are celebrating, and that they would like to see the wine list. The *directeur*, having finally understood, springs forwards with the list, dismisses me and then stands proudly as the Mine-Owner looks blankly at the pages. The *directeur* goes through the motions of talking through the wine list himself, as it is Monday and Franjo is not working today either. I am not close enough to hear the conversation, but it is clearly not going well, with lots of ''Ow you say?' as the *directeur* fumbles for words. In no time I am called back over by the *directeur*, who is slightly red in the face and most certainly embarrassed. Incapable of communicating properly in English, he is unable to guide the Australians in their choice.

He explains to me hurriedly: 'They must not take these wines from the front pages. These wines are below someone of such stature. But I do not understand what they say. You must do it. Advise them one of the wines towards the back. One of the *grand vins de France*.'

It is the wife who speaks first. Her voice is sharp and nasal. She has thin red hair, drawn-on eyebrows and red lipstick that is painted, for the most part, onto her face and not her lips.

'Let's take the Châteauneuf-du-Pape. That's a good wine,' she crows.

'But the tall man here doesn't seem to think so,' said the Mine-Owner, nodding towards the *directeur*.

I can't help but smile.

'*Qu'est ce qu'ils disent?*' What are they saying?

I tell the *directeur*, and he smiles awkwardly with a little bow. Having understood that they had called him a '*un grand homme*', a great man.

'You are sharing a *côte de bœuf*, no?' I ask.

'We are,' says the wife proudly. 'It's my birthday.'

'Happy birthday, *madame*. Well, for a birthday, the tall man here may have a point. You are right, *madame*, the Châteauneuf-du-Pape is indeed a great wine...' She looks at the Mine-Owner with an I-told-you-so look. '...but this year, 2008, was not so great.'

The lies slips off my tongue like oil.

'If I may.' I take the wine list from the Mine-Owner and to the *directeur*'s amazement begin flicking towards the back with an assurance that surprises even me. He remains silent, but I can feel his eyes on my back. I scan the pages, desperately looking for something that stands out. I've never seen any of the wines this far back. Most are over €400 a bottle. Finally, one jumps out. I instantly remember the sommelier's description, or at least enough of it to make it sound convincing.

'A-ha!' I exclaim.

I feel the *directeur* bristle over my shoulder. As I pass the list back to the Mine-Owner, he and his wife peer at the names and numbers as if they were written in Arabic.

'Let's not go too crazy, hey,' the Mine-Owner says under his breath, having seen that some bottles are comfortably five-figure sums.

'The Chambertin, Clos de Bèze.' I pause. '*Madame* was correct in her choice of accompaniment for the beef.' As she smiles I can almost feel the notes sliding into my pocket. 'Such a fine piece of meat deserves a noble wine. The Chambertin is often considered the little brother of Châteauneuf-du-Pape, but the Clos de Bèze, to those who know at least, has always been considered far superior. And this year, 1990...' – I am in full stride – '...what a year! The wine really came into its own. It became an instant collector's wine. And that was twenty-three years ago. You cannot imagine the taste today – imperial, deep. You can taste the centuries of France within it, the Dukes of Burgundy, the monks—'

'Well, I guess we'll take that, then,' says the Mine-Owner, cutting me off. He hands the book back to the *directeur* without looking at him, and we both hurry off. The *directeur* insists I come with him to the *cave* where the *vins d'exception* are kept under lock and key. Another blank on my mental map of the restaurant is being filled in. A narrow stone staircase leads down far below the building. I am finally in the famous wine cellar. As I should have suspected, it is nowhere near as vast or impressive as the waiters have made out. Nothing like the endless underground warehouses, hewn out of the limestone below Reims, where Pommery keep their champagnes. The cellar is impressive nonetheless, purely by virtue of the amount of valuable wines there. The ceiling is low. The old stones of the building are cool to the touch. We crouch near the dirt floor and the *directeur* draws the bottle out of the rack as if he were removing a stick of plutonium from a nuclear reactor. In the half-light from the single bulb I can't see his lips, but he is muttering something, perhaps some reverent phrases to his god of viticulture.

'An excellent choice. Magnificent. *Quel vin. Quel vin!* Perhaps I underestimate you, *l'Anglais*.' He hands me the bottle. 'You do the honours. You will open and serve it. Let me remind you how…'

'It's OK,' I says. 'I know.'

'Please, I will not have you ruining this wine with your ignorant methods.'

I assure him more firmly that I know how, and as we walk back up to the dining room the sommelier's words go around and round in my head: 'Always with one hand. Hold the bottle here – like a woman, around the waist, not the neck. When you remove this foil, you cut below the raise at the top of the neck. Why? If we cut here – like most people – then we risk having tiny shards of metal when we pour… you will know instantly if it is corked… you do not even need to try the wine; the cork tells you everything… it must not smell wet… a simple gesture of wafting it under the nose will be sufficient… for the tasting, you pour a small amount, then offer the bottle as the client tries it… he is not tasting the wine, he is checking if it is corked… he must be able to see the label, so you cradle the wine like a child in your hand… the other, you must keep behind your back... don't look at him... next, if it is OK, you will serve the other guests and finally fill the glass of the person who tasted it... the cork you may leave on the table so that the customer may smell it... ensure that the label of the wine is turned towards the person who chose the wine when you leave the bottle on the table... I tell you this because in certain countries they turn the label to the room so that the other tables may see... this, in my opinion, is completely unacceptable... vulgar.'

I open the wine with Sal's burnished *limo* (*a waiter's friend for a waiter's friend*) and pour it with great success. The Australian Mine-Owner nods that it is not corked and proceeds to compliment his wife on her choice. While they wait for their *côte de bœuf* the *directeur* informs me that I can wait their table for the rest of the meal. If I didn't know better, I would have said he felt a kind of paternal pride in my work.

'Whatever they leave is yours,' he says, as if a man of his upbringing were above money.

For the entire meal I am the most courteous of waiters, more like a valet. Always on hand and happy to give them advice about the city. I smile the smile of a seasoned waiter, each movement has a little bow, a gesture of servitude. I am already spending the money in my head. How much does a billionaire leave as a tip? Fifty? One hundred? More? Everything I have learned since I arrived I put into practice. I am the model waiter. When they leave I even have the audacity to collar a hostess and demand that she call a taxi, as if I was the Billionaire's very own private secretary. This I do as much for Lucien and De Souza, who are close by, as for the Australian Mine-Owner. In the hostess's eyes I can read that she wants to tell me to fuck off, but the appearance of the *directeur* bowing and thanking the Mine-Owner stops her. And the way the Mine-Owner warmly shakes my hand and pats my back feels like he is personally welcoming me to waiterhood.

In the little black leather book the Australian Billionaire has left ten euros. There isn't a chance in hell the others will believe me. However, on a more positive note, they have barely touched the bottle of wine. I pick it up and hurry to the Pass to find Lucien.

'*Mon ami.*' Lucien looks like he might begin to cry when he sees it.

'Wait.' He leans down and barks into the Pass. 'Nimsath! Two wine glasses. The nice ones.'

They appear on the metal surface. Deep crystal bowls. Lucien pours the wine slowly, almost religiously. We raise the glasses, touch them together. I knock it back quite quickly. But Lucien savours the moment, rolling the velveteen liquid around his mouth. I've barely swallowed when he spits it out into the bin of food slops.

'*Putain de merde. Il est bouchonné.*' It's corked.

He puts the glass down and turns to leave. 'It's worth nothing. Nothing. Throw it.' And with that he is gone.

I look at the half-full bottle and his barely touched glass. It isn't *that* corked. Not to my ignorant English nose at least. Piotr soon arrives and has little problem with wine being corked or not.

'It's still got alcohol in,' he smiles.

By the time we leave the Pass a couple of seconds later the bottle is empty.

At the end of the service the *directeur* comes and finds me.

'*L'Anglais,*' he says. 'Well done today. I was impressed. Tomorrow you will serve on the terrace. OK?'

Music fills the air as night falls that evening. The elderly saxophonist, leaning against a wall under the arches, is tonight butchering the theme song from *The Godfather*. As I smoke my cigarette on a break, I smile. Here I am, in Paris, in my tuxedo, my red socks and pocket square, enjoying my first smoke as a Made Man. At last, I have been accepted into the brotherhood. I am certain things will be different from now on.

I have finally, after six months, become a waiter.

THERE'S ALWAYS A NICO
AT A HOUSE PARTY

After service Lucien and I are sitting in the *bar-tabac* near the restaurant, which is closing. Lucien announces that we should go to the Marais and find a house party in order to celebrate my ascension to the brotherhood.

'We can't sit here like this. Look at us. We should be with girls our own age. Clotilde there must be what, seventy?'

'We should change first. I stink,' I tell him.

'Not at all.' He stands up and looks at himself in the faded mirror behind the bar. 'We look good. We look chic, that's what we look like. Stand up. See? A quick freshen-up in the toilet, and all is good.'

I can't tell if he is talking about Adrien's merchandise, or quite literally washing. Lucien orders two shots of cheap whisky and then we set off. For the best part of an hour we walk up and down the quiet streets of the Marais with our necks craned, 'street beers' in hand *à la* Salvatore, with occasional bar stops for shots of cheap whisky. We are close to giving up when we hear the unmistakable sounds of laughter and music echoing off the walls.

'There.' Lucien is pointing up at the windows of a large-looking apartment, its lights ablaze. At the windows stand groups of people smoking, their divine laughter pouring down like celestial music from the heavens.

'How do we get in?' I ask.

'Easy, follow me.' Lucien counts the windows of the buildings and the floors. Then, when he is convinced we have found the right door at street level, he gives me a cigarette. 'Now we wait,' he says.

We don't wait long. Almost immediately a group of people come out of the building, having clearly just left the party.

'*C'est au quatrième, c'est ça?*' It's the fourth floor, yeah? Lucien asks casually.

'*Oui, bâtiment B, puis quatrième à gauche...*' a girl with dark green eyes and a leather mini-skirt responds. Directions to Parisian apartments are inordinately complex; fortunately Lucien's fine-tuned waiter's short-term memory absorbs all the relevant information.

In the caged lift that runs up the centre of the stairs we agree on a backstory. At Lucien's insistence we are actors in town from London.

'What's a Shakespeare play with two male leads?'

'*A Midsummer Night's Dream?*'

'With the fairies?'

'Yeah, but there's also two guys, Demetrius and Lysander.'

'They're cool?'

'Well, they like these girls in...'

'Playboys, perfect. You know that song by Jacques Dutronc, "Les Playboys"?'

He begins to try and sing it, which tells me nothing apart from how drunk he is. He is in his element again, possibly because of the chance to impress with his acting skills. Outside the front door the music is loud.

'Ready?' Lucien asks.

'Of course.'

'Just follow my lead.'

He rings the doorbell and lights a cigarette. A guy opens the door and looks at us suspiciously.

'*Hé, salut,*' Lucien says amiably.

'*Oui?*' the guy asks sceptically.

'We're friends of Nico's.' Lucien has already started walking forwards before he's finished speaking.

'Cool,' is all the guy says.

Once in the apartment, which is a luxury affair replete with questionable contemporary art, cream sofas and dark wooden floors, Lucien turns to me with a smile and says, 'That's another thing you should know. There's always a Nico at a house party.'

We spend most of the time in the kitchen where the champagne is, as we've decided to keep a low profile until we have been accepted as part of the guests. We begin chatting to one girl, a petite brunette called Margaux who oozes the kind of elegance that only a French girl can. When Lucien excuses himself to go to the toilet, having helped himself to another bottle of champagne from the fridge, Margaux comes up close to my face and with a smile says, 'I'm impressed.'

Not following completely and taking it as a compliment on the promising trajectory of our acting careers that we've been telling her about, I decide to respond with a cool, 'We're nothing special. Lucien, he likes to talk.'

'Oh, but you are. You convinced me.'

I realize that she has rumbled us.

'You were doing well,' she continues, 'until you said you were friends of Nico. You see, Nico – he's my brother.'

I look in the direction she is now looking. Nico, it turns out, is the hulk of gym-hewn muscle currently doing shots of Get 27 and vodka with four equally rowdy friends who are cheering him on. From the other room the music has stopped, mid-song, and what sounds a little like what Lucien was trying to sing in the lift comes on.

'Jacques Dutronc?' I ask Margaux.

'Yes. "Les Playboys". Are you worried?'

To suggest that Nico and his friends are intimidating types would be an overstatement. However, at this hour in the morning and seeing their current state of inebriation and excitement (they are chanting at two others who are engaged in a race to down shots), it is probably an idea to get moving.

'Don't worry. I won't say anything. I find it funny. His friends are all boring anyway. So, what do you really do?'

'Honestly? We're waiters.'

'I should have guessed it. The suits. Him, it was more obvious.

But you threw me. You don't look like a waiter.' She takes a long drag on her cigarette. 'Waiters. Ha!'

'You live here?' I try to change the subject.

'No, it's my Dad's place. He's out of town. Lucky, too. I wonder what he'd say if he knew a couple of waiters had broken into his place. I could call the police, you know.'

We look across the apartment. It is a scene of decadent carnage. There are couples embracing, people smoking, drinks being spilled, bottles and glasses on every flat surface. The music meanwhile gets progressively louder. Nico dispatches one of his friends to turn it down. It stops abruptly. The friend returns with a look that tells me we are in trouble, as Nico and the others immediately go out of the kitchen looking pissed. Sensing the drama, most of the others in the kitchen follow.

'I think your friend may have landed you in trouble,' Margaux smiles and follows the others.

I run after them to find Lucien in the middle of the sitting room, surrounded. Nico has him by the collar.

'Nico? You're friends of Nico's, are you?' Nico shouts.

His friends laugh.

'Teach him a lesson.'

Lucien, to his credit, does the best he can to talk himself out of the situation.

'There's the other one.'

Before I can react, someone behind me has put their arm around my throat.

'You a friend of Nico's, too?'

'Not yet,' I say foolishly. 'Friends with Margaux.'

Margaux, however, is nowhere to be seen. We are soon bundled out of the apartment in a frenzy, with a couple of sloppy punches thrown in our general direction and the door is slammed shut behind us. The music comes back on and we hear a cheer from behind the door.

'How's my eye?' Lucien asks.

'Fine. Why?'

'The bastard got me good.'

On our way down the stairs we pass four policemen coming up.

'Finally, guys,' Lucien says.

'Are you from the party? We've had noise complaints,' the first one says.

'No, sir. We live in the building next door. We went to tell them ourselves that it was too loud. We can't sleep. And you know what, they were very rude. I'd say it's louder now. How are we meant to sleep? Some of us have work tomorrow.'

The policemen look at us suspiciously, then continue on their way.

'Nico,' Lucien shouts after them.

'What?'

'Nico, that was the gentleman's name. Most unpleasant character.'

We wait in the stairwell silently. We hear the knock, then the door open and the music spill out. There is shouting, the music stops, finally we hear the policeman ask, 'Who's Nico?' And with that we run down the stairs and out of the building.

'Did you get her number?' Lucien asks.

'No. You?'

'Damn it.'

'I think Jacques Dutronc might have ruined it for us.'

'We are not the first guys to lose a girl to him.'

We walk back through the Marais singing "Les Playboys" and drinking a bottle of champagne that, at some point during the party, Lucien has had the foresight to sneak outside and leave hidden behind a potted plant on the floor below. As usual we speak about cinema and what we'll do when we are in LA. When we part company Lucien's eye is swelling up a bit so we use the now not-so-cold bottle against it.

The next day he turns up to work, clearly wearing make-up, much to the amusement of the waiters who say that, having failed to become an actor, Lucien is now moonlighting as a transvestite cabaret dancer, and has an act going with the *directeur*. Lucien does, however, manage to keep far enough away from the management for them not to notice.

PART 6
LE DESSERT

SISYPHUS

It's late and the terrace is almost empty save for a table of French women whose staccato laughs occasionally carry across the small square in front of the restaurant like salvos of machine-gun fire into no-man's land. Just in the doorway, illuminated by the red heater, stands Piotr, like some skinny royal guard. Above him, visible through the large windows of the dining room, the silhouettes of the diners, the flickering candles and the occasional passing of De Souza, like a spectre, with trays of *digestifs* or cheese. After a moment he appears at the entrance next to Piotr; they exchange a few words before De Souza hurries along the terrace and disappears down into the dark eaves of the arcade. Piotr, having looked at the table of drinkers, goes inside; a moment later I see his unmistakable shadow passing in front of the windows.

De Souza hasn't seen me. He's pacing up and down, even on his break, smoking quickly. His shoulders hunched up, small steps, fast pace, just like in the restaurant. De Souza is a career waiter. He's been doing it his whole life, and as far as I know he'll be doing it until he keels over.

'De Souza.'

'Oh, *l'Anglais*. I didn't see you there.'

He sits down next to me with that familiar groan.

'What do you make of the new guy?' he asks.

'Piotr? I like him.'

'Hard worker.'

'Says he's got his own restaurant,' I say. 'In Gdansk.'

'Told me he's the silent partner of the *patron*. God knows what he's talking about. Half the people in this profession are crazy. That's one of the reasons I love it: the people. They're either crazy, stupid or running from something. This guy, Piotr, I think he might be crazy, stupid *and* running from something.'

'Adrien says he told him he just got out the French Foreign Legion. Seems plausible: he has that scar on his face. And the tattoos.'

'I told you, *l'Anglais*. Crazy, stupid or running from something.'

'Which are you?'

He ignores me; he's thinking of something else.

'I was meant to see my daughter tonight. It's her birthday. Three years old.'

'What happened?'

He doesn't answer immediately.

'At six, Corentin tells me I've got to stay. Just like that.' De Souza exhales. 'I guess that makes me stupid.'

There's a silence. I wonder how he does it. How he takes it. How he lets them just take his time away from him like that.

'But I made decent money,' he continues. 'I'll get her something nice. That's the thing about this place. The tips are better than anywhere. And it's beautiful.'

'How much?'

He purses his lips. 'For the entire day? Perhaps...' – he does a calculation in his head – '...one hundred and sixty.'

'What's the most you've ever made?'

He smiles at me in the darkness. 'A lot more. You know... once... I was working... I was probably about your age, and I had this table of Arabs – you know, the rich ones – anyway, there they are enjoying their meal. Everything was perfect – I was looking great, the food was fine. But there's this woman at the end of the table who says nothing all meal...' He smokes. '...She looks *misérable*. Of course, the men ignore her, you know how it is. *Bref*... So, sometime during the meal she goes into the restaurant, I assume to go to the toilet or whatever. But, actually, what she had done was go to the bar and drink three neat shots of vodka! In her head scarf and everything.

'Now, the barman, this guy, puts these shots on the bill. But he doesn't think to tell me. Later, the head of the table asks me for the bill... *Bref*, it turns out that the woman who had drunk the vodka was his wife! But I didn't know this yet. So, of course, I bring him the bill. It's long and very expensive, and I don't really look closely at it – it was late, I was tired, you know how it is. Of course, when you've brought the bill you must leave the customer with it.

'So, I'm at the Pass taking the last of the plates back from another table when suddenly I hear shouting. I go back, and can you imagine? The barman is standing there, and he is arguing with the man. With the *putain* Sheikh! He tells me – in front of the whole restaurant – "This man is calling me a liar, De Souza. He says that his wife didn't drink three vodkas. I know she did – I served them!"

'You can imagine the scene. With the husband and wife both denying this. Of course, I still didn't know she'd drunk them, the barman was an alcoholic, so he'd always try and hide drinks on people's bills to cover up what he was drinking. Anyway, I take the barman inside after assuring the clients I will sort out this mistake... In the end I go back to the table and say that there's been a huge mistake, that his wife didn't drink any vodka and that the barman is a drunken fool. They were not happy, but when I was ruder about the barman from Marseille they laughed some. When they left I could see they'd left nothing on the table. Can you believe it? That piece of shit barman ruined my tip from a table of Arab princes. I was so angry. But then... and you won't believe it... this other Arab I have never seen before comes back and shakes my hand and thanks me for what I did, says he is the Sheikh's driver or something, and he is thanking me, shaking my hand, telling me that it was an important business meeting, then he leaves with a wink... and in my hand he has left a five-hundred euro note. Five hundred euros! Have you ever seen one? They're big. Big and purple.

'Naturally, I said nothing to the barman. I pretended they'd left nothing, said I needed to go and smoke. And I just looked at it. Five hundred euros. Like this, in my hand. In one day, I'd paid my rent. But I didn't do that – no, no, no, no. No, I bought my lady presents. I spent it all! In one weekend, five hundred euros. Bam, just like that. I felt like a Sheikh, too.

Those days remind me why I love this job. The people, the money, ah!'

'Now it would be different. You know what I'd do now? It's for my daughter, all of it. That's why the slow days hurt so much, or when that bastard Renaud steals. Because I'm thinking about her future. Or about Christmas. I'm sick and tired of the credit-card debt, *l'Anglais*. This year, my fiancée and I agreed: no more credit-card debt at Christmas. We've already started saving. Every month we put some money aside. The wedding isn't helping. If anyone tells you a wedding is cheap, you give them a friendly reminder from me. Corentin knows it. That's why they know they can get me to stay on nights like this. My daughter's birthday. Man...'

'I admire you, De Souza. You're a good waiter.'

'Good waiter; bad father.'

'Excellent father.'

'*Merci, mon ami*. I love them so much, you know; it scares me. I worry that I'll lose them.' He lights a second cigarette, then points at the square. 'Do you ever try and imagine the things this little square has seen? The people who may have crossed it at some point in their lives? Maybe a king, maybe just small people, like us. But it's beautiful. Not many people can say that about where they work. I sometimes imagine an office job. Impossible. All day locked in a room staring at a screen. No, thank you.'

'What about becoming a manager? Would that help?' I ask.

'I'd have a better salary, probably better hours. But I wouldn't be doing what I love. I'd miss the buzz of being in the *salle*. The human contact; the game for the tips, of course. I think they make less, maybe.'

'Head waiter?'

'Adrien's job? Forget about it. Wouldn't take it if they forced it on me. It's his. No one could do it better. Besides, I think Jamaal and Renaud have their eyes on that...'

'But if it wasn't here, in another restaurant?'

I worry he's almost been institutionalized. He seems to love his tormentor. As far as I can see, the restaurant doesn't care for him. They'll use him until he can work no more, then they'll replace him.

'*L'Anglais*, I have a kid; soon a wife to support, too. If I change job, who's to know what it will be like? Maybe the new restaurant fires me after a week. Then what? Here they know us, they look after us. I don't worry about losing my job. Anyway, I like it here for the moment. When I want to leave, I will. That's what's great about waiting. You can go anywhere. And you meet so many different people. Like you. My first English friend.'

We shake hands. I finish my cigarette and get up, touched by De Souza calling me his friend.

'*L'Anglais,*' De Souza calls to me. 'Talking of overtime. Don't think I haven't noticed how much you're working either. Listen, I know it's hard, but just remember to smile.' He performs a slow-motion right hook, then shadow-boxes for a moment. 'Give as good as you get.'

'You box much at the moment?' I ask. The other waiters say he never boxed, just uses it as an excuse for his broken nose. That or memories of a glorious youth.

'No. But I will. I love waiting, but you know what? In the end, I'd like to open my own gym. That's the plan. Nothing special. A few bags, a ring. A place to train, to teach kids... you know, that kind of thing.' The effort of describing his dream future quickly loses steam.

'I've never seen a five-hundred note.'

'It's because the criminals have them. You can get 25,000 euros in a cigarette pack using five-hundreds. They use them for the big deals.' He looks at his pack of cigarettes. 'Imagine. All that, in here. It could change your life. And it fits in your hand.'

'How do you know that?'

'Adrien.'

'Adrien. Of course. He seems to be getting nervous about his speech.'

'I hope you can make it, *l'Anglais.* It would mean a lot to me.'

'To your wedding?'

'Of course! You're one of the boys. You have to be there.'

My excitement at this invitation is obvious, which De Souza appreciates. From my reaction you'd think it was the greatest thing to have yet happened to me.

'Do you think I can get the time off?'

'Use some of that overtime they owe you. It will be great. We can be together. Enjoy a party for once.'

De Souza would always say that, as long as we can smile to ourselves, then it is not so serious. He was the very essence of Camus' Sisyphus, not me. He had learned to love the job. The repetitive, backbreaking nature of the work, the precarity – although less so now he had a daughter and, soon, a wife. De Souza was the incarnation of loyalty, so much so that he wouldn't even entertain the thought of replacing his friend, even if it helped his family situation. His attitude was admirable: he was rarely down and almost always positive. Yet on the nights when he was held back and would once again miss picking his daughter up from nursery or putting her to bed or even her birthday, he may have smiled politely to the management but in his eyes you could see a true sense of sadness. He'd been going around on a treadmill that he could never get off, and he knew it. Dreams happened when you slept, but in restaurant work you were too exhausted to dream. His talk of boxing was nothing more than a distraction, and he knew it. Boxing was something he'd done in his youth, now he didn't have the time. And though he was happy to stand at the Pass talking about bouts between locals, or shadow-boxing and correcting our stances, he wasn't the boxer he may have once been, and he wasn't going to become it any time soon. Talking about his boxing just allowed him to pretend that there maybe was another future once he'd succeeded in finally getting the rock to the top of the hill without it rolling back down.

De Souza didn't have a bad bone in his body. He wished ill upon no one and wouldn't hurt a fly. He didn't even aspire to become a *maître d'*; he was happy with his station in life. It afforded him the necessary luxuries, and the state would provide his child with an education and healthcare. That's how he saw it, perhaps. The truth was that he'd been doing it so long he didn't have a choice. He had to look at it that way.

If there's any reason to leave a waiter a tip, then it's for people like De Souza.

Piotr

Piotr lived in a kind of refined squalor, in a hovel up by the Porte de Saint-Ouen, near one of the overpasses of the Périphérique. It was shambolically decorated and felt more like it had been transplanted from occupied Paris than the Paris of today. And though his apartment was accompanied by the constant hiss and rumbling of the ring road – of which his kitchen offered an excellent view – the floor was parquet, he had painted wooden shutters, and in one of the rooms there was even a kind of carpeting on the wall and an open fireplace, which would 'keep the bills down in winter, and dry out the mould in the ceiling', he assured me. It was an Orthodox priest's property, he said. 'Cheaper than what you pay, *l'Anglais*. And 100 per cent bed-bug free.'

'How did you know?'

'I had the same marks on my wrists when we were stationed in Guiana. Used to burn them with my cigarettes they were so big. Fuckers would be crawling up the wall. It's bad?'

I lifted my shirt. My torso was covered with the bites. You could almost trace the route they'd taken across my body. My sheets in the morning would be covered in little trails of black – bed-bug excrement.

'*Ah ouais, quand même.*'

'My landlady said I brought them.'

'You know you can't get rid of them. You have to burn the bed.'

'That's what Lucien said.'

For all dining-related items, such as serviettes, plates and cutlery, Piotr had equipped himself liberally with everything the restaurant had to offer.

It's quite normal to steal a few things (bread, wine, coffee), for there's a tacit agreement between the waiter and his employers – the restaurant gives him little, and the waiter cheats his way to whatever he can. What was impressive was the sheer scale of Piotr's operation.

At my best guess from what he had recounted, Piotr had worked his way to Paris following stints in Marseille, Nice and Lyon. And it seemed that, wherever he had gone, he had landed on his feet. In the restaurant, he still maintained, depending on whom you asked, that he owned a restaurant in Poland, was an actor, an aristocrat and also a part owner of Le Bistrot de la Seine. Since I had become friends with Piotr, he had omitted all this, replacing it with the more plausible version of having recently left the French Foreign Legion. Of course there were still vast holes in his past, which he didn't speak about, but I liked him. What Piotr wanted from life wasn't a question. He lived for the present and would deal with the future tomorrow. 'It can't get worse, *l'Anglais*; if it does, we keep going,' he would always say during a hard service. Like De Souza, he was a man of positives, no matter what the situation; and as for his current living arrangements, he felt like the King of France. The only thing that irked him was the informal market that took place twice a week in the underpass down below his place.

'You cannot imagine it, *l'Anglais*... the *merde* they sell. This one man, he has a shoe and then a cable for a kettle – that is it, *putain*! Who buys one shoe? But you should see them all – fighting each other. Hundreds of them some days.'

I know the people he is talking about, having seen them doing their rounds when I was in the Hôtel du Simplon. The 'other' economy. The recently arrived immigrants without papers or family in the city, the homeless and the Roma. The aspect of Paris the other tends to pretend doesn't exist, except when it's convenient for them, such as getting rid of things quickly by leaving them in the street.

Most of these people, especially the Roma, live just outside the capital in numerous shanty towns that have grown up around abandoned railway lines, motorway verges and industrial estates. Rows of shacks made from materials picked up around the city: abandoned door frames, shelves, tarpaulins. One shanty town isn't too far from where Piotr lives, hence the informal market. It sits in a depression alongside the busy inner ring road on the former railway track that encircles Paris, La Petite Ceinture, the little belt. The huts all made from chipboard and tarpaulin with thin metal-pipe chimneys poking out the top that smoke all day. On the makeshift roofs are abandoned objects: rotting clothes, plastic tubs and children's toys – black with the soot from the chimneys. In Paris, if you want to get rid of something, you leave it in the street: no matter what it is, it will go, and most of it ends up in these places.

A regular sight for me when I was in the Hôtel du Simplon were the groups who would wait at the bins behind the big supermarket at the times when they knew things would be thrown out. They'd all be there at the end of the day and early in the morning, groups of (often) women in headscarves sitting around chatting and gossiping. When something was thrown out, they would descend on the bins and, in an orderly fashion, begin rifling through for anything edible. There was a hierarchy among them, and even if most of what was discarded ended up on the pavement, they were respectful to each other. Often, if an outsider arrived (a homeless man, for example), the women would admonish him if his conduct was considered too boisterous or competitive.

In typical Parisian fashion, on the other side of where Piotr lives is the famous antiques market, la Marché des Puces, where we sometimes walk together. I can never be sure which of the markets annoys him more, this one or the informal one on the other side of the neighbourhood.

'Look at this, *l'Anglais*. You see the price?' he will say to me as we stalk the covered aisles with the small shops either side brimming with expensive antique furniture. 'I'm telling you. We take a van, you and me, and we drive all around Eastern Europe... The *merde* they sell here – old chairs and cupboards – the people in the East, they can't get rid of it quick enough. We pick it up, free of course... then, when we come to Paris with a van full of "antiques", we set up one of these shops and we sell everything. We say that they are from pre-Revolution Russia. Pretend you're English expert; they believe you, not me with my accent.'

'We could say you're a White Russian.'

'We'll be rich. I'm telling you! With the money we set up a small restaurant, you and me. An Englishman like you out front, it will be the talk of the town. I manage the kitchen and the waiters, make sure they don't steal anything.'

'You can never trust a waiter.'

'Never,' he smiles.

'What about your restaurant in Poland?'

'Yes, yes, of course, but ours will be much chicer. Polish people don't have enough money anyway. We can sell the same food as in Poland but for four times the price. Five times even.'

'Where will we open it?'

'Rive Gauche. Or, we go to Switzerland. I hear it is even more expensive there. There was a Swiss guy in our regiment. Imagine, they sell pizza for thirty euros there. Thirty euros! *Putain.*'

Conversations go around and around like this for some time. It is the same with all the waiters. We discuss what we are going to do in the future, but it is more like some kind of game, for I'm not sure that any of us really believe it will happen. These things happen to other people; we are just invisible observers who hover by their shoulders for a moment while they eat.

Piotr is adamant that I should meet the aforementioned Orthodox priest. And the temptation to move again is quite strong. Especially now the bed-bug problem is getting progressively worse; what started as a few irritating marks on my wrists in the mornings has developed into something severe. Now, if I come back from the restaurant late enough, they've already come out and are crawling across my sheets looking for me. Going to sleep every night feels like lying down on a sacrificial altar.

TALES FROM THE WOODS

Piotr and I are sitting in the weak morning sun enjoying a cigarette before the Sunday lunch service. His eyes are a blistering red, he smells strongly of alcohol and his hands are shaking slightly – he looks like a man who hasn't slept, if you bother to look closely enough. Fortunately most diners rarely look at their waiter.

'How did it end up?'

'Ah, it's so long ago, I do not remember,' he says, with a forced smile.

'And tonight?'

'I never make plans that far ahead, Englishman.'

'The back of your jacket is covered in dirt,' I say to him.

To this he says nothing, just burps, swallows and then spits a horrible red-brown globule of saliva into the gutter. We are near the door of the kitchens and the smell of shallots caramelizing in pans keeps wafting out. After a moment Piotr gets up, stands between two cars and vomits. He wipes his mouth with the back of his hand and sits back down next to me. Two well-dressed women who witness the entire scene continue walking as if nothing has happened. If he were a rich man, Piotr would be described as eccentric, or perhaps a *bon vivant*, but because he is a waiter, unfortunately, he is neither. The last time I'd seen him was in Pigalle at 3am last night. We were celebrating, having both made decent tips.

'I do not work like a dog all day to sleep like one!' Piotr had said when he came out of the back office having handed over his money after the service. 'I work like a dog to fuck like one. And tonight, *l'Anglais*, you come with me. I invite you. You cannot say no. It is rude, and Englishmen are not rude. Besides, we earned this together.'

He opened his waiter's wallet which was stuffed full of dirty notes.

'One drink,' I told him, and I meant it, as all I wanted to do was sleep.

'One drink, good. We go to Pigalle. I know a place.'

Two hours later we were in a tiny subterranean den with low red lighting drinking expensive, room-temperature beers. The girls in their tired clothes looked as poorly fed as Piotr and me, but he wasn't deterred.

'Look at her breasts,' he whispered, before beckoning her over to sit on his lap.

The girl looked at me without curiosity. 'My friend is over there. She likes you. You want to spend the night alone?'

'I've got him, thanks.'

'Come, *l'Anglais*, that is rude. I pay. You,' he said to the girl, 'you come with me. We do private dance, yes?'

The girl took Piotr behind a screen just next to me so that I could see his feet poking out. We were the only two in the bar apart from the bouncer in the long leather jacket standing at the door and the weathered woman behind the bar. The girl who had been sitting at the bar drinking water came over.

'You want dance?'

'No, thanks.'

'You don't like me?'

'I don't have any money.'

As I spoke I could hear Piotr from behind the screen. 'Go on, just touch it,' he kept saying. Meanwhile, I was having a conversation with the other girl about how easy it was to walk from King's Cross to Russell Square.

It wasn't much longer before Piotr's girl reappeared and the tall bouncer who had been watching us limped over. I could see Piotr's feet still sticking out from behind the screen. The mountain of a man went over and hauled Piotr up, telling him that he owed two hundred euros for the two beers and that if he didn't pay he'd '*éclater nos gueules*'. Shatter our faces. The threat didn't have time to sink into our alcohol-soaked brains before Piotr caught the bouncer by surprise with a lightning-fast headbutt. The bouncer went flying back onto the floor clutching his nose, whereupon Piotr landed a kick in his stomach. This was the last thing I saw, for I was already running up the tiny stairs and into the street. The screams of the women chased us up the steep stairs. The two of us ran for quite some time along the boulevard until, with lungs bursting, we stopped in hysterics.

'Fucking Bosnian, smash our faces... I smash his face. Piece-of-shit Bosnians.'

'Bosnian? What do you mean? How could you tell?'

'You can tell them a mile off.'

'All Polish guys know this?'

'You ask too many questions, *l'Anglais*.'

'Just admit you're not Polish. We all know it.'

'I am Polish. My name is Piotr.'

'Sure. You better tell me your real name one day.'

Since his arrival Piotr has galvanized the restaurant with his work ethic. No one works as hard as him; he is like an ox. And no matter what they throw at him, he absorbs it, the waiters included. After a while he becomes known as someone who can get things done, even if the others find him a bit of a joke. For example, for Piotr, having the table at the far end of the terrace is not a problem, he relishes the challenge. On his first day, when I was a runner, after being shafted with the faraway tables, he handed me twenty euros and didn't say anything. I worked with him. At the end of the service he handed me another twenty. This was a true professional, and from then on I stuck with him through the services regardless. We worked well together, and the only time he reproached me was when I was limping slightly because of two giant blisters on my right foot.

'This is nothing, *l'Anglais*. In the Legion they gave us an old pair of boots and 22-kilo rucksacks, then told us to march a hundred kilometres without stopping. They gave boots at random. You don't choose size and mine were too small. A hundred kilometres – think about it. Now tell me if your feet hurt.'

Whether Piotr's Legion stories are true or not, they provide me with immense entertainment during low times in the restaurant. They include everything from North African brothels and jungle training camps to his comrades' daring escapes. But having him seen him floor the Bosnian bouncer, despite the state he was in, I am more convinced than ever that he may have been in the Legion. It is the most plausible of all his stories and might go some way to explaining the new identity.

'We need to find girls, *l'Anglais*,' he had said that night, having just bought a pack of cigarettes from a guy selling them in the street. He ripped the filters off them when he smoked, which I always found quite impressive.

We dropped into a few other bars which were populated by sad-looking men until Piotr announced that if we wanted real girls we would have to go to the Bois de Boulogne. There, he said, the roads were lined with women and a man could have all the pleasure he sought. What he went on to describe was a place with old vans parked along the dark forest roads, vans with bin bags in the windows, women standing under streetlights in the woods.

'Different roads, different women; whatever your taste, you find it. It is great, you walk along, you see the girls, you talk, then you choose. But you have to be careful.'

'Yeah?'

'There's this one area and if you didn't know you could make a big mistake.'

'Why?'

'They're not girls. Just Latino men.'

'A friend told you about it? That area?'

'Fuck off.'

As with all these things there was a code, which Piotr readily explained: 'If they have a scarf tied to the wing mirror, then they are busy. If not, they're probably sat in the front seat. Not all have cars. Some have these tents in the forest. Tarpaulin. It is quite nice. Especially in the evening with the mist. Very naughty place.'

'Sounds like a horror film.'

'*Mais non, l'Anglais!* Even the French politicians, they go there.

That's why it's where it is. Just next to the 16th arrondissement. Either they go after work, or after dinner. I'm telling you, it's tolerated. This is why France is a great country. Criticize the French, but admit, there are some things they understand. So, you come?'

'Not tonight, Piotr.'

'Fine. But next time.' We shook forearms at the Place de Clichy, where Piotr took a taxi for the Bois de Boulogne.

Piotr takes his jacket off, dusts it back down and rips the filter off, then lights another cigarette, a different pack from the one we bought four hours earlier.

'I'm in love,' he finally says.

'With who?'

'This girl, from last night.'

'So, you do remember last night?'

'How could I forget? The Bois de Boulogne. You should have come... she was magnificent. Different. Very beautiful.'

He sucked on his cigarette with intent, as if he couldn't believe it himself.

'You fell in love with a prostitute, Piotr. Come on.'

He slaps me around the back of the head. 'No. She wasn't a *pute* like the others. It was her first time working – she said so herself. I actually found her on the Pont de Suresnes wearing a red dress. No joke – don't laugh. As we drove past, I thought I was imagining things. This wasn't your usual girl. She could have been one of the hostesses. In fact, she probably is, but in a different restaurant. I could tell she was sad, you know; maybe problems with her husband. Why you laughing? I'm serious. This girl... I can't stop thinking about her. *Bref*, we spent the whole night together. Not only like you imagine. Of course, that first, but then I couldn't leave her; I couldn't stand the idea of her being with other men, not this girl. So we went into town. You know the restaurant, Au Pied de Cochon? Open all night. You should have seen me, *l'Anglais*... champagne, oysters, more champagne. She must have thought I was successful businessman. I spent everything I had. I was still wearing my suit and I told her I come from gala dinner at the Elysées Palace. Can you believe that? She didn't speak much. But she drank the champagne and ate the oysters and laughed at my war stories. I told her she can be my wife and that she will be able to work in my restaurant. Look.'

Piotr takes his waiter's wallet from inside his jacket and shows me the contents.

'Nothing,' he says proudly.

True enough, his wallet is completely empty.

'I spent it all. Everything. And I would do it again. I will do it again.'

'Will you see her again?'

He fishes around inside his jacket until he finds a piece of paper with a scribbled phone number on it and the name 'Carmen'.

'I wanted to go see her tomorrow night. But I need money first. I'm broke.'

Sensing an opportunity, I ask Piotr if he'll take my shift on the night of De Souza's wedding. He agrees. He'll inform the *directeur* or Valentine after the service. Part of me wants to be there when the Rat bursts into the Pass looking for me, and instead finds Piotr.

'Next time you come, too. She said she has nice friends,' Piotr says.

When we have finished smoking we stand up and go back into the Pass. The lunch service is about to begin, and Piotr will now be in that fine dining room on the other side of the swinging door, serving *vitello tonnato* and *filet de bœuf* to people dressed to the nines, completely unaware that only a few hours before he'd been spending all his money buying oysters and champagne for a girl from the Bois. And he hasn't even had time to shower.

Raki and Loukoumi

The infestation of bed bugs has become so severe that I am beginning to look like I have a serious case of measles. Also, since working out that I am not actually a student, Madame Maury has become intent on getting rid of me. She'll wait at her door in the mornings and call me all manner of names. Accusing me of having lied and cheated her and infested her building with bed bugs. This is patently not true, as what I initially mistook for the squished, bloodied remains of mosquitos on the wall were clearly the last resident's futile attempts at beating back the tide of bugs as they advanced forth under the cover of darkness. I decide I will take Piotr up on his offer to meet the Orthodox priest, Father Milan, whom he's described as quite a colourful personality. To meet him I need to go to an Orthodox church in the north of Paris – not too far from the Hôtel du Simplon, incidentally.

Inside the cool church a baptism is taking place. The child is crying, the mother crossing herself in the Orthodox fashion and the father looking stoically up to the painted ceiling. A few family members and friends are lined up watching. Behind them stand two aggressive-looking men in leather jackets – one small and round in thick-rimmed glasses and a bald head; the other tall, thin and handsome. However, when they began to sing, it is delicate and light, celestial almost. Hard to believe it is coming from such people. In the centre of the scene stands a small, bearded priest in Orthodox robes and wire-framed glasses.

After the baptism I hang around by the entrance where an elderly woman is begging. Eventually the family file out amid lots of crossing and kissing of icons, then finally Father Milan appears. He leads me into a small room off the church and offers me raki – an anise-tasting *eau de vie* – and loukoumi, which looks a little like Turkish delight. As I eat and drink, the priest removes his ceremonial robes – wafts of incense fill the room. Finally, he sits down and pours another round of raki. He seems even smaller without the hat and golden robes.

'Balkan Turkish delight,' he says with a chuckle, pointing at the loukoumi. 'But let's not talk about the Ottomans – a complicated history for us Serbs. Now tell me. You are a friend of Goran's, so you are a friend of mine. You need a room, it is so?'

'Goran?'

'Yes,' he says pensively and stares at me.

'Piotr? He said you might be able to help?'

The father raises his bushy eyebrows and goes silent. 'Yes, Piotr. Piotr,' he says, nodding his head. 'Quite a life.'

'Yes?'

'Man can know nothing of the judgements of God,' he says evasively.

'How do you know him?' I try.

'Ah, that is a long story.' He leans forward and refills our glasses. 'The first time we met was in a monastery on Mount Athos. Many years ago.' There is a silence as he savours the alcohol. 'Another life. You've been? I would recommend it – especially the Georgian monastery. Wonderful food.'

For the remainder of the conversation about our mutual friend's past Father Milan alternates between calling him Piotr and Goran. From what I can ascertain, Piotr was previously called Goran. Until 'something' happened, and he joined the French Foreign Legion. I can't wait to tell Camille everything I have learned. Eventually our discussions move on to the room, and, once that is concluded, another round of raki is poured. The priest assures me that, if I want the room, which is in a flat share, I can have it today. The raki burns as it goes down. On an empty stomach the hard alcohol is starting to have quite the effect, and between the two of us we've polished off most of the bottle, which Father Milan informs me is home-made back in Serbia and 'most certainly above 50 per cent'.

'Now I show you the room. It is not far.'

I follow the little priest as he hurries across the 18th arrondissement. There is something incongruous about the little old man in his black robes, like some kind of Byzantine presbyter threading his way through the crowd. It is market day, incredibly busy. Occasionally I lose him among the mêlée and smoke and shouting, only for him to reappear in the distance a few seconds later. If it wasn't for the Parisian architecture, I could have been in fourteenth-century Constantinople. The priest moves quickly, with little movement, as if he was floating. I lose him one last time, this time I think for good, but eventually find him next to a rusted-out Fiat Panda 4x4 with rosary beads hanging around the rearview mirror. When he starts the motor, the stereo erupts into life to the sound of a men's choir chanting.

'Beautiful,' he says.

We cross the 18th in record time.

'I learned to drive in Serbia… but perfected it in Greece,' he says when we get out the car, which he has parked in a way that would make a Roman envious.

What he offers me is a room in a large apartment divided into three bedrooms. The other two residents are there when we arrive in what has become the sitting room: a sickly, pale-looking boy sprawled across the sofa staring at the ceiling and smoking rollies and a neatly dressed girl who only seems to sneeze in groups of three and whose main concern is whether I like cats. The boy, Auguste, speaks vaguely about having a job in classical music, and the girl, Maud, describes herself as an art critic, though the fact that they are at home doing nothing on a weekday suggests otherwise.

'And you?' Maud asks.

'A waiter.'

The room is perfect. In the sense that it is clean. It has absolutely no furniture, however, just a mattress on the floor. Piotr, I am sure, can help me out here. We shake hands on the spot and, as my two new flatmates serve the priest and me tea, a German neighbour knocks on the door and comes in. He introduces himself as Klaus, saying that he is a German philosopher. He lives in the roof, he says. The conversation seems to oscillate, quite naturally for him I will learn, between the burial place of Alexander the Great's father and two Spanish women he had met in the local public swimming pool the previous day. Klaus, it turns out, is fluent in several languages.

Before I leave Klaus invites me up to his room – he wants me to read over something he's written in English. After I've made a few suggestions, he enquires as to whether I, too, write. I tell him the usual spiel that Alice listened to a million times over. That many an unpublished writer has uttered.

'You have something in mind?'

'About the restaurant, maybe.'

'If it's important to you, then do it.'

'Yeah, maybe. Not sure who'd want to read it.'

'Just do it and send it off.'

'Where?'

'I don't know. You'll find something.'

It is impossible arguing with a philosopher, so after a time I beat a retreat. I need to get my belongings from Madame Maury's without her noticing. Then wash everything I have in a laundrette, drop it off back here and get to work. As usual, doing anything else is easier than thinking about my future.

I also have a more pressing issue: what to wear to De Souza's wedding. I can't go dressed as a waiter.

De Souza's Wedding

It's late afternoon. I'm waiting on the corner in front of the Gare d'Austerlitz for a lift that Lucien says he's sorted out. Eventually a small black Peugeot arrives; Lucien beckons for me to get in. He's drunk and boisterous. I squeeze into the back with two other men I do not know. We introduce ourselves. The girl driving says she is an old friend of De Souza's; they worked together in a restaurant some time back. The other men say the same. As we slip out of the city, drinks are passed around; Lucien smokes and talks belligerently while dropping ash in his lap, telling us that waiting is a loser's game and we'd be better off getting out, but the atmosphere remains ebullient. The driver turns up the radio, and the other men tell Lucien to shut up and open the window some more. The warm air of Paris rushes in. We're heading out of the city, the warm spring sun at our backs. It's a journey that takes us through the eastern suburbs.

Eventually we arrive at the town hall of Vitry-sur-Seine. A red-brick building of little charm bedecked in *tricolore* flags. Outside a small group has congregated. Furtively smoking and making small talk in Portuguese and French. Pauline is there, and Adrien, and a nervous-looking De Souza soon arrives. It's strange to be together in our civilian clothes, or versions of them. Everyone seems younger. We are no longer so similar, we have identities, and as such are almost strangers again. As waiters we have no identities, that's the job: to remain in the background – only the initiated can tell us apart. The conversation between us initially slips into the familiar, jokes about Renaud and Jamaal, tales from the day's services, but here, outside of the restaurant, it feels hollow and is soon dropped as we go about getting to know these different versions of ourselves. The mood between us is completely changed, a different kind of fraternity. On the town hall those three words again: *Liberté – Egalité – Fraternité*. Perhaps it's our proximity to them on the façade of the building, but for the first time I feel all three. Even if the liberty is fleeting, for I'll be back in the restaurant the day after next. The *egalité*, now that we are no longer all dressed the same, now that we are all individuals, seems to solidify. We all feel it. The positions that the restaurant has imposed upon us, titles meant to separate us, have been swept aside, they are meaningless. Head waiter, runner, waiter, they mean nothing. Here we are simply friends.

As we smoke, others arrive, groups of men and women in small cars, most talking Portuguese. One of the men comes around and pins white flowers to our lapels. Eventually a girl comes out of the town hall and tells us to come in: 'She's arriving soon,' she says.

We file into a drab-looking room and take our seats. At the front, behind a large wooden desk, a local official wearing a *tricolore* sash stands impatiently. Painted above her again: *Liberté – Egalité – Fraternité*. As far as ideals go, it's hard to knock them. The hope of the Revolution, as the *ancien régime* was swept aside, must have been something to behold. These days, unfortunately, they are mostly nothing more than decoration, something written on walls. But today, the day of De Souza's wedding, they come to life.

After some time, the bride arrives to a collective gasp. She and De Souza stand with their backs to us as the civil vows are exchanged and the witnesses sign the documents, including a particularly proud-looking Adrien. Finally the representative of the Republic signs. When it is done there is a cheer and we all file out.

Back outside, one of the bridesmaids gives out handfuls of dried rice. The newly married couple appear into the bright red evening sunshine and are hastily covered in rice and kisses. The atmosphere is cheerful. De Souza has tears in his eyes. Eventually, the wedding party makes its way towards the cars, which have now been decorated with small white bows around the aerials and plastic flowers hanging from the wing mirrors. In convoy we depart. Horns honking, men standing through sunroofs shouting at passers-by, bottles of champagne are passed around, beers froth into laps and spill as the convoy brakes and accelerates; the warm evening air of Paris, the sky a violent red, people waving from terraces. '*Vivent les mariés!*' an elderly man with a cane shouts at the car, and the convoy replies with a salvo of honking and cheering.

The Wedding Party

We reach the gates of the city; the traffic has crawled to a stop. Cars everywhere, red lights ablaze in the fading light. There are no more Haussmannian buildings here: we are firmly in the waiting room of the great city. The further we drive, the quieter the roads become until, finally, we reach an old industrial estate with rows of long single-storey buildings, like barracks or warehouses. The place is deserted.

The party is being held in the basement of one of the warehouses. Everything has been pushed to the sides so that there is room to dance. Someone has even rented lights. There's a smell of dust. As we wait in the silent basement with the red lights pulsating, Lucien tries, a little too heavy-handedly, to chat up Pauline. A guy I don't know comes over and asks if everything is all right, Lucien says it is and tries, after a few attempts to get the flame close enough, to light a cigarette.

'Eh! Not in here,' someone whispers.

Lucien ignores them, mutters something about it being a party and not Vichy France.

'It's good you came, *l'Anglais*. He'll appreciate it,' Adrien says. 'And you're not working tomorrow either. Nice work.'

'Thanks to our Legionnaire I'm free tomorrow. You?'

'Of course not.' He hands me a shot of something. '*Santé.*'

Conversations continue in the darkness, drinks are poured; finally, someone silences us.

'*Ils arrivent! Ils arrivent!*' they cry. There's a bustle of excitement. We hear the dull thud of car doors closing and eventually the side door upstairs opens with a metallic creak. After a moment we can hear De Souza's voice.

'...*je ne comprends rien,*' he's saying. 'I thought we had booked a restaurant?'

'*C'est bon, viens,*' a female voice assures him.

They arrive and the lights go up. There's an enthusiastic cry of 'Surprise!' and the music begins. De Souza looks genuinely stunned. We go over and hug him. Everyone present has put in some money for this party to happen. We can't hear De Souza now because of the music and dancing and shouting, but we can see that he is crying his eyes out – overwhelmed, relieved; probably both. To see him out of his waiter's suit, and the quite garish one he'd chosen for the civil part of his wedding, he looks like your regular guy from the *banlieue*.

'My wife! My wife! Isabel...' De Souza shouts in my ear later. 'I didn't know about the party. Her surprise! I can't believe you all...'

I kiss her on the cheeks; she's small like him, with a tan face and dark hair.

De Souza is drunk and happy and puts his arms around us both.

'Our daughter, Maria, is the most beautiful girl in all of Paris. You know why? I'll tell you. Because she looks like my wife. Look at my wife. Tell me she is not the most beautiful woman in the world. Imagine my daughter, she will be magnificent also.'

'As long as she takes after her mother,' I say.

'Bastard. Look at us both. Here like this. Did you ever imagine? When you arrived in winter we said you'd last a couple of days. Now look at you. A real waiter, hey. I love you. I love you all!' he shouts, to which the party all cheers back.

There's such warmth. I'm a complete outsider, yet everyone welcomes me. It's probably the incredibly strong punch that we've been drinking, but I, too, feel pure love for these people I work with. And speaking with De Souza and his wife I finally realize that I've been accepted. I am a waiter. I did it.

'Why are you smiling like an idiot?'

I turn. It's Camille. Bright blue eyes, elegant green dress, her hair down.

'I'm in love with you all, that's why,' I say.

She takes my face in her hands and plants a kiss on my lips.

'Boys only say that when they want to sleep with you,' she says with a smile. 'Is your dancing as bad as your French accent?'

Among the heaving crowd, hot bodies bumping into one another, the music loud, the air heavy with cigarette smoke, the floor sticky with spilt drinks.

'Where's your boyfriend?'

Camille closes her eyes, leans her head back. 'Not tonight,' she eventually whispers.

Later in the evening I'm at a table with De Souza and his wife when Lucien arrives and says something rude about the party. Isabel excuses herself after whispering something to her husband.

'Hey, mate, slow down on the drink,' De Souza says to Lucien.

'It's a wedding. We're celebrating. Drinking is what we're meant to do.'

'Yeah, but you're annoying people.' De Souza's laugh is awkward, but Lucien doesn't notice as he's wasted. 'Not me. I love you. I'm glad you're here.'

'I'm not annoying anyone.'

'Let's go outside,' De Souza proposes. 'Even I need a break from this old Portuguese music. It's hot down here.'

We wind through the dance floor, the mass of moving bodies, the air thick with sweat and cheap perfume; finally, we're up the stairs and into the cooler night air outside. It smells of summer, summer in Paris. A soft wind is picking up.

'What were you talking about with Camille?' Lucien asks.

'Nothing,' I tell him.

'Nothing?'

'I was talking about being a waiter, if you must know.'

'Well, this is waiting. This is how we live.' He gestures to the deserted industrial estate that we are in. 'Seen enough yet?'

De Souza interjects: 'I was actually thinking that here would be a good place for a boxing club. Could have competitions on the weekends. There's enough space.'

'Like *Fight Club*, you can do it in the basement,' I say.

'I have the poor man's version of Brad's body in that film.' De Souza laughs and pats his belly. 'But, once I get back down the gym a bit more. Once I get some time off...'

'Stop with this boxing talk, De Souza,' Lucien says.

He is just to the side of us. Standing in that way drunk people do, legs slightly too far apart, head hung forwards.

'Look at us. Look at how we spend our days,' he continues. 'We're slaves. Pieces of shit. We run around all day hoping that other pieces of shit will toss us some coins they don't want. We're no better than beggars.'

'You know, Lucien,' De Souza says, 'when I was at school, the other pupils called us Portuguese kids *les concierges*. Because most of our parents were concierges. But we didn't become concierges. That was our parents' generation. We got out of that. Our children won't even know any of that.'

Adrien arrives, his crab's gait even more exaggerated than usual. '*Ey*, what's going on, Lucien? There's some girl down there all upset. I don't care, but her brother is looking for you.' He laughs. 'And he's pretty ripped.'

'Whatever. Can I have a bit more?' Lucien asks Adrien in the kind of secret way that only a drunk person thinks is secret.

'Sure, *mon ami*.' He hands Lucien a small wrap of coke and turns to us. 'Maybe that will straighten him out.'

Lucien proceeds to unwrap it and in doing so pours most of the contents on the floor.

'You idiot.' Adrien slaps Lucien around the back of the head.

'Fuck you, Adrien.'

'What's his problem?' Adrien asks us, having decided that Lucien no longer merits talking to directly.

'Just pissed,' De Souza says.

'I'll get him a lift home,' Adrien says. 'Ruining the party. Not cool.'

'I'm not leaving. If you don't like what I'm saying, that's your problem. But it's the truth. We've got no future. Look at us. This is it. I'm sorry, but *putain*, we've fucked up. We're going to be waiters for the rest of our lives.'

'You need to go home.' Adrien is more assertive now. 'De Souza, go and find someone to drive him to the station.'

'It's cool, he can stay. Lucien, just chill out a bit, have some fun.'

Adrien insists that De Souza go and enjoy his party.

'Do you like it? This life? Honestly?' Lucien asks Adrien. He's beginning to sound teary.

'Just sit down. How much have you drunk?'

'He was wasted when he arrived,' De Souza says. 'But he's good. You'll be OK, yeah?'

'Did something happen to him today?' Adrien asks.

'Today? No, I'm talking about the last ten years,' Lucien says. 'Where have they gone?'

'Right, I'm going to go and find someone,' Adrien says to me. 'You stay with him. Don't let him out of your sight.'

Adrien and De Souza go back inside. I sit with Lucien on the stone steps. He doesn't say anything. We look at the empty parking space and the closed warehouses, the plane trees by the road rustling in the wind. In the distance the orange lights of the main road and the hissing of cars and the glow in the distant sky where Paris is.

'Give me some of your beer,' Lucien says. Then, 'Got a smoke?' he asks, even though there's a cigarette behind his ear.

'Here.'

'I've fucked up, *l'Anglais*.'

'What's happened?'

'You know it's my birthday today?'

'Why didn't you say? Happy birthday. We should celebrate. How old?'

'Celebrate. What have I got to celebrate? I'm thirty.'

'Thirty's not old.'

'Oh, and they called me about the film today... I didn't get the part.'

'What did they say?'

'Does it matter? It's always no.'

'Keep trying. Isn't that what you—'

'You want to know something?'

'What?'

'Do you know how long I've been waiting tables in this city? I worked it out this morning. It's actually ten years, not eight. My entire twenties. And the whole time I thought it was temporary. That I was really an actor.'

'You still can be. You are an actor, in fact.'

'You know how it works.'

There's a silence between us.

'You're right in one sense. I am an actor, I've been acting at it for a decade.'

I try reasoning with Lucien, but he doesn't want to know. He's put all his hope into this film, all his chips – and the house has won, again; and now, with all hope gone, he has to face the reality that he is in.

Adrien comes back with an elderly couple.

'Lucien, these are De Souza's aunt and uncle. They're going back towards Paris. They'll drop you off at the first Métro. You do anything stupid, you'll pay. Now get out of here and stop ruining it for everyone. This is De Souza's day.'

The old couple walk arm in arm across the car park towards their car.

'Is that it? I have a few drinks, which I paid for, and I'm asked to leave?' Lucien says to Adrien.

'Why are you so special?' Adrien snaps. 'You're not special.'

'Some people are. Not us. You and me, all of those people down there in that basement... we're nothing. We're here so that other people's lives are better. Not ours. Ours aren't important. You like what you do, Adrien? You telling me that this is what you dreamed of doing as a kid? Picking up plates of half-eaten food and slopping it into bins? Didn't you think there was more to life?'

Adrien says nothing.

'Well, there is...'

'You're pathetic. That's what you are. Little kids dream of becoming actors. Or footballers. Grow up. It isn't going to happen,' Adrien snaps.

Lucien stands up and gives Adrien a glazed look, but says nothing.

'Make sure he gets in that car. I can't deal with him anymore.' Adrien walks back inside. As the door opens we hear the music and then silence again.

Lucien puts his hand out: 'Well, it was a pleasure.'

I offer to head back into town with him, but he refuses. 'I want to be on my own. To think. Besides, I'm working tomorrow... I shouldn't have come. And don't think I didn't see you with Camille. You bastard. I always thought there was a little spark... me and her. I'm wrong about everything.'

'What about Pauline? She's here.'

'Pauline. Hah. I don't think that's the solution.' He takes in the industrial estate and stares at the door down to the basement where the music is coming from. 'This isn't you, either, by the way. Don't forget that. I mean that in a nice way. Don't take it personally. Do us all a favour. Get out, show us how it's done; give us some hope. Write, I mean it.'

'Sure.'

'I'm serious. You always say you've got nothing to say. That no one wants to listen to you. Write about this, then. Write about us.'

'I couldn't do you justice. No one would believe it.'

Lucien smiles.

'You sure I can't come with you? We can go for some drinks. For your birthday,' I continue.

'*Non, non*. It's good. I need to sleep. I'm pissed. And you need to dance with a pretty lady.'

'I'll see you later then. Don't do anything stupid,' I say as we shake hands.

Lucien doesn't reply. I watch him walk awkwardly across the shale car park then, having opened the door, turn and bow ceremoniously like a stage actor, before finally getting into the car.

Back in the basement it's hot, humid, decadent and loud and everyone is dancing and singing. Camille is sublime, her dress shimmers in the disco lights, her lips taste of cigarettes and beer. Music alternates between French, Portuguese, Italian and even Arabic, and everyone, regardless of nationality, erupts into song and stands arm in arm even if they don't know all the words – although most do. De Souza talks excitedly of his plans for his boxing gym, says a place like this is perfect. At one point someone puts on 'La Marseillaise', and everyone puts their arms around one another and shouts the words at the top of their lungs. Camille and a Tunisian waiter laugh as they teach me the words. It feels like that scene in *Casablanca*: here we all are in some forgotten outpost, waiting to get somewhere. The only difference is that there are no Nazis. *We'll always have Paris.*

Later we bump into Pauline outside as we smoke. She's drunk and flirty and her mascara is smudged. A cool wind has picked up and ink-black clouds are running low across the skyline.

'Where's Lucien?' she says.

'Why?'

'Nothing like that. I don't date waiters.'

She casts a disparaging look at Camille and tries to be seductive, but doesn't manage. Striking me instead as a little tragic.

'And Salvatore?'

'That pig.' She stops and looks at me. 'I'd never sleep with a man like that.' She laughs. 'I'm sure you loved him; everyone did. Often, it's those ones who are the unhappiest. The funny ones.'

Pauline is a woman of few illusions.

'I think he went to Egypt.'

'Egypt, Italy, Antarctica. Who knows, who cares?' She pauses. 'By the way, we've missed the last trains.'

I look at my watch. It's 4am. Camille laughs.

'If I find a lift, do you guys want to come?'

Back down in the party a guy comes over with some drinks and leads Pauline into one of the corners. Eyes follow her, just like in the restaurant. Camille and I stay by the bar talking to whoever and accepting shots. Of the Portuguese people, most are family of De Souza's and Isabel's, while the rest of us are somehow affiliated to working in restaurants. There are people from all corners of France and then the rest of Europe, North Africa and beyond. We listen to De Souza talking to a cousin of his wife about his boxing club, asking for advice. The cousin has that flighty, fidgety way of moving that suggests he's struggling a little psychologically. He keeps removing his glasses as he speaks and rubbing his nose or doing up his top button and undoing it again.

The cousin is a hairdresser; he says he'd owned his own salon, but that he lost everything for it – including his health.

'And his hair,' Camille quips.

'I was full. You wanted a haircut, you had to call weeks in advance,' he is saying. 'Tell me why I only had one thousand euros a month to live? I'll tell you. The first three weeks I had to give to the government for taxes and then for rent. That meant it was only the last week of the month that was mine. And then what? What if I want to go on holiday for a week? I can't. For four years I didn't take a holiday. The day I went to court to declare my company bankrupt, there were twenty other small companies there for the same reason. And you want to hear the best part? After I was declared bankrupt, I got a bill from URSSAF [the French social security office] saying I owed 10,000 euros. Where will I get this money from? And you tell me the new government will change things. Sarkozy said the same. He got rid of one tax and replaced it with another one. But not for the big companies. Not Airbus, not EDF... They say they want entrepreneurs in France? Until they get rid of URSSAF, forget about it.'

As the cousin speaks, the enthusiasm drains from De Souza's idea.

'Stick with waiting,' the cousin says. 'At least they can't tax your tips.'

'I like it anyway,' De Souza says with a smile. 'Look at all these wonderful people. Look at you!' he shouts. 'I love you all!'

There is an eruption of cheering. Indochine comes on the speaker. We each sink a round of Get 27 and vodka, which is like drinking toothpaste, and dance the night away – hidden in a basement, away from the splendour of Paris as she glows quietly on the horizon.

DIRECTION PARIS

It has started raining again not long before dawn, just before we climb into the car. Not a heavy rain – one of those light melancholic summer showers that seem to lighten as the sky brightens, only to darken again and stay like that. Small cars pull out of the car park and disappear in various directions, the white ribbons on the aerials fluttering in the wet wind. Apart from the driver only I am awake. Camille sleeps against me – completely still, like a doll. The odour of the night's excesses on our clothes, the smell of summer rain through the crack in the window. The radio is on, something about the new government: '*La France va toujours mal, mais...*' France is still not well, but...

Stopped at a red light, the indicator ticks quietly. With every occasional sweep of the wipers the city reveals itself like a greying watercolour before blotting itself out again. It is industrial yet residential. I didn't notice yesterday. Occasional tower blocks rise up out of the concrete housing estates and into the clouds. Over to the right is what looks like a building site, or perhaps factories, with heavy machinery, smoking chimneys, pirouetting cranes and menacing-looking towers of steel. An enormous dirty truck crawls past in front of the car, leaving a trail of dirt along the road like the track of some animal.

'*On est où, là?*' My throat is starting to hurt from all the smoking and shouting over the loud music.

'Near Vitry-sur-Seine.'

'Ssshhhh.' The guy who has Pauline in his lap in the front seat stirs, then goes back to sleep. He is a waiter in the Marais, he's said.

Pauline's eyes are completely black from her smudged make-up, the wrinkles around her eyes exaggerated in the morning light. Her skin looks tired, almost grey. Eight years, that's how long she's been here, she eventually tells me, having arrived fresh from the south-west. It seems such a long time to have been in the restaurant. I can't imagine where I'll be, or who I'll be, in eight years. Since arriving in Paris, I have changed. Over the last eight months, as I've disappeared into the world of waiting, I've lost contact with people outside of it. Part of that is necessity; the stress of being reminded where you aren't and what you don't have requires it. Mine is a world in which the boundaries get tighter and tighter until you can't really see beyond it. I was so desperate to become a waiter that I stopped looking at the bigger picture. Lucien was right: I've seen what I came to see; now I have to get out. I need to start hassling newspapers again. I need to get something published. Just to prove to myself that I can. That I'm not living in a fantasy, that I am different from those people I met with Alice all those months ago, who'd sit around calling themselves writers and photographers while living off their parents' dime.

Looking at Pauline, and the tired mask of make-up, I realize that nothing really changes. Especially the restaurant world. It is still just as Orwell described it. It has always been the same; only the faces change – like the city. I feel sad for Pauline. It must be the same for her every year. Her Salvatore of last year leaves unannounced, and then she waits to be seduced by the next handsome waiter. Where does it end? What is she waiting for? Perhaps Lucien has a point.

We follow a long, graffiti-covered wall for some time amid more of the same cityscape. To our left are the types of houses I am becoming accustomed to outside of Paris. The architecture of post-war France. Brick two-storey dwellings, painted an off-white, with closed flaking-metal shutters on the outside. Even the newer ones look the same, the only difference being that the gardens have nothing in them, just patches of dirt or concrete. There are very few trees here. Nothing like the great boulevards of the city. Here it is a verge of patchy grass by the road decorated with discarded cans and bags. It is hard to tell if the place is in the process of being constructed or dismantled. Not a soul stirs in the streets, only the lorries travelling in both directions, wheezing out plumes of cloudy black smoke that will slowly dissolve into the rain. The signs overhead always say the same thing: *Direction Paris*.

After half an hour of driving, the Seine comes into view. We follow it into the city. Intermittently the car is filled with rumbling as we drive along roads of *pavés*. The cobblestones are always there, in fact – when they're not, they've simply been covered with bitumen. Slowly the suburbs give way to the metropolis. It is a Tuesday morning, late August, and the city is sleeping, too; the abandoned city, its denizens at distant beaches. Emerging into the grey dawn with no one about, it looks like the elaborate set I've come to know so well, with its wide boulevards lined with poplar trees, the Haussmannian façades, the familiar trilogy of signs along the boulevard that glow in the dawn rain: the red glow of the *tabac*, the green cross of the pharmacy and the yellow glow of the baker's baguette.

The car pulls up at the side of the road just after the Gare d'Austerlitz, in front of the Jardin des Plantes. The indicator ticks softly and the wipers swipe across the window at strange intervals. The rain has now turned to drizzle.

'*Bon. J'y vais à* _____ . *Il faut descendre…*' Right, I'm going to _____ . You need to get out, the driver says.

He has spun round and is looking at me. Camille stirs but sleeps on.

'Where do you live?' Pauline asks.

I tell her.

'It's easier if you get out here. We're not going that way.'

The coarse light of morning. Paris, the great museum. Its breath cool on my neck. Camille's tired head on my shoulder. The sound of a scooter, like a wasp, accelerating off up the boulevard. We watch the car drive off as we stand in the warm rain. The park is still closed. For some time we wander. The city is ours, it feels eternal. We discuss our plans. What we will do, who we will be. I don't mention what Lucien said, she doesn't mention her boyfriend. We speak about writing; what it means to write something of meaning. That is all that matters, she says. I feel a pang of shame at calling myself a writer, yet the kernel of what I want to write is now inside of me. It was planted when I walked into the restaurant.

We keep walking. We feel alive and happy, wrapped in the elegance of the city as she wakes from her sleep. The smell of baking bread and croissants on the air; the metal shutters of a *boulangerie* sliding open like thunder. Fresh croissants and coffee on a green wooden bench. The rain has stopped. The world is still.

'What if we got out of town for a few days?' she asks.

'Where?'

'I have an aunt, in Provence. She's away...'

Hopes, dreams and plans. The empty, narrow streets of the Marais; Camille's heels echoing off the ancient, sloping walls; the saccharine smell of perfume, rain and cigarette smoke on her dark, tousled hair. The sparkle in her eyes as she speaks. The odour of the rain drying on tarmac. The night is dead; the day is beginning.

'I'll use my overtime. I must be due at least a week off by now. Maybe more...' I tell her as the plan comes together in my mind. The thought of summer, of holidays, of France. 'I'll ask tomorrow.'

We walk like this for some time. The storm has passed, the sky is lightening, a washed-out blue. Camille removes her heels; I give her my shoes and walk in wet socks.

'I should go home,' she says. 'He...'

She doesn't need to say any more. A final kiss, a smile. We part at the Métro, with promises and plans.

'Phone me when you know which days you get off.'

Finally collapsing into bed. Falling asleep to the sound of the awakening city. From my bed the sound of a scooter in the boulevard below, like a dying breath, making its way north out of the city, leaving silence in its wake. The city is awake now. Beyond the thin curtains the same yellow light as earlier. Silence interrupted in the immortal city.

A few hours later, my phone rings violently. A waiter hasn't turned up for work. It's a miserable day and a Tuesday, when many museums are closed and tourists want to eat. I have an awful hangover to boot. I finish after midnight, a non-stop fourteen-hour shift. I collapse straight into bed when I get back, like a poet in a self-dug grave.

LOSING TIME

The waiter who hasn't turn up to work after De Souza's wedding is Lucien. He doesn't turn up the following day either, and after two days of goodwill, at the *directeur*'s insistence, he is chalked down as MIA. Ill-will among the waiters has been growing since the first day of his absence, from none more so than myself, who suffered the most, having to fill in for him after De Souza's party. Despite my best efforts, Lucien will not answer his phone. I even go to his parents' restaurant and some of our regular haunts, but he is nowhere to be found: clearly he doesn't want to be. Maybe he's even left Paris.

The Tuesday he disappears, the day after the wedding, is a Tuesday unlike all others, where chaos reigns supreme. We're faced with a non-stop barrage of disgruntled diners. They never stop coming, wave upon wave of them. There is disorder in the kitchen and discord among the waiters, and as a result the service and food are noticeably below our usual standard. With the number of old hands low – as the likes of Adrien and De Souza and everyone else who's been at the wedding are not present – the ranks have been filled with the student waiters who are becoming a more frequent sight in the restaurant, as the schools and universities have broken up for the summer and the crowds in Paris swell. For them the job of waiting is just a bit of fun, a temporary thing, and whether or not things go well is of little interest to them. Piotr, Renaud, Jamaal and I have to carry the service; however, Renaud's open hatred of Piotr and me – for what he perceives as having been part of his humiliation when Adrien tripped him up – only makes things worse. Whenever he can he sabotages orders by stealing plates – Nimsath says he's watched him put entire side dishes of Piotr's straight into the bins from the Pass. He bad-mouths us to the student waiters, who are convinced that Piotr is behind their missing tips and resolve to get back at him whenever they can by messing with his orders. It is chaos, through and through. And the diners are more than aware. Once one table storms out, it's only a matter of time before others start complaining. The mood has changed, and the previous one is irretrievable. The Rat, unable to control the car crash, is looking for culprits, too. It is a huge blame game. Having Lucien there would have helped all of us. I can't for the life of me work out if he's simply cut loose the night before and overslept, or he's genuinely taken his final bow and walked out. Perhaps he couldn't take it? Knowing that the others would know he'd failed to become an actor? Perhaps he's actually gone abroad?

All that gets me through it is my dream of Provençal days with Camille. It is all worth it, I tell myself, the suffering, the blisters, the shouting – I am banking overtime. Time that will be spent as a *flâneur* in Provençal markets; wandering among the cobblestone streets of hilltop villages; lazing in bed, the sunlight dripping through the pergola and half-open pastel shutter, dappling the sheets where Camille sleeps and I read the local paper and drink coffee.

I work straight through, without stopping, from 8.30am until midnight. At the end of the service, I decide to enquire about my overtime. I have calculated that I am due at least a week off – surely a lot more, although the other waiters tell me to be realistic. I decide that I will accept four full days, with pay. Buoyed by my impending freedom, by the mass of hours and days that have been accumulated, noted and sorted, and are now ready to be paid out as dividends, I make my way to Corentin's office. I am there to cash in my winnings: Provence, Camille, summer, freedom…

The Rat's hovel smells of carpet cleaner, cigarettes and incense sticks as he tries, in vain, to remove the stench of the rotting detritus he's found underneath his old sofa. I find him reclining on the sofa in front of a fan, the radio on, a slowly unrolling banknote on a tray on the floor by his fetid shoes, a cigarette on the go, his jacket off and sweat-stained shirt open at the neck.

'What a day!'

He sucks aggressively on his cigarette and eyeballs me: 'What do you want, *l'Anglais*?'

'I wanted to see you about my overtime...'

'Overtime?!'

Unable to contain his rage he springs up from the sofa, pulls down a large blue folder from the shelf above his desk and starts flicking through the pages. According to him, these are my hours from when I began in the restaurant, back at the beginning of the year. He can't help himself: what starts off with him simply reading them out escalates into shouting them, the spit from his mouth covering the page:

'...Thursday 12th, five hours; Friday 13th, six hours...!'

This goes on and on and with every week that passes his voice gets louder and angrier.

'Four hours? That's bullshit and you know it! No one works four hours in this place.'

He ignores me and carries on.

I take it all in. Corentin, in his tight, shiny-grey suit trousers, the shirt with the yellowing patches under the arms and tasteless black buttons, his long arms and hands with hair on the back and the vulgar glistening earring, his narrow face, small mouth and beady little rodent's eyes – it fills me with an all-consuming hatred for the man. As he speaks, he is rewriting my entire past. He is an insignificant middle manager, a sadist who abuses his position for whatever means suit him. Here, I am nothing but a simple instrument. I will be used until I break, and then tossed aside. Better still, I will be used until I break and then leave of what I believe is my own accord. They will have got what they wanted, cheap labour that asks no questions, and I'll be replaced within seconds of stepping off the premises.

The Rat begins shouting something about lack of respect and trust.

'Trust?'

Though they act as if they are above us, the management are probably only marginally more trusted than we are. We are all part of the same punishing system. The difference is that to get where they are, with their pitiful little offices and small privileges, they've stepped on people. When we are hungry, or our feet ache, or we are denied a break, or have to work three weeks without a day off, it is because the management consider us acceptable casualties when it comes to carrying out their duty and hopefully getting promoted. Even if they disagree, they know that, to retain what little power they've accumulated, they must support the system that gave it to them. Because, deep down, they fear losing it. They are not in any way qualified for what they do, nor are they better than the people below them; ability is immaterial, for they have status. And their status depends on the survival of the system that provided them with their privileges.

Sensing my anger, and inability to contradict what he is saying, due to the imbalance of power and a still-limited vocabulary in French, Corentin stops and looks at me. After clearing his nose and swallowing the globule that has lodged there, he asks if I want him to carry on.

'These aren't my hours,' I say.

'It's what is written down here,' he smirks.

'You told me when I started that you write down my overtime.'

'Noting supplementary hours is the waiter's responsibility.'

'Not me. No one works for four hours in this place. Today I did fifteen and a half.'

'We only know what these pieces of paper tell us. And it tells us that you have no overtime,' he laughs, a nasty little laugh that bares his long front teeth. 'What are you going to do about it? If you don't like it, you're free to leave – at any time.'

Of course, the curse of the waiter: paid enough to survive, never enough to be free. If I walk out now, I'll have nothing. In a month, six weeks tops, I'll be out of money.

The Rat stands over his desk, lips curled, breathing heavily. There is nothing I can say, nothing I can do. I feel completely and utterly trapped. I see the space for what it is, a place where small-minded people make decisions that impact the lives of those below them in a bid to climb higher and obtain more for themselves. When viewed through the prism of the restaurant, French society – the darker side at least – seems to be built upon a vindictive sort of one-upmanship. *Other people's failure, your success.*

As I am leaving, he shouts, 'Just as I thought, *un lâche*.' A coward. 'Like all the English!'

Never have I been so conscious of how little of my own free will I have. I am to all intents and purposes a slave, locked in servitude with no way out. Lucien was right. The restaurant can treat us as they wish, and we can do nothing about it. Unless you have something else lined up, which is unlikely as you never have any time for that, you are stuck. And they know this and take full advantage of it. The fact that I know even less than the average employee, being foreign and not speaking much French when I arrived, has allowed them to use me to their heart's content. How many others here are in the same situation? All those guys in the kitchens? The Tamils? They probably have absolutely no idea of what their rights are, of what is right and wrong, they've come from war-torn countries, from poverty; this inequality, as far as the restaurant is concerned, is a gift they are being given. They may not have job security, or any of the other privileges that the people who eat in the dining room have, but they have a job. They should be content. Now multiply the situation in this restaurant by all the other restaurants in Paris, in France, in Europe, in the world. Le Bistrot de la Seine isn't necessarily the same, but it isn't much different either.

I go back to the dining room where Piotr is preparing for the dinner service.

'Fucking management,' I say.

'You only just learn this?'

'No, but still...'

'What you going to do about it? At least we're not cooks. You'd be lucky to have a job at the end of the week.'

He is right; there have been rumours about it for some time already – fewer fresh food deliveries; whole meals coming in pre-made, in plastic boxes, frozen in preference to fresh – but now it is obvious. Half the stuff we are currently serving is industrially made, which means bigger margins and less need for cooks. Whereas before the lower kitchen was bustling, now it is working on a skeleton crew. The ping of microwaves replacing the clatter of pans. As for the waiters, I am starting to agree with Renaud and Jamaal; sure, it is getting busier, but we are woefully understaffed and suffering. We are putting in sixteen-hour days without breaks, and our complaints are ignored. It is the usual response: you want out? You know where the door is.

I've known it all along – but like everyone else here I've put any qualms I have about this kind of behaviour aside as, faced with the prospect of poverty and in the pursuit of my own goals and needs, I've ignored and absorbed the injustices. And in doing so, by keeping my head down, I have sacrificed any hope of change. I have been a tacit partner in their oppression. In exchange for what? For the machine to keep turning, to make me want it to accept me, then to let it grind me down and eventually spit me back out?

The whole system is built on a bunch of arbitrary rules, handed down from generation to generation and enforced by people like Pauline or Corentin because it gives them slight privileges over others – and all this happens because we do nothing about it. Sure, there are laws against it, but what does that matter? The lawmakers are in the dining room being served by people working in an industry that operates in the dark. The two worlds touch, but no one will admit it.

I may have been oblivious to it, naive even, but now I know. My head boils with the frustrations of it all, and a desire to do something about it wells up inside of me. About Corentin, the system and the injustice of the whole damn thing.

London Calling

Old newspapers and skipped meals. Hazy mornings. The city elegant, with an attitude. For over eight months I've been living in a bubble. Playing my role as a waiter in the great piece of theatre that is Paris. The nights are now long and warm, and my world is continuing to shrink. I exist between the four walls of my room and the four walls of the restaurant. When we can, Camille and I see each other. Stolen moments between services; a bottle of wine drunk from plastic cups on the banks of the Seine after work; lying on the lead roof of her apartment, still warm from the sun, the ice cube floating in the cloud of pastis; her shower next to the bed, just big enough for two. But it isn't to be. Her boyfriend eventually returns; things are serious. 'We've been together for over four years...'

After De Souza's wedding we never speak again of Provence. I wait for her to mention it, to change her mind, see sense, give into the temptation that we both feel. Part of me even wants her to suddenly announce that we are leaving, just so I can walk out of the job. Start again, find something in Provence. Meanwhile Paris remains abandoned. It is August and the summer exodus took place weeks ago. The city is now populated by tourists and waiters, or so it seems. Eventually Camille leaves, too. Announcing suddenly after service that she isn't coming back, that she's just quit, that it is finished. Something about going back to school, business school. I can't say I am surprised, even if I am a little sad. I watch her go as I'd watched her arrive, the silk skirt that clings to her hips, the quiet beauty, the slender arms and elegant gestures – she is incomparable. A glimpse of another life. Though I hardly know her, her absence feels complete. I feel as alone as when I started. Salvatore has gone, Lucien, too. I've tried repeatedly to track him down. Unlike Sal, his number still rings, but he never picks up. No one anywhere has seen or heard of him since he left. After a couple of weeks, I let it go. *A waiter's exit must be dramatic,* as he had said; perhaps that was it, then.

New men join the ranks. At first to replace Lucien and Camille, then after that just to deal with the increase in diners that the weather brings. Ambrus is one of them, a large, heavyset Hungarian. He can carry two trays fully loaded without breaking a sweat. Back and forth he travels, his powerful, brutish strength propelling his enormous mass up and down the terrace like an ox. With his wide face and large volume, he is almost the opposite of Piotr, who is drier and sinewy, with his thin face, the unmissable scar running down it and arms covered in tattoos. The restaurant brings in even more student waiters, part-time boys and girls with cheeky smiles and a carefree attitude. They seem to speak solely about what the future holds for them, of what they are going to do with their lives. To them I count among the old guard now. Another player in the waiting game. What a difference eight months can make.

Of course, we are rude to them. We are jealous. And scared, also. To each of us they represent something different: dreams that never were or have been lost; failed school careers; lost youth; futures of certain hardship. It has been four years since the recession. Perhaps these kids are right; perhaps there are jobs waiting for them when they finish studying.

I begin to remember how I felt a year ago, the anxiety I had about my future. It is Camille's departure and her mention of going back to school that do it. The presence of the student waiters only compounds it. I don't want to be faced with it again. I've thrown myself into the world of waiting as a last recourse, but also as a way of cutting myself off from these thoughts. Now these students are here, and they are reminding me. It is the beginning of something that I don't want to think about. I push the thoughts down deeper and get on with the job. It is easier to knock around the Pass making jokes about the student waiters, talking lecherously about the hostesses and being as slimy as possible in order to make tips than it is to answer the question: what am I going to do with my life? Besides, I am busy trying to sow dissent among the waiters as part of an all-out revolution. 'The August Revolution' is what I am aiming for, a small incident at a prestigious Parisian bistro that unifies the waiters of the world against their corrupt employers. One that will eventually be joined by the diners as they demand not only fair treatment for staff, but greater transparency when it comes to what they are eating...

Since the seventeenth century the bistro has been at the heart of Parisian life. A place where revolutions start and affairs end; where careers have been made and lives destroyed – and that's just in the kitchen. There is no reason for my own revolution not to succeed.

One evening Piotr, Ambrus and I are working the terrace, De Souza is in the dining room. It is midweek and fairly quiet. A warm evening with a sad summer wind; candles dripping wax and flickering on the tables. The air is fragrant with the perfume and sounds of summer and makes one think about a world outside the Bistrot: evenings with friends, dinners in restaurants, sitting by the canal drinking cold beers – all the things people do in summer, apart from waiters. While the Parisians who have stayed in the city laugh along the banks of the Seine under a full summer moon, I am watching the sorrowful ceremony of an elderly Russian lady slicing and piercing her food. She comes every week without fail, in the same outfit, and always orders the same meal: confit of duck leg with *foie gras* and celeriac accompanied by a bottle of Saint-Émilion with two glasses; her husband's favourite meal – when he was alive. The tragedy is that she never even seems hungry but pushes on out of obligation, weighed down by her jewellery and her memories. De Souza says the hardest is at Christmas: she sits at her table until closing time, when one of the waiters has to ask her to leave. Despite our best efforts, she never seems to want to speak: Piotr even tried in Russian, but the lady, though clearly understanding him, said, in French, that she refused to speak Russian. Piotr was a little disappointed as he is convinced that this lady, who he is sure is some kind of aristocrat, has lots of money and no heirs, and thus could sponsor him. He reasons that it would make her happy to see him enjoying her money in ways that she can't. Because, according to him, no one would be a better rich man than him as he's spent so much time thinking about it.

'The rich don't know how to live,' he says in his heavily Slavic-accented French. 'I do.'

When Piotr speaks about 'investments' he is invariably talking about the French Loto, of which he is a religious player. Camille would often tease him by telling him that the lottery was just 'maths for idiots'.

The Russian lady reminds me that we are more than people who transport food, we are the human touch between the diner and the kitchen. No wonder the older waiters are so proud: they have a job that is sociable, one in which people seek their opinion, or place their trust in them. The waiter, as a construct, is something noble. Something to be proud of.

At the Pass Ambrus is talking to Nimsath in stilted French, trying to tell him that he should be working in the South of France in the summer. The South of France is bad, Nimsath is saying. Bad people, bad pay. Ambrus disagrees and assures Nimsath that he has a job lined up there and could put him in contact with the manager if he wanted. It is the usual chat between restaurant staff; there is always a better opportunity around the corner. They just have to wait for it. It reminds me of Salvatore's promise of a job in Sicily if I wanted it, which if I had any way of contacting him I would certainly have entertained. It also reminds me of Provence and Camille; what was and what would never be. Paris in August, everything so bitter-sweet.

For what it is worth Ambrus loves waiting, much like Piotr and De Souza. He has travelled the world and plans to keep doing so. 'Summer by the sea, winter in the mountains' is his motto. And it has taken him everywhere.

'I get bored easily. Even if I'm settled, with an apartment, a TV, a girl... I leave. I save my last month's wages and tips, then I go. I go wherever I hear is good. Waiters always have good addresses.'

Ambrus has worked on boats in Italy and in Canada and crossed the Atlantic twice on them. He says that he likes people, that's why he does it. 'Everyone should be a waiter at some point in life; it should be obligatory. Think of what you learn. About service, and people, and life.'

'No one knows how hard it is either,' I say.

'No. But hard work is good.'

Ambrus has sensed my discontent with the work and the institution and has consequently taken it upon himself to remind me of its merits. For him, waiting is life. At forty he has been in the game for a long time, but with no money saved he is starting to worry. His mother back in Hungary is showing the first signs of dementia, and he is certain he will have to return to look after her.

'You'll go back?' I ask.

'That's life.' Ambrus has large, watery eyes with long eyelashes that remind one of a calf.

'What will you do?'

He looks out over the small square and sighs. 'I've done many things in my life: waiter, barman, hotel work, museums, bouncer, tea rooms – you name it, I've done it. But where she lives, there's nothing like that. It's countryside. Fields and barns. That's what you find there. As far as the eye can see.'

'So, you'll do farm work?'

'My father was a farmer. And my grandfather, and his father, and his father. It's what we do. Look.' He holds out his enormous pawlike hands. 'Made specially for picking potatoes out of the soil,' he says.

'Do you want to?'

'You know what, yes, I think I do. And you? What will you do?'

'Next?'

'Yes.'

'I don't know. I mean, I'm not sure. It's not easy.'

'What?'

'Knowing what you're meant to do in life. Knowing what you're good at.'

'If it was easy, it wouldn't be worth doing.'

'Like potato farming?'

'Yes, the challenge will be something...'

Piotr comes in, his worn leather soles skidding on the flagstones.

'*L'Anglais,* English people. You take them?'

'Sure.'

'Four-zero-three. Just drinks,' he says.

I make my way over to the table. I can see their backs. Two boys, fairly well dressed, with confident voices and in-jokes. I hover near their shoulder and without looking up at me the blond one says to the darker-haired one, in English, 'What you having?'

'Not sure,' he replies. 'What you thinking?'

'We've had wine. Let's move on.'

'Gin and tonics?'

'Yes. Two gin and tonics.' The blond one glances up at me and hands me the menus before carrying on his conversation. 'Oh, and lots of ice!' he shouts in English as I am walking off.

Once I've put the order through, I hang around away from their table trying to catch a glimpse of the other one, the dark-haired one. When I finally do I am certain.

'Piotr, can you take the drinks to four-zero-three?' I say.

'Why? I give it to you.'

'I want to smoke.'

He looks at me suspiciously.

'You can have the tip. It's all yours.'

'They look like good tippers. Nice watches.'

'I want to smoke.'

I sit in the shadows far away from the restaurant and watch the two silhouettes of the English boys on the terrace. Piotr arrives, hands them the drinks, pours the tonic in, they touch glasses, one lights a cigarette. My mind is racing – have they recognized me? Surely not. With the candlelight they won't have got a good look at my face. Or have they? Perhaps they won't remember me. It has been a good few years since I've seen them, maybe six, and I hardly knew them. For some reason I feel ashamed. Back in the restaurant I avoid them as much as possible. They'll be gone soon enough. However, this optimism doesn't last long. Ben, the brown-haired one, hears my footsteps as I am passing with a tray of dirty plates and turns around suddenly.

'*Monsieur!* Ice. You forgot the ice.' I see his dark eyes searching my face, then his round face smiles. I curse Piotr for forgetting the ice.

'Right away,' I say, turning obediently and hurrying to the Pass.

Nimsath gives me the ice, but neither Piotr nor Ambrus is there. I wait until I can wait no longer. Valentine even comes and admonishes me for standing around.

'Your table asked me again for ice,' she says. 'Why are you standing here just holding it?'

'I'm going. I'm going.'

I can see the two of them talking. I feel sick in my stomach. As I approach, the fair one, Ollie, lets Ben know I am coming by tapping him. He turns briefly before they both sit up straight and look the other way, clearly waiting for me. I set the ice down on their table and go to leave.

'Excuse me,' Ollie says, 'but, um, I think we know each other.'

I look at him with my best impression of uncertainty.

'Definitely,' Ben says. 'It's you. Do you not recognize us?'

'First year, we did history together.'

'Of course,' I say. 'Of course. How are you?'

'We thought it was you. Ollie said he was sure. But it wasn't until you brought the ice over that I was certain. What on earth are you doing here?'

'Working.'

'I can see. But why?' They both laugh at this.

'We hardly recognized you in that fancy suit. That's a pretty tidy hair-cut,' Ollie says.

'Yeah. Well, we kind of have to. It's uniform.'

'You look completely different.'

'It's been a while,' I say.

There is a silence.

'What are the chances? We were just out for dinner around the corner at this place. What's it called, Ben?'

'Some French name. Le Carry On, or something.'

'Le Carillon,' I say.

'That's it, you know it? Not bad, right?'

'I know it,' I say.

'It's just around the corner; of course he knows it. It's bloody good.'

'What brings you to Paris?' I ask, keen to change the subject from the restaurant I've never eaten in.

'Here for the weekend. Just decided to take the Eurostar over. Boys' weekend. Maybe meet some nice French ladies...'

'Talking of which, if you know any...'

'I'll have a think.'

'Anyway, the waiter at the other place said here had a nice view. Then we bump into you.'

'So, what is it, then? Evening job while you study? You doing a PhD or something?' Ollie asks.

'Yeah,' I say vaguely. 'You? What are you guys up to?'

'We're brokers. Ollie's in insurance, I'm in shipping. Do you like it here, then? I've always thought Paris dirty, and the French rude. Not sure I could do it myself. So much graffiti, too. How many years since we last saw you?'

'Maybe six.'

'Must be at least five,' Ben adds.

'Cigarette?' Ollie asks, holding out a full pack.

'Can't, I'm working.'

'What time do you knock off? Join us for a drink. What's your number?'

'I don't know it,' I try.

'Give me your phone.'

I take my phone out.

'What's this?' The two of them laugh at the small grey Nokia.

'1996!' Ben says.

Valentine taps me on the shoulder. '*Excusez-moi, messieurs,*' she says to the boys, then to me she whispers that another table is waiting for the bill.

'I'm coming,' I say.

'Duty calls,' Ollie says.

'She's not half bad,' Ben adds lecherously.

I nod and go to leave.

'Oh, when you have a moment, two more of these. Forget about the tonic, we've got enough.'

'Sure.'

Ollie hands me back my phone. They laugh as I leave and then keep watching me and whispering as I work. When I bring them the drinks they carry on:

'Really is a pretty smart look you've got there.'

'We were just admiring the red socks and matching pocket square.'

Valentine comes up and hands me a fresh ashtray. I switch it with the one on the boys' table.

'What about that drink, then? What time do you finish?'

'Not sure.'

'Who decides? Is it that woman? Bring her along too. She looks all right.'

They are drunk and both laughing and decide to call Valentine over.

'*Madame*, how about you let him go so he can have a drink with us?' Ollie brays.

'You come, too. *Vous venez avec nous,*' Ben says.

Valentine gives an awkward laugh and responds in terrible English: 'He must be doing his working now.'

'Come on, we're old friends. Just let him off for a cheeky drink. For old time's sake.'

'Come on, love, it'll be fun. You can show us the haunts. Bet you know where to go out.'

Valentine stands next to me, staring at them blankly. She has no idea what they are saying.

'*Qu'est-ce qu'ils veulent?*' she says under her breath.

'*Rien.*'

'We leave you now, OK,' she says, bowing slightly and reversing away, her long silk dress trailing.

I follow her, my humiliation complete. Behind us the loud, obnoxious English voices fill the evening.

'Yes, mate.'

'Classic.'

'You know them?' she asks me angrily at the Pass.

'No.'

'English. Drunk as usual and causing a disturbance.'

Ambrus comes in.

'This is their last drink, OK? Any trouble, Ambrus, you tell them to leave.'

Ambrus grunts in understanding.

'They're your friends, no?' he asks me when Valentine has left.

'Not really.'

'They know you.'

'What makes you say that?'

'They keep talking about you.'

'You speak English?'

'I speak Hungarian. Of course I speak English.'

'Can you do me a favour?'

What?'

'Can you serve that table from now on? You can have their tips.'

'Yes. But listen. Who cares what they think?'

I think about his question. The bubble has burst. For the last week the pressure has been building inside me: first Lucien, then Camille, then the student waiters, the Rat, my overtime... Tonight, the outside world has finally found its way into my new one. I stay in hiding until they leave. I realize that, despite everything, despite all my efforts to obtain this coveted position, there is an uncomfortable truth: when tested, I was embarrassed to be a waiter. I know that, deep down, it is not me.

La Chute

'Adrien, can you come with us?' The *directeur* speaks quietly. He is accompanied by two plainclothes policemen with grave expressions.

We have been getting ready for the lunch service. Piotr, De Souza, Ambrus and I. Adrien doesn't ask any questions; he looks at the *directeur* and understands immediately. The three men accompany him down to the locker room in silence. When the kitchen staff realize there are policemen around, they go silent and try to disappear into their work for fear of being noticed. Even the Tamils keep to the shadows of their small room. From the bottom of the steps we watch as best we can. Jamaal soon arrives, out of breath.

'What are you smiling for?' De Souza asks.

'Nothing. I'm not smiling,' Jamaal responds.

'Didn't want to miss the spectacle?' Piotr says.

'I saw two police come in: of course I ran in.'

'First time I've seen you move so quick,' De Souza quips.

'Piss off.'

The police make Adrien open his locker and then begin to search it. Adrien, who is usually so proud, stands deflated.

'What are you looking at?' one of the policemen shouts at us, causing us to scurry back upstairs.

At the Pass no one says a word. It isn't long before Adrien is marched back past with the police on either side of him. One of them has a plastic bag in his hand.

'As we agreed,' the *directeur* says to them before they reach the door.

'Don't worry. No cuffs,' he says. 'You won't do anything stupid, will you?' he asks Adrien.

The two policemen then remove the orange armbands that say 'Police'.

Adrien says nothing. He looks humiliated. The tables eating an early lunch don't seem to notice as he is led out of the restaurant and into a waiting police car.

In the kitchen everyone is quiet. No one works. Eventually people begin to speak, rumours begin to fly. The cooks say they've seen a gun put into the policeman's bag; others say it was a knife. In the low-ceilinged room the *directeur* sits behind the cluttered desk, flanked by Corentin and Valentine. They are speaking in hushed tones when De Souza comes in, demanding to know what has happened.

'They got a tip-off,' De Souza tells us back at the Pass.

'About what?' Piotr asks.

'The coke,' De Souza says.

'What did the *directeur* say?'

'Nothing. Where is he?' De Souza says.

'Who?' Jamaal asks.

'The only person who wasn't here when they came.'

'You think Renaud was behind it?'

'Who else?' De Souza asks.

'He's on the terrace,' Piotr says. 'The dirty little rat.'

Before long the *directeur* returns with Valentine and Corentin. Renaud follows them in.

'You all saw what happened. It concerns none of you. It was a simple check. Adrien will be back later.'

'A simple check? Why didn't they check my locker then?' De Souza snaps.

'We have a service now. Let's focus on that. If you have any questions...'

'Yes, I have a question. What happens to waiters that rat out their colleagues to the police?' De Souza sends a searing look in the direction of Renaud, who sneers back:

'Stop talking about things you don't understand.'

'Enough!' the *directeur* says. 'Behind that door we need to serve over five hundred dishes. You will not ruin this. Anybody does anything stupid, they're gone.'

Everyone is nervous. The entire house of cards looks set to fall down at any minute.

On the terrace Piotr and I discuss what has happened, but the only thing he seems preoccupied with is the fact that he's been given the VIP area again and it is a slow day.

'Do you think he did it?'

'Renaud? No doubt.'

Jamaal soon sidles up to us. You can feel the heat emanating from his mass: he's been running up and down the kitchens trying to find out what has happened and, of course, start spreading some rumours of his own. What is most surprising is that he believes he is now finally in with a shot at becoming head waiter.

'Who do you think will take his place?' he asks.

'The *directeur* said Adrien is coming back,' Piotr says and walks off.

'He's not, *l'Anglais*. My brothers downstairs told me what happened.' By brothers he means two of the Algerians who are now working in the kitchens. 'Want to know?'

I don't want to give him the satisfaction of wanting to know, but alas, I do. Jamaal's version of events is that the police were called after a bunch of fashion people had been caught in possession of cocaine and had given Adrien's name as the supplier. This is, of course, ludicrous but confirms that what they had come looking for was his cocaine, which means that someone in the restaurant tipped the police off. It certainly wasn't the management, seeing how much they valued Adrien's extracurricular contribution and how the *directeur*'s position now looks uncertain.

Apart from his take on what happened, there is one thing useful that Jamaal finally gives me, and that is a reminder to go to the hammam he told me about. This time he writes it down on a slip of paper in his notepad and hands it me.

Back in the Pass and down in the kitchens the small printers begin to chatter again. Orders are flowing, and soon the pressure to get the plates out is all we can think about. To replace the Untouchable, the Rat has stepped in. Relishing taking control of the situation. Renaud, it seems, was more than happy to oblige. The *directeur*, meanwhile, loiters in the wings, biting his nails and clutching the phone.

The Hammam

At Barbès the streets around the station are lined with groups of young Maghrebi men talking hurriedly, exchanging money, black-market cigarettes and dope. The place has an edge – you pass through hoping not to be noticed as eyes size you up. A man leaning against a wall clucks; another hisses and furtively opens his hand to reveal a phone. 'Eh, *monsieur*. Look,' he says.

The street is a mess, strewn with paper and sodden cardboard boxes. Overheard the Métro rumbles across stone arches covered in black grime from the unceasing traffic below. At the crossroads, the cars wait in line as the young men constantly walk between them shouting to one another, occasionally fighting. A taxi driver with his window slightly open is speaking on his phone when suddenly one of the men on the street leans in, grabs it out of his hand and runs off. The crowd engulfs him, violent shouts erupt up the street, whistles, heckling. He's nowhere to be seen. Meanwhile the taxi driver is out of his car shouting, his palms towards the sky. The men taunt him. They saw nothing, they say. But he begs. He looks distraught, like he's lost everything. 'You don't understand,' he laments, 'how will I work now?' The young men along the street are laughing at him; they spit on the floor and point, hoicking up thick phlegm. Now more shouting. The traffic lights have gone green and the drivers of the cars behind have grown impatient. Horns, then shouts. There is no law here. This is a brutal, dirty world and no one cares about you. This is the truth and, having learned it, the driver gets back in his taxi. The lights are red again and he edges up to the crossroads, where most of the hard-looking boys stare at him. His windows are closed now, the doors locked. But he's not safe, and he knows it. The groups of men are rough-looking, untrustworthy: if he tries something they'll ruin him. They are in charge here. There is a police station on the road parallel, but this is of no use to him.

I hurry down the pavement, past phone shops, discount clothing stores, a bakery and kebab shop with women haggling over bread. I count the numbers above the doors as I walk, trying to look like I know where I'm going. Then I find it, number fourteen. It's a large double door painted a faded pink in between two miserable-looking phone shops.

'You won't find it in the guidebooks,' Jamaal had said as he wrote the address. 'It's the only way to get rid of this...' – he made a motion that took in the Pass area – '...and that.' He pulled my shirt collar and looked inside. 'You shower?'

'Piss off. I shower.'

'Not enough to get rid of the restaurant. This is the only place you can go,' he said, tapping the piece of paper.

A couple of rough-looking types are leaning against the door. One spits on the floor, and they both look at me. There's a buzzer with 'Hammam' written above it. The plastic fisheye of the camera has been completely scratched over, the unseeing eye. I ring the bell and wait: nothing happens. I push the heavy door, which gives slightly, but doesn't open. The men stare at me as it heaves back to its place with a bang.

'*Ça va, frère?*' one says.

I try the buzzer again and push the door repeatedly. It doesn't budge.

'Oh!' the young one says as he sucks harshly on the last nub of a joint. He's small, with a hard, ugly face and receding hair. 'What do you want?' he asks.

I press the buzzer and try the door again. The two men are concentrating solely on me. Their heads hang forwards; one looks at me through one eye. I stay leaning against the door in case it opens.

'Hammam,' I say, trying to act nonchalant.

They spit on the floor again in recognition.

A police car glides past slowly. There are four of them in it. You can almost see their faces in the shadow of their car, looking at us; are they grinning? The men by my side talk to each other in Arabic, clicking their tongues and raising their chins in the direction of the car. I remember Stéphane's comment about the only time you see a policeman out of a car is when he's buying a kebab.

'You sure you're at the right place?' the taller one asks when the police car has gone.

'Maybe it's closed,' says the other.

'Maybe you're not meant to be here.'

'Maybe it's the wrong time.'

'Do you have the time?' the taller one asks with a grin that bares a mouth of bad teeth.

'No,' I say.

I have nothing of any value on me. My wallet is empty save the fifteen euros for the entry, and my phone wouldn't get more than a tenner in the phone shops next to us, but I still feel uneasy. I stand out, I'm not one of them and we all know it.

I press the button marked 'Guardian' instead. Finally, an indistinct voice answers with a crackle; I can't hear what it says because of the street noise. But suddenly the door shifts under my weight and I'm deposited into a cool dark alley with a low ceiling and cobblestones. The heavy pink door closes behind me and the noise from the street has gone. There's a cold, damp stillness. At the end of the alley there is a small courtyard with a flight of stone steps that leads up to the doors under the sign 'Hammam'. To the right an Arabic hairdresser. Three women sitting in the middle chatting in silence behind the glass as they count out strands of black hair extensions. To the left a man is standing guard by another door that leads into a block of apartments. He looks me up and down, then ignores me. The reinforced glass is cracked and most of it has been boarded up with pieces of metal crudely welded together. By the guard's foot, leaning against the wall, is a metal bar bent into a weapon. I go up the steps and in through the front door; in doing so I pass another threshold and finally enter a different world.

The lighting is dark, a world of shadows. The smell hits you immediately – cardamom, spices. At the old till a woman is counting coins to pass the time. She gives me a key, number eight, and raises a hand towards a staircase. At the bottom of the stairs an attendant hurries over and gives me a black shawl to wrap around me. The air is humid, the room entirely tiled. As I remove my clothes at the locker I become aware for the first time of how truly dirty I am. But also how skinny I've become. The heavyset men around me, changing in silence, are potbellied and darker skinned. My body is deathly pale, and bony, and the smell of the kitchens, of sweat, of everything I've absorbed in the restaurant these last months seems to emanate from every pore. I look and smell like a dead man. Which seems apt, as the changing room feels like a morgue with its pink-tiled walls and blue-tiled floor and numbered lockers along the walls. As in the restaurant I hang up my clothes, but here I take nothing down: I am naked save for the black shawl wrapped tightly around my waist.

Now the walk. In the first room, in beds on either side, men are laid out like cadavers; motionless, wrapped in white robes, even their faces covered, they have no eyes. The attendant leads me through the room. In one corner a man is praying towards Mecca. The attendant speaks to me in Spanish.

'*Se limpiar. Ahora.*' He points and leaves me at the threshold to the next room.

A long, tiled space. Warm, humid with men sitting on the benches that run along either side, wearing nothing but their black shawls and washing themselves from small sinks with plastic buckets. They eye me suspiciously as I move through and find a place by one of the free sinks at the end of the room. In front of me is a rectangular tiled table on top of which lies a man on his back, his arms outstretched either side with a messianic smile, calm like Buddha's, across his face. His eyes are closed, he does not move. At his feet kneels one of the attendants in nothing but a robe, washing his feet. The attendant has a hard, sinewy body. To the sound of buckets filling and water slapping against tiles I begin to wash myself. The attendant continues to work the man's body, scrubbing it diligently. The other men have stopped looking at me. Apart from the occasional glance, avoiding eye contact. Now we clean ourselves, slowly, methodically. Time seems to slow; a certain lethargy takes over. The man on the table is motionless as the attendant begins to scrub him violently.

Clean, I move through to the hammam. A room of cardamom-smelling mist that bellows out of metal sinks full of branches. The forms of potbellied men appear among the steam, like ghosts. Reclining against the walls, lying face down on the tiled tables or on their backs. It's hot; movement is reduced to an absolute minimum. Occasionally one will rise from his cloud table and spray it down with the cold hose. As I sit there, I dissolve into nothingness; old and young, everyone looks alike here. Faded outlines of humans, dark shadows where eyes should be. Immobile figures that disappear into the wall of searingly hot vapour, only to reappear again as if they were floating upon it. It is dark, but also light. A completely flat light that emanates from the steam. Whispers of Arabic, spitting, slapping of water on the blue and pink tiles. We're all faceless. Beads of sweat drip down my forehead, trail down between my shoulder blades. After an eternity the attendant comes to fetch me.

'*Vamonos.*'

I follow his stooped figure out of the hammam. The prone man is no longer on the table. A young boy in a pair of swimming trunks is throwing water on it from a plastic bowl. The attendant spits on the floor and shoos him away. He throws more water on the tiled surface, then motions for me to lie on it, face down. He talks to me in Spanish as he scrapes my back with a coarse exfoliating glove. Occasionally he shows it to me with delight – it's completely covered in what I understand to be dead skin. It feels like he's slowly removing layer upon layer of it, getting deep down to the dirt, removing me from it, or it from me. Next, he kneads my muscles, wrenching them violently from the tendons and my skeleton. When he's done, he slaps my back, then throws buckets of cold water on me. The shock of the dousing pulls me from my half-sleep, and I'm soon following him back through the room with the potbellied men with sloping shoulders and receding hairlines who are washing themselves by the sinks with the plastic bowls. Once outside, the attendant removes the black shawl and wraps me in white, leading me finally to lie among the faceless in the dark room I passed earlier. As I drift into oblivion, I promise myself that I will leave the restaurant. That I must leave. I must find a way out.

I understand that I'll never be as good as the others at waiting; it's not me. But I've proven to myself what I came to prove: I can do it, I know how to wait, I know how to work. Now I have to prove something else, that I can write. That I can tell these people's stories. That is what I must do – tell these people's stories.

My body feels empty, new, reassuringly clean. There is a way to remove the dirt of the restaurant, and of Paris, and of everything outside these walls. One must first go to the least alluring part of town, pass through the double gates and descend even further.

FREEDOM FIGHTERS

Since Adrien's arrest the atmosphere in the kitchens has turned vile. Because of the events of the past month – including the way Corentin has continued to talk of taking the *directeur*'s job – everyone has split into factions based on racial, ethnic or even ethical lines. Adrien hasn't returned, and it doesn't look like he's going to. De Souza is rallying support for a retributive strike against Renaud. Even Jamaal can regularly be found down by the bins talking thick and fast with his two Maghrebi friends who were brought in following the sacking of two African cooks who the Rat decided were stealing food. As a result, Jamaal has become more vocal in his distrust of the Africans and uses every opportunity to talk of the plight of his '*frères*' down in the kitchens and the African conspiracy to get them fired. It is thanks to his brothers, Jamaal assures the management, that theft in the kitchens has diminished, and they would do well to promote them if they have any idea what is right for them, as the two boys were both waiters at prestigious hotels in Algeria and Tunisia before coming to Paris. That they really expect the restaurant to run effectively when the kitchen is staffed by '*les Blacks*', he informs us, tells us everything we need to know. Piotr is mystified by Jamaal's attitude and regularly reminds him that he also comes from Africa. Jamaal assures him that it is not at all the same, and that most of his own country's problems are caused by Africans, not Maghrebis.

'In Serbia, I always say that people are homophobic because we spent so long being fucked by the Turks. Maybe this is the same in your country, Jamaal?'

The unsubstantiated claims of thefts that Jamaal makes increase until the inevitable happens and he goes to the management to claim his phone has been stolen and that he knows who stole it. A kangaroo court is hastily organized, which sees the poor cook in question summarily found guilty under the watch of the *directeur*, Corentin and *'les Arabes'*, as they are now being called by the other waiters. No one stands up for the accused, and for the entire time it lasts the other cooks do their best to disappear into the wet floor by staring at it as hard as possible. With judgement passed and the judge and jury picking their way up the narrow stone steps to the Pass, Jamaal can be heard suggesting the name of his cousin to take the dismissed cook's place. Once in the Pass Jamaal proudly shows us the returned phone as evidence of the treachery that is going on below. Despite no head waiter having been appointed, Jamaal is beginning to talk about himself as if it were already him. Following the sacking of the third cook in the lower kitchen, Femi comes to find me in the Pass after a service, looking a little worried.

'You've got to help me become a waiter, bruv. It's bad down there.'

I had spoken about Femi to Adrien, who said he'd help, but now he is gone, and I know that the Rat is in no mood to start hiring people from the lower kitchen as waiting staff – he has a low enough opinion of the waiters as it is. He is of the mind that he needs to replace everyone if the restaurant is to return to its former glory. And any recommendation coming from me would only be a curse for Femi. As far as Femi is concerned his days are numbered – the management are looking for any reason to sack cooks.

It isn't long after this that the Rat marches into the Pass to inform Nimsath that spot checks are to be carried out in the Pass area due to 'the blatant mismanagement of the restaurant's resources'. It turns out that, during the search of the locker room in the hunt for Jamaal's 'stolen' phone, a number of bottles of alcohol were found. The number turned out to be quite large as, when two of the student runners were sent down before service to clear the locker room out, they returned an hour later with five bin bags full of empty bottles that had been hidden in assorted voids behind the lockers and in the walls and ceiling. Whether or not any matched those being served in the restaurant is immaterial; the Rat has convinced the *patron* that the restaurant is riddled with thieves and has taken it upon himself to clean it up. He has finally been given the power he sought from the beginning. By all accounts he is now the acting *directeur*.

'This is a restaurant, not a black market, and anyone found stealing will be fired immediately and expected to pay the menu value of whatever it was he had taken, food or drink,' is how he finished the last pre-service briefing. The *directeur* stood by him mute, deflated. By the looks of things, it is true: he is on the way out. The kingdom is no longer his, although whether he is being given another posting in the *patron*'s empire is never shared with us.

With regards to the stealing, Corentin is at pains to make it clear that suspicion has, of course, fallen directly on the Tamils, and his investigations will be conducted with that in mind.

It is as Nimsath recounts this to Piotr in a fit of explosive rage that Piotr simply raises his fist and, smiling, says, 'Tamil Tiger, Freedom Fighter.' Piotr knows better than anyone that the last people to steal in this place would be Nimsath and his Tamil brothers.

After Piotr has raised his fist, Nimsath, then Baloo and finally Mani, who appears out of the back of the Pass, do the same. It isn't long before De Souza and Ambrus have joined us, and the repetition of 'Tamil Tiger, Freedom Fighter!' has slowly escalated into an all-out battle cry. Like a wave, we hear as the commotion is picked up down below; one of the cooks even activates the intercom so we can hear the chant, not only booming out of the stairwell, but also crackling over the speaker. We are all jumping up and down with our fists in the air, screaming, 'Tamil Tiger, Freedom Fighter' as loudly as possible when eventually the Rat appears with Jamaal at his shoulder and, in a terrified near-squeak, demands to know what is going on.

We stop, but of course the echo from the bowels of the restaurant continues for some time afterwards, like the dead wanting to make sure they are being heard.

Out of breath and red in the face, Piotr informs Corentin that 'duty calls'.

'Yes, it does. Five minutes ago,' the Rat responds, clearly missing what has just taken place and scurrying off to the lower kitchen to restore order there.

It is in this rowdy act of defiance and union that the revolution I have been dreaming of is, in my mind at least, seeded. Of course, we aren't about to start coming to work in red armbands or crucifying members of the management on the terrace each morning – and I don't think anyone considers writing a manifesto and pinning it to the door; that would require reaching some kind of consensus – but it feels like a step in the right direction. Despite the crushing and increasingly divisive actions of the management as they jostle for power and financial saving, for the first time since I arrived we are unified. They may have denied us *liberté*, worked hard to create a world devoid of *égalité*, but they can't take away the one thing that is truly ours: *fraternité*.

Adrien's arrest has acted as a catalyst; all that remains is to see how it plays out.

COMEUPPANCE

A few days later the subject of the thefts hasn't been let go and the Rat has taken to pursuing other lines of inquiry. He is now of the opinion that everyone, no matter who they are, is in some way trying to rip off the restaurant. It doesn't help that the *patron* has blessed this absurd project and therefore elevated the Rat's previously temporary status to something more permanent.

'They think that everyone who works in this restaurant is a thief,' De Souza is saying, having just returned to the Pass following an interrogation by the Rat. As self-appointed Internal Affairs Detective, Corentin is certainly taking his job seriously.

'Which they are,' Piotr assures him.

Piotr, despite the complexity of his personal operation, seems unfazed by everything.

'It's the cooks,' Jamaal assures us.

'What are they going to steal? Haricot beans?' De Souza says.

'Thieves,' Renaud erupts, 'I'll tell you who the thief is. This restaurant, that's who. Work me like a dog, then give me the shit tables and expect me to make tips with the *merde* they serve as food.'

'It's all pre-made now. Even the carpaccio!' Jamaal adds.

'They're thieves, that's what this restaurant is.'

'The restaurant is not a thief,' Piotr smiles. 'It's a conman. And a very good one. People know when they've been robbed. Our diners leave happy. My diners at least.'

'Call it what you like, Piotr. But if we don't have decent food, what do we have? Hey? It's the last part of our culture, of French culture, and we're outsourcing it to underpaid immigrants in factories.'

It appears that Renaud, for all his scheming, does have some values. Although I can't say whether his problem is with the deterioration in the quality of food being served in French restaurants, or the fact that it involves foreign labour.

As Corentin's investigations advance, the waiters' few privileges are squeezed to nothing. His visits to the Pass become so regular that even the bread rolls are no longer stored there, thus cutting off an important supply chain in the waiter's limited resources when it comes to fuelling their assaults on the terrace and dining room during service. Coffee has been stopped almost entirely, too. In addition, the pressure on the staff is being ramped up with supplementary hours, and weeks now pass without days off. To add to this heady mix of overwork and undernourishment, the city itself is being besieged by what the French call *une canicule*, a heatwave.

The heat is oppressive and there is no escape from it. During the day, it is reaching the high thirties. Even the nights offer no respite as the buildings continue to warm from the heat they've trapped during the day. No one is sleeping properly; the day is hot before the sun is up. We are working non-stop with nothing to eat and no coffee to stifle the hunger. All things considered, our energy reserves are increasingly depleted and our nerves jangling uncomfortably. Piotr's eyes are ringed black from lack of sleep: a Vietnamese family has moved into the building next door to him and is hosting nightly parties that involve blaring Vietnamese pop music so loud that it feels like the entire family, and sound system, are in his bedroom. There is nothing he can do. All night he lies there in a hot stupor, calling out melancholically as he slaps the heavy wall in frustration; it is impossible to get to their door as it is in another building. He's called the police, but they say they are too busy. It is for this reason that, while we are speaking outside the back of the Pass, Piotr is using some twine to attach an old paint bucket to a bamboo stick that he's bought in the market in the underpass. His plan is to fashion something that he can swing out of his window and smash into one of the Vietnamese family's windows so that he can finally get their attention. With his bloodshot eyes he has something of the madman about him.

'They're trying to break us,' Jamaal is saying. 'It's clear. They want us to leave. Cheaper to hire students. It's Corentin's plan.'

'I thought they were making you head waiter, Jamaal?'

'Piss off, *l'Anglais*. I wouldn't want to be head waiter here anyway.'

'Really?'

'Yeah.'

'I'm already looking elsewhere,' Renaud says. 'I'll be gone soon enough. If they think they can run a restaurant without real waiters, I don't want to be here.'

'I'm going down to my cousin's place. In Nantes,' Jamaal replies.

'You guys make me laugh,' De Souza says. 'Professional waiters. When was the last time you polished your shoes, Renaud?'

'No one looks at my shoes. They're under the table,' Renaud announces smugly.

De Souza shakes his head. Piotr meanwhile is still busy with the old paint bucket, bamboo and twine, a filterless cigarette clamped between his lips, muttering something about heat and sleep and Vietnamese people. Coupled with the unmistakable scar on his face and the tattoo he could have been a veteran from the Indochina War. That said, Piotr's style has improved markedly since his arrival and his suit now has a silhouette that Salvatore would have appreciated. In a move that was seen as quite radical at the time he has also started wearing a mohair waistcoat, black, with just a hint of it above his buttoned jacket. The *directeur* approved, but now Piotr, more than any of us, is suffering in the heat. True to his character, he never complains or removes the waistcoat; instead he has rigged up an ice bucket in the Pass with a serviette in the water so that the waiters can wipe their faces in between dropping off plates. The problem is the smell. At the end of the day he smells horrific, but no one wants to say anything as we are probably all just as bad.

Because the Pass has now been equipped with a camera, we've taken to standing outside the back door on the small side street to smoke between shifts. Trust between the waiters and the management is at an all-time low, and the understanding that we smoke separately has been eschewed in favour of collective fag breaks. It is part of the French spirit to protest, and the management even seems to accept it. Besides, with Adrien gone, who is meant to organize it?

The instability created by the management has created instability among the waiters, too. Piotr and De Souza's take on why we are working longer and more often is slightly different and more reasonable than Jamaal and Renaud's, and doesn't hint at any secret plan by the management: it is summer and the restaurant has more people coming, hence the additional hours. Piotr doesn't mind – more work means more tips, which means he'll be back sooner with Carmen. But De Souza has been left a little rudderless since Adrien's departure and is struggling to find meaning in his work now that he knows, from the way they treated the former Untouchable, that the restaurant doesn't really care for him. Sure, Adrien was dealing, but at heart he was a waiter, and a good one. He dealt because the management bought, and because they paid him so little. If the Untouchable could be sacked, any of us could. The realization that De Souza could lose his job, and just after his wedding, is hard for him to swallow. The shock to me is that he's spent so much of his career believing that the restaurant has his best interests at heart. Renaud, too, picks up on this. For all his faults, I can't disagree with his cynicism.

'They'll sack you if it suits them,' Renaud says. 'You're an idiot if you think they care about you.'

'The *directeur*'s been good to us.'

'The *directeur*'s as good as gone,' Jamaal puts in.

'If he's so good to us, why aren't you a manager, then?' Renaud asks. 'They didn't even make you head waiter when Adrien left. You're expendable. Adrien thought he was untouchable. At this new place I'm going to be *maître d'hôtel*. Pays twice as much as here. And I'll do half as much.'

'No one would make you a head waiter.' De Souza is getting angry. 'After what you did.'

'Get over it,' Renaud responds. 'Adrien was caught doing something illegal. Selling drugs in a restaurant. You think because he's your friend he's above the law? This is the problem with France. You guys think the rules don't apply to you.'

'You guys?'

'Yeah, you guys.'

'I'm as French as you are. Didn't have you down as Front National,' De Souza says, referring to the right-wing political party.

'Front National?' Renaud laughs. 'The things you say. So, you're Portuguese when it suits you, then?'

'What if I said that it's your fault Adrien was sacked? We all know it. Why don't you admit it? You like rules so much. Honour, honesty... Admit it.'

'Admit what?'

'That you're a *balance*.' An informer. 'And now we're left with you and Jamaal fucking things up and none of us earning tips. That's what.'

'Bullshit.'

'Bullshit? Someone should teach you a lesson.'

'This guy thinks he's a fighter. He's all bark, no bite,' Renaud says to Jamaal, who sniggers.

'You find that funny, Jam?' De Souza says.

Jamaal walks back inside, saying something about not needing to be involved in De Souza's *conneries*.

'Just drop it, De Souza,' Renaud says.

'I won't drop it. I won't drop it because I'm sick of working with you. How can you show up here after what you did? You've got no shame. Things are hard enough without people like you trying to make them worse. A guy lost his job because of you. Think about that a minute.'

'Did what? What did I do? Hey?' Renaud with his round head and dark eyes and horrible little teeth grins sadistically as if the whole thing is a huge joke to him.

For the first time since I arrived, I see De Souza raise his fists, but this time it is not to shadow-box while he waits for plates to arrive.

'You know what? Put them up.' De Souza is standing square in front of Renaud.

'Give it up. I'm not going to fight you. Guys, seriously...' Renaud looks to Piotr and me, and we ignore him.

'Put them up!' De Souza is angrier now. 'You think you're so clever, don't you? Think we don't know.'

'This guy, he's crazy. You going to tell him to stop acting like a kid from the *banlieue*? It doesn't suit you, De Souza.'

'I am from the *banlieue*.'

In his baggy suit Renaud raises his open hands and bobs his head, the black eyes searching De Souza's with that horrible smile still across his face. 'You finished with your drama yet, Little Boxer?'

Piotr looks at him and, having exhaled a large plume of smoke, simply repeats in his heavily accented French, 'Just put them up, Renaud.'

'He speaks!' Renaud says. 'I thought you just carried plates. You saying you believe this little Portuguese man? You think I'd do that – grass on a colleague? What do you care anyway? You didn't know the guy. He was giving you the shit tables. Taking the good tips. I didn't do anything anyway...'

De Souza has moved in close now, his fists up by his face, his shoulders hunched. Renaud, unsure, steps backwards, uttering something indecipherable. He finally stops protesting his innocence when De Souza has backed him up against one of the parked cars and he can move no further. Eventually he pushes De Souza back. De Souza, who is coiled tightly, unleashes a flurry of punches which land on the hands in front of Renaud's head, then retreats quickly, always bouncing on his toes. Renaud pushes himself off the car and takes a couple of sloppy swings in De Souza's direction, which he ducks with ease.

'Is that it?' De Souza says, mocking Renaud by lowering his guard and giving him a clear swing at his face.

'You're crazy...'

'*T'est un mouchard. Une balance. Et un voleur.*' You're a rat. An informer. And a thief.

'*Ferme ta gueule,*' says Renaud, telling de Souza to shut the fuck up.

Again, Renaud launches himself at De Souza, who waits until the last minute and gives him a deadening uppercut in the chest, then spins him around and pushes him into the parked car. Winded, Renaud remains leaning down, then he stands up, spits in De Souza's face and tries to walk away. Piotr blocks his path.

'Move!' Renaud shouts. 'Stupid Pole, or whatever you are – get out my way.'

Piotr pushes him back: 'Finish what you started.'

'Started? He started it. You stupid Eastern European. What about you, *l'Anglais*? You going to stand there like a coward?'

'Coward?' I say. 'I don't scheme with Corentin to call the police on my colleagues.'

'If that was true, why am I leaving, then?'

'Because he used you, too,' I say.

'Just admit it and you can go, Renaud.' De Souza this time.

Renaud turns around and snaps: '*Bon*. I did it. You happy? I called the police. I told them that your pathetic little boyfriend was dealing coke in the kitchens. Why are you protecting a dealer anyway?'

'He wasn't just a dealer. He was one of us. A waiter. A friend. A brother. And you... you broke it.'

De Souza's response is as rapid as it is powerful; a jab to the right eye, and though his right fist is raised for a cross, there is a flinch, then a moment's hesitation as he restrains himself, which is fortunate for Renaud as it would have floored the miserable waiter. Renaud falls back onto the car with a groan and then slides down to be sitting on the pavement. When we walk away, he begins hurling abuse. We are barely in the door when Jamaal runs around the corner and into us.

'Your friend is looking for you,' Piotr says dryly, which takes Jamaal by surprise as he's always seen Piotr as a figure of ridicule. 'If you have any sense, you leave.'

'What?' Jamaal says.

'Maybe I say it differently. If I see you back here tomorrow, I break your face.'

'You can't... I'm going to be head waiter...'

'You're nothing,' Piotr says.

At the Pass Piotr gets ice cubes from the Tamils, wraps them in a serviette and hands them to De Souza. 'For your hand,' he says. 'Nice punch. For a lefty.'

'You box?' De Souza asks with a smile.

'We had to do something to amuse ourselves in the Legion. I can't stand fighting lefties.' He turns to Nimsath, who is oblivious to what has just happened outside. 'If that rat Renaud asks you for ice, you give him nothing. OK?'

'Yes, *chef*,' Nimsath says.

'*Chef*, I don't like that. Comrade, that's better.'

'Careful, you're starting to sound like Salvatore,' I say as he turns and walks into the restaurant.

'Everyone talks about this Salvatore. I never met him.'

On the terrace all is calm. The first lunch customers arrive and slump into their chairs after ordering iced drinks which are half melted by the time they reach the table. But no one complains. The heat renders everyone lethargic.

'That Legion stuff true, do you reckon?' De Souza asks me later. A great weight seems to have been lifted from him. Perhaps he's finally got the rock over the hill?

'I once saw him take down a guy twice the size of him.'

'I always thought he was just bullshitting.'

'I think the restaurant in Gdansk was bullshit.'

'And the acting. He told Adrien he was an actor.'

'And Lucien. He told Camille he was an aristocrat.'

'Engleeshman, what happened?' Nimsath asks. Trapped in the Pass, he and the other Tamils are desperate for the full story.

As I tell him, his eyes twinkle and he smiles. 'But you know, Piotr, he is not who you think he is. He once told me.' He leans across the Pass and says in a whisper, 'He is not even Poland man. No. Piotr, he is Serbian special forces, assassin; and he come to Paris, to restaurant, to hide. Bad people want him dead. I know soldier when I see one.'

As Renaud struggles through the lunch service his eye continues to swell. By the time the dessert orders have been taken his eye has completely closed up and is going a colour not too dissimilar from the *tarte aux myrtilles*. Despite keeping his head down and trying to work through it, he is flustered; his service has gone to pieces, and De Souza and Piotr are making a show of taking his tips from recently vacated tables while he is busy dealing with other tables angry about what has happened to their orders. All of the tips they take they put in a cup at the end of the service and give to the Tamils. The *directeur* has just told Renaud to go home and not to return until the swelling has gone down.

That evening the Tamils join us all at the bar for the first time. I've also invited Femi in a bid to help him become a waiter. He turns up with a couple of the other cooks. Impressed with Femi and his warmth, at some point in the evening both De Souza and Piotr promise him they'll make it happen. They will speak to the *directeur* tomorrow, they say.

'I already asked him. Said they don't need any waiters at the moment, like,' Femi tells me later.

'I think there might be two new places just opening up.'

'Yeah, but that Corentin guy hates me.'

'The *directeur* is leaving because Corentin took his job, so he'd probably just do it to spite him. Besides, it will be good for me to have someone to share his hatred.'

We share ideas of small tricks to play on Corentin over the coming weeks when Femi becomes a waiter.

De Souza, meanwhile, has managed to hijack the small radio in the bar and turn up Nostalgie FM. It is Jacques Dutronc, but this time the song is 'Il est cinq heures, Paris s'éveille'. Which seems fitting, as it's about Paris waking up at five in the morning. The waiters sing the chorus and try, unsuccessfully, to teach it to the Tamils and the cooks, none of whom have much interest in it.

'Tamil Tiger,' De Souza says and raises his fist in the middle of the bar.

'Tamil Tiger, Freedom Fighter!' we all shout. Louder and louder.

'Quiet down,' the woman behind the bar says. 'This isn't a discotheque. And shut the music off.'

There is a joyous, almost triumphant mood, and we spend every single penny we have. Such a rabble of men, from all corners of the world, none of us French in the strict sense of the word, but all of us Parisian. From the ruins of the old family of waiters, a new one has arisen. We're exhausted, dirty, drunk, but happy. The air is stifling, and the city is empty. We leave the bar in the early hours. Paris is ours.

THE COLLAPSE

For three days on the trot the temperature has continued climbing. The heat in Paris is now unbearable, with record temperatures being recorded on a daily basis. Nothing changes at the restaurant – we stay open; only now even more people are being driven in, seeking shade beneath the cool arcades. The city is so hot that the mayor has announced some of the parks will be kept open all night so that people can escape their tiny furnace apartments that have been heated by the wrath of the sun all day.

The parks at night are strange places: otherworldly, with silhouettes stalking around or lying in the grass. I have been going to the Buttes-Chaumont Park in the east of the city, not far from my new apartment. Originally an abandoned quarry, it was converted into a leisure space for the working classes who lived in the neighbourhood in the nineteenth century; now once again it is providing them with respite. The higher I climb, the cooler it gets. As you ascend the Avenue Simon Bolivar, the temperature begins dropping by degrees, then there is the smell of the trees, the plants, then the water and you know you are close.

Often, I just lie there, half asleep, half dozing, but it is better than the oppressive heat of my room. And quieter, for on my street what usually takes place inside and occasionally spills outside has become a purely external affair. The residents are so lethargic with the heat and the disturbances so regular that we've completely stopped gathering at our windows when the screaming or cries float up. Unless, of course, it is particularly violent and we can hear windows smashing or a street brawl, there is little interest now.

After a night dozing on a grassy knoll under a full moon, just before dawn, I climb to the highest point in the park. Paris lies before me, an open book. The distant lights, twinkling like shores of a foreign land, waiting to be explored. As I listen, in the distance I can hear the prolonged wail of a siren somewhere in the city, no longer so foreign sounding; closer by, the rumble of a car, perhaps a taxi as it goes down the road.

It has been an incredible few months. A little under a year ago I arrived here, looking to call it home; now it is. The last few weeks have been intense. The in-fighting, the literal fighting, the extra hours, the lost free time, Adrien's sacking. It has started to feel like we are all really nothing but fodder in a violent machine. But there is hope, there is spirit – that is clear from the green shoots of friendship that have blossomed in these last few days. There is a family of sorts, and we have each other's backs. And try as they may, the people who uphold the system – the Corentins and *patrons* of the world – can never truly crush the spirit of the people they use. It is a brutal, thankless existence. One that everybody in the city uses, but no one cares for. The men and women working in the service industry are considered acceptable casualties for eating cheaply.

I've spent the last years casting around for a story to write, and it turns out it is staring me in the face: the waiters – there is something heroic about them, working against such injustice, day in and day out. Someone needs to tell their story, strike a blow against Corentin and the system that makes people like him. This is the story I will write. This is how I will do something of meaning.

As day breaks, the city emerges from its grey mass of night. To the east, behind me, the sky shows a streak of pink that slowly dissolves into the darkness above. The resonances of the capital and the glow of the city begin to change, gradually giving form to the now-familiar sketches of Paris – all greys and blues in the morning light and haze. I can see the squat outline of Notre-Dame, with her high front looming into something tangible and weighty as the light writes life into her structure. An hour ago, she was merely a dark thought, a breath that drifted on the night air. Now, the heavy, flat front thrusts upwards to the sky like an axis around which the whole of Paris turns. The back of the building is more beautiful, where the fine buttresses, like stone fingers, sink into the ground and hold her in place. Almost as if she were digging herself in, so as not to be swept away by the most romantic river in the world, the Seine. I think about the small shrine at her source in Burgundy, built by the Romans, that Lucien told me about. Of all the places the river flows past on her way to the sea: the ancient forests, medieval villages, battlegrounds, castles, cathedrals and more – of France. Below me the last nine months play out like a dream, as I run my eyes up and down the roads, I think of the places I've lived, the streets I've explored, of Camille and Salvatore, the house parties I snuck into with Lucien. Finally, my gaze returns to the immortal Notre-Dame. From here she looks so tall and flat and delicate that she could be pushed over with a flick of a finger.

A desire to go out of the city, to walk in the countryside, with the smell of the earth and the sunlight filtering down through the trees overcomes me, until the sound of a woman's heels clipping along the pavement just outside the park me brings me out of my reverie. It is nearing six: if I want to walk to work, I need to leave shortly.

The route down from the Buttes-Chaumont to the restaurant is the same as when I lived with Alice. First down the Rue de Belleville with the last of the night's Chinese prostitutes hanging around smoking; gone are the fake-fur jackets, replaced with cheap-looking silk scarfs. The smell of croissants as I cross the Marais sets my stomach grumbling, but I've never seen the *boulangerie* where they are being made, so I don't stop, I stroll right through. In the lingerie boutique the screens are illuminated, but the cleaner is not there. There are more people in the streets than before – the light mornings bring them out – but there are still the tired night workers heading home, still the heaps of flattened cardboard boxes where the homeless are sleeping. A bin truck disappearing up the road leaving a trail of scattered bins in its wake. Down on the Seine the horsechestnut trees are dense and green, yet the smell of the river has not changed.

Then the restaurant. Already the first rays of sunlight are creeping along its silent terrace. The little square in front emerges from the night, as the shadow of the building slowly recedes. It is still and empty, but not for long. I walk along the terrace, the first steps of the day on its polished flagstones; my feet no longer hurt, or at least they no longer register the pain. The soles of my shoes have been stuck on using double-backed masking tape, which squeaks in the silence of the morning. The front door is open, and I step in. Valentine is at the bar, reading the newspaper and drinking coffee.

'*Salut,*' she says.

I continue towards the door, you know the one. It's at the back of the restaurant and it gives onto a world you know quite well now.

'Ingleeshman.'

And so the day begins. Just like the hundreds of others that preceded it. We prepare, we work. From first thing in the morning the terrace is open and already hot. The Rat insists we keep our jackets on, at least until lunch. The heat beats down with fury, absorbed by our black suits; the dirty polyester shirts stick to our backs; beads of sweat run down our necks, accumulate beneath our arms, between our shoulder blades. Before the lunch service, during the briefing with the *directeur*, De Souza asks if we can remove our jackets for the service. He's just arrived and hasn't been working all morning. The *directeur* agrees it is a good idea, but when he sees the state of our shirts as we remove our jackets – and, with some of the waiters, notices the smell – he decides that it's best we keep them on. Ambrus's shirt is so wet it's transparent. Piotr's face, meanwhile, says nothing, but with his waistcoat he will suffer immensely today. The briefing is short; half the waiters cannot attend as they are busy on the terrace already serving diners who have arrived early. There's no time to eat, there hasn't been since yesterday morning. I should have bought something this morning, I think to myself. I should have, for once, gone looking for the *boulangerie*. There's still no coffee at the Pass, nor bread rolls – these the Rat guards at his own station.

As the pressure at the Pass mounts during the service, so too does the temperature. In between picking up or dropping off plates the waiters are wiping down their faces or eating ice, although by mid-service we're told to stop eating the ice as the restaurant is running low. The sun's heat is relentless; so too is the service. The queues of people at either end of the terrace seem never-ending. Renaud hasn't shown up since the fight with

De Souza, and Jamaal has heeded Piotr's threat, so Ambrus and Piotr have divided their tables and I've been asked to cover the drinks terrace as well as the two *rangs* beside it. The work of three waiters. Femi has been brought on as a runner as a trial. The rest of the *rangs* are filled by seasonal staff.

The sheer volume of people means no one can stop. It also means that no one is happy. The diners who have been waiting longer than they were told for a table are already annoyed when they sit down; the waiter is annoyed as he hasn't had a break since breakfast; the Tamils are annoyed because the service is a mess; the diners are even more irritated because their orders aren't arriving at the same time; so the irritated waiter is going back to the Pass to steal more plates on their behalf, and the waiters are arguing with one another, and the Pass is screaming at the lower kitchen for replacement dishes, and they in turn can't keep up with the orders, let alone the replacement ones, God knows what is going on in the upper kitchen – if it's hot here, then it must be hotter than the sun up there – fortunately they're not running around, too; the managers, meanwhile, are keen to get more people in and more people out and as a result increasing the pressure on the waiters, which in turn irritates the diners... all the waiters know there will be no tips today, and yet we plough on. Each man for himself, lips sealed out on the terrace, but elbowing one another, name calling and stealing from the others as soon as we're in the Pass. Everyone is at it. Piotr tries to be too clever and take two tables' worth of plates to the other end of the terrace on two *plateaux* – one in each hand. It looks impressive, until Ambrus swings round and knocks one and it hits the ground with a splendid crash, right in front of the table it was destined for.

'Didn't you hear me? I cried *chaud derrière*,' Piotr grunts.

'I heard nothing,' Ambrus says. 'Say it louder next time.'

'You idiot. You need to listen—'

'You need to shout properly.'

Their argument is contained by the arrival of the *directeur*, who assures the table that replacement dishes will be brought immediately. I am dispatched to reorder. Nimsath doesn't listen. I scream at him, telling him that he needs to reorder the 704 and the 709; he calls me a *punday*-something. Ambrus and Piotr are on their hands and knees on the terrace, picking the smashed crockery out of the mashed remains of fish, a salad and sauces and vegetables and whatever else it was before the fall. I arrive with a dustpan. Meanwhile, with three of us doing this, plates are stacking up at the penny-pusher Pass, all of us are aware that the other waiters are taking advantage of the situation and stealing from our orders; we can feel the looks of our tables as they try to catch our eye to ask where their drinks are... or if they can order... or if they can have menus. The unrelenting Parisian sun beats down. Heat comes at us from all sides. We're moving as quickly as we possibly can through the inferno without breaking into a run. All of us are exhausted, hot, dehydrated, famished, overtired. In short, it's a chain reaction of purely bad events. At some point we completely run out of ice, and Femi is dispatched to beg in neighbouring restaurants for more.

At around 4pm the service eases for the first time in seven hours. I walk down the steps and into the shade of the arcades. The first shade in seven hours, my heart beating, my head light. There are no longer people queuing, all of my tables have been served. I plan to simply smoke a cigarette as quickly as possible and sit down with my jacket off in a cool place. I light the cigarette. My vision goes black and white, I feel dizzy, my mouth is dry...

The next thing I know I'm being hauled up by my shoulders by a French man asking me repeatedly if I'm OK. I can't string a sentence together but manage to sit against a wall. One of the hostesses comes over to see if I'm all right, and upon seeing the colour of my blood-drained face darts into the restaurant. She returns some moments later with a plastic cup of warm Coke. In the meantime, I have ascertained that the hand I had been holding the cigarette with doesn't look like it should and that one of the bones is pushing up in a way that it normally wouldn't. I try to explain this to the hostess, and then to Piotr, who arrives sometime afterwards. Still, despite my best efforts, I cannot string a coherent sentence together. Piotr refuses to listen about the hand and instead tries in his own way to see if I'm concussed. With three staff members missing it is, of course, only a matter of time before the Rat arrives. By now I'm semi-coherent and have convinced the other two that my hand is definitely broken. They explain to the Rat that I fainted and have probably broken my hand in the process. The Rat is so angry that he can't bring himself to look at me and simply tells Piotr to pick me up and deposit me at the nearest medical centre.

'...I'll have to call other people in. Do you realize the shit you've put us in? We are fully booked tonight. And you do this. *C'est n'importe quoi.* If it's not broken, then I expect you back here straight away. Piotr, as soon as he's there, come back. *Putain. Putain!*' the Rat screams out as I'm led away.

Piotr drops me off at a place not far from the restaurant.

'*Courage, mon ami,*' he says.

'*Merci, Piotr.*'

'*Non, merci à toi.*' He squeezes my shoulder and looks directly into my eyes. 'You know how to fucking work,' he says in English. 'Today, I've never seen anything like it.'

'You speak English?'

'Enough.'

He takes a look at my hand and says, '*C'est bien cassé, ça.* At least you're not left-handed.'

'I am.'

'Ah, well it's a good opportunity to, I don't know, learn to do things differently.'

To help me get used to my new situation we have a final cigarette together, which Piotr kindly removes the filter from for me. We smoke in silence.

'*Bon, à plus,* Piotr,' I say when we are done.

'If I see you again in that restaurant tonight, I'll personally march you straight out.' He looks at me and smiles.

'Fuck that restaurant. I'm done,' I say.

'You've got that look, *l'Anglais.* It's in your eyes. Tells me you're up to something. You're not done.'

I force a smile; my hand pulses in pain.

'Everything that comes in fresh leaves rotten,' I say.

'Everything that comes in fresh leaves rotten,' he replies. 'Félix.

Our very own philosopher. *Au revoir, l'Anglais.*'

'*Au revoir, Piotr.*'

And with that Piotr leaves me. I watch his thin frame tramp off up the street in the direction of the restaurant. He has his jacket off, his shirt sleeves rolled up and his waistcoat open. He doesn't turn back, just carries on with that unmistakable walk of his: the walk of the Legionnaire. I stand there and I know, with a strange certainty, that we will never see each other again.

PART 7

LE DIGESTIF

THE MUSEUM

The following morning, I awake in a hospital bed with my arm bandaged and an X-ray of my hand with two new bolts in. Light streams in the window; everything is calm; I am immensely tired. The surgeon appears, declares the operation a success and hands me a piece of paper attesting to the fact I cannot work for three weeks.

'I'm obliged to tell you that you can stay as long as you feel is necessary, but, well, like I said last night. We need the beds.'

I thank the doctor, get dressed and make my way out. It is just after seven o'clock in the morning. A beautifully bright summer's day. With my bandaged hand I make my way towards the canal and sit there for a coffee. I order a *tartine*, a croissant and then a *pain au chocolat*. I feel a strong sense of liberation, tinged, I must admit, with a touch of guilt, too. In a matter of hours my former colleagues will be arriving at work and finding out they are a man down and that the place is fully booked. For the rest of the day my name will be evoked in the same way that Guillaume's, Salvatore's, Lucien's and all the others had been. It is a ritual in itself: a means of burying the name of the departed under a pile of insults.

The waiting job was finished, I knew it. The minute I missed my next shift, it was over. In a sense that was a good thing, I had achieved what I came to do: I had become a Parisian waiter, I'd been accepted. My experience with these people had changed me. I had discovered a world hiding in plain sight; one we interact with daily, but care little for. It was the one that Orwell had written about; the very same world, for it has changed so little. A world populated by incredible characters; people I could now call friends, colleagues and comrades. And though my time with them was over, I still felt a duty to them. One I could repay in my own way, now that I would have the time. And, of course, the confidence.

My next job was as a security guard in a museum on the Boulevard Haussmann. The work was boring and the hours long. Despite the beauty of the paintings, after over a hundred hours even a Canaletto or Van Dyke loses most of its interest. The days were quiet, however, and apart from elderly visitors asking for directions to the toilet, I was left alone. It was in these moments, then, that I began to write up my notes from the restaurant, fuelled as always by Café Richard from the employee coffee machine downstairs.

When the museum tearoom got wind of my previous job as a waiter at Le Bistrot de la Seine it caused quite a stir, and when my hand had fully healed I was asked to join their waiting team. To go from the chaos of Le Bistrot's hundreds of covers each service, with thousands of dishes, to the sedate world of the tearoom was easy and, thanks to my experience, I was considered a pro.

Amusingly the waiters – who in the tearoom were all female – would regularly complain of the same things: the rush, the customers, the stolen orders. They were also keen to show their surprise that a guy could work the job as well as them. They were no different from the guys at the Bistrot de la Seine in that respect. At times I missed the restaurant. The tips in the tearoom were non-existent, and the work was never adrenaline-fuelled or exciting. But the hours were more humane, and with a night-time job as a barman I was making enough to live, if perhaps sleeping less than before. They also gave us lunch breaks.

In the meantime, and much to my surprise, I'd received a response from *The New York Times*. Instead of trying to contact them for a job, I'd sent them an article. The reply simply read: 'Thank you for your submission. We would be very interested in publishing it.'

Before I knew it, it was published in print and online. The article was entitled 'Notes from a Parisian Kitchen'.

Whatever happened next, at least I could say I had been published in *The New York Times*. Certainly an improvement on sitting on it in a hotel toilet as I try to grab some sleep.

CODA

Salvatore: You know why, in Italia, we drink Amari after dinner?
Me: Digestion?
Salvatore: No. Because no matter how sweet the meal was, the bitterness
of the drink, it reminds us that we must return to our lives... until the next
meal, that is.

Of course, I know now that I was never truly in the same situation as the
characters I met and worked alongside – I was merely a spectator passing
through on the way to somewhere else, even if at the time I didn't realize it.
My being there was part economic reality in a post-financial crisis world,
and part belief that by perhaps going and actually doing something, by
living my life differently from what was expected, I could succeed in what
I believed in: to experience something truthful and to write something
of genuine meaning. The poverty and humiliation I felt in these jobs will
never come close to those of the people I encountered, for they are not
living a job, but a life. They do so day in, day out, and often with a smile.
And though they will spend a life dreaming of something else, the reality is
that they will never get there; the cards are stacked against them. I'd been
to university, I was middle class, English and White. For what ended up
being most of my twenties I genuinely had no idea what I'd do with my
life and if I'd ever get out of the hole I was in. I was in a constant cycle of
dead-end jobs in Paris. My notes from this time reflect that anxiety, but
writing them up today, with the benefit of hindsight, I can see that, though
I'm still making my way through life, I've certainly come a long way.

And that, even if I was completely lost when it came to work, I was incredibly happy to be living in Paris. It made everything that much sweeter. (Well, apart from dealings with URSSAF.)

This book was never meant to be about me, so it only seems fair to finish with the story's real heroes. People I can say that I admire and respect, people who work harder and longer than anyone else I've come across since.

When I left the restaurant, I respected the archaic rules of the waiters and never went back, yet I always wondered what had become of them. Adrien I know about, for it wasn't long afterwards that I ran into him in another of the *patron*'s restaurants. Our conversation was brief as he was working, yet I could clearly tell that he felt a little uneasy at seeing me. Was it that I was out of my uniform and therefore, in a way, above him? Or was he simply worried that I still worked at Le Bistrot de la Seine and would tell the others where he was?

During the initial writing of this book, the restaurant was still open, and after much thought I finally decided to go back. But when I got to the entrance, I could not bring myself to cross the threshold. I still felt that I would be dishonouring my former comrades, breaking the rules of the waiting game. Instead, over several days, I returned and watched from a distance. There was no sign of the *directeur*, Valentine, Pauline or the Rat, but I did see De Souza with a suit looking finer than his last. He was working the VIP tables with a smile and managing the other waiters (including Femi) like a true *maître d'*. But imagine my surprise when from out of the double doors came striding the person I least expected to see in the dove-grey suit of a manager: Piotr. Perhaps his restaurant does not overlook the Black Sea, but the view here isn't half bad and the food is certainly overpriced. When there was a lull in service I stood as close to the terrace as possible so that I could see in behind the Pass. The angle was acute, but by straining, at first, I could hear, then see, the powerful hands – then finally, as he leaned forwards to growl at a new waiter, I saw his face. Nimsath. That will be sixteen years he's worked there now. Sixteen years of that small, dark cramped space, right in the centre of Paris, still no doubt dreaming of going to London. Of Renaud I never knew what happened: no doubt he'll be serving you someday you're in Paris. Jamaal possibly went to Nantes. Camille, I saw from LinkedIn, gave up on her dream of social justice through journalism and now works for a secretive defence firm. And Salvatore, well, there's nothing about him on the Italian free-diving websites. Wherever he is I hope the tomatoes taste good.

One person I of course didn't see was Lucien. I had long given up trying to contact him. I decided now to look him up online. Imagine my delight when I saw his face on a talent agency's website, although my delight soon faded as I read that he still had no acting credits to his name since those TV appearances as a child. The next link I clicked on was more sobering: it was his self-employment tax status – which is open to the public in France. It read: Lucien Fabre, domiciled in the 18th arrondissement. Domain of Activity: *Restauration*. Profession: Waiter.

Acknowledgements

I would like to thank the Aurand family for that initial roof over my head. And, indeed, all the other people over the years who have let me sleep on their sofas, cellars and floors.

Simon Kuper for replying, and then later encouraging me to write this book.

Gordon Wise for his patience and perseverance.

Jake Lingwood for his unfailing enthusiasm.

Sybella Stephens for getting rid of the cadavers.

And, most importantly, Morgane Lequand, for everything, notably living with someone writing a book.

This monoray book was crafted and published by Jake Lingwood, Sybella Stephens, Caroline Taggart, Jaz Bahra, Two Associates, Jeremy Tilston and Allison Gonsalves.